RESTRUCTURING INDIAN FINANCIAL SYSTEM

RESTRUCTURING INDIAN FINANCIAL SYSTEM

In Response to International Financial Flows

By

NIDHI JAIN
Reader
Department of Financial Studies
University of Delhi

ANMOL PUBLICATIONS PVT. LTD.
NEW DELHI - 110 002 (INDIA)

ANMOL PUBLICATIONS PVT. LTD.
4374/4B, Ansari Road, Daryaganj
New Delhi - 110 002
Visit us: www.anmolbooks.com

Restructuring Indian Financial System

First Edition, 2002

ISBN 81-261-1111-9

PRINTED IN INDIA

Published by J.L. Kumar for Anmol Publications Pvt. Ltd., New Delhi - 110 002 and Printed at Mehra Offset Press, Delhi.

Contents

Foreword

For a long time, applied research on Indian economy had reflected the inward looking emphasis in developmental economics thought and policy making. Though the last decade of the last century has dramatically altered the perspective for research on Indian Economy. The new perspective of globalisation of markets has just begun to impact academic research work in India. Dr. Nidhi Jain's work on **Restructuring Indian Financial System In Response To Financial Flows** is among the first set of research work that partly reflects the new perspective. She has made a pioneering effort at dealing with a number of concerns that naturally arose in the minds of Indians used to a largely closed-economy regime as the Indian economy began opening up in the early 1990s. Dr.Jain's research establishes the urgency of further research work to aid the design of future reforms to enable the Indian Financial System to face the challenges of rapidly globalising and integrating financial market environment.

The author has contributed to our knowledge base in at least four broad areas. First, a framework has been established to analyse the impact of external financial flows on major components of the domestic financial system. Second, she provides an excellent overview of the nature, composition and trends in international financial flows, especially of private non-debt flows, especially to emerging markets and India. Third, the empirical analysis of the impact of external financial flows on India's macro-economic variables and different components of the Indian Financial

System is the main contribution of the book. Finally, she provides an indication of the gaps in data that constrain rigorous research in these areas.

Using statistical tools, the author finds very weak correlation between FII investment and percentage variation in money supply (M3), between FII investment and percentage variation in WPI (inflation rate) and between FII inflows and current account deficit as percentage of GDP. The author observes that real exchange rate in India has depreciated during the FII inflow period.

With regard to the capital market, the major findings are that though net FII investment affected equity price indices movement with a lag and share returns are positively correlated (but not so high) with FII investment, FII investment has not increased share price volatility during the study period. Also, only about 5 per cent volatility in share return is explained by volatility of FII inflows.

With regard to the banking sector, Dr. Jain finds that India has not experienced rapid credit expansion during periods of strong FII inflows and there is no significant difference in investment as percentage of GDP during FII flow period as compared to pre-FII flow period. According to the study, the overall financial sector vulnerability has not increased.

Some of these conclusions are contrary to the apprehensions generally expressed at the inception of economic reforms and also to what the author refers to as theoretical expectations. To my mind, the conclusions are not surprising given that the magnitude of FII inflows so far have been very small relative to the size of the Indian economy and that the policy making and regulatory authorities have worked successfully in introducing reforms to contain the risks of opening up to FII inflows.

The author has made a comprehensive set of suggestions for further reforms to enable the Indian Financial System to attract and sustain larger foreign portfolio investment inflows and minimise the risks associated with such flows. While many of the suggestions are already under implementation, the research findings reported in the book will facilitate our understanding of the requirements of the overall management of the financial sector and the macro-economy in the face of progressively larger foreign portfolio investment in India. Since we have already entered the era of rapid globilisation of financial markets aided by information, internet and telecommunications technologies and rapid spread of risk management products, further quantitative research work is needed. I earnestly hope that Dr. Jain's book encourages greater interest among economists in research work in this area of research. Therefore, I commend the book to both policy makers, practitioners and academicians.

Basudeb Sen

DR. BASUDEB SEN

Chairman & Managing Director

Industrial Investment Bank of India Ltd.

Preface

The Indian economy was in the grip of foreign exchange liquidity crisis in 1991. This forced the government to undertake radical structural economic reforms in the field of foreign trade policy, industrial policy and continue the fiscal reforms with an emphasis on reducing 'fiscal deficit' in addition to reducing the revenue deficit and monetised deficit. It was realised, however, that these structural reforms will not have their intended impact on the economy unless the financial sector is also reformed on the lines of supply side economics philosophy. It was felt necessary to introduce reforms in the financial system consistent with the reforms introduced in other areas.

Restructuring process of Indian financial system was undertaken partly in the light of rigidities and weaknesses that had developed in the financial system. These had to be addressed to enable the financial system to play its role in ushering in a more efficient and competitive economy. The restructuring process aimed to correct distortions and weaknesses that had crept in, maintain and sustain growth and attain international competitiveness on account of globalisation. International integration was another factor that motivated the process to restructure the financial system.

The process to restructure Indian financial system - an integral part of the macroeconomic stabilisation and structural change program - has been accompanied by a surge of financial flows to India. With the relaxation of restrictions on foreign investments since 1991, India's equity market has attracted significant non-debt financial resources from FII's such as mutual funds, pension funds and insurance companies seeking international asset diversification. Driven by a number of factors (external and internal) these financial flows pose risks to financial systems. These flows can cause a meltdown, like the South-East Asian meltdown in 1997, if domestic financial institutions are not properly supervised or if short-term borrowings are used for long-term investments. Several countries that have received substantial financial flows have faced costly banking crisis. Therefore, it is necessary to restructure our financial system so that it can absorb too much inflows, cope with sudden outflows, can handle risks posed by these flows and can avoid costly banking crisis.

Indeed, the process to restructure the Indian financial system shall not be complete in the absence of policies to attract, absorb and sustain these flows and to deal with the risks posed by these flows. Thus, to make sure that the process of restructuring Indian financial system takes place at optimum pace, it is necessary to analyse the impact of the global financial flows at macro level.

The present work attempts to study the impact of international financial flows on Indian financial system. Based on the analysis, the work attempts to spell out restructuring that is needed in Indian financial system in response to financial flows.

The book consists of *ten* chapters. Chapter one introduces the concept of financial flow and financial system and gives an overview of the study. Chapter 2 analyses the changing nature and composition of international financial flows, recent trends in international financial flows and issues concerns raised by international financial flows of the 1990's. The trends and patterns in financial flows to India since the 1990s particularly private non-debt flows have been examined in Chapter 3. Chapter 4 reviews some of the studies on financial flows and its impact on financial system. Chapter 5 examines the impact of the flows on Indian financial system. An overview of India's attempts in 1990's to restructure its banking sector is presented in chapter 6 and chapter 7 gives insight into Indian initiatives in 1990's to restructure its capital markets. Chapter 8 presents the restructuring that is needed in Indian financial system to attract and sustain international financial flows. Chapter 9 covers the Indian experience on the management of financial flows and the restructuring that is needed in Indian Financial System to minimise the risks posed by international financial flows. The final Chapter 10 summarises the findings of the study and contains the concluding observations of this study and tasks ahead to ensure financial system stability in the light of financial flows.

I record my deep sense of gratitude to Prof. V.K. Bhalla, Faculty of Management Studies, University of Delhi without whose guidance this study would not have been possible. I am also grateful to Prof. Shirin Rathore, Joint Director, University of Delhi South Campus, Prof. Muneesh Kumar, Head, Department of Financial Studies, University of Delhi and Prof. S.P. Gupta, Dean Faculty of Management Studies, University of Delhi for their continued support and encouragement.

I also express my thanks to Prof. L.C. Gupta, Director Society for Capital Market Research and Development and Prof. P.K. Jain, IIT Delhi for their valuable comments.

I am also thankful to Prof. R.S. Nigam, Former Head, Department of Commerce, Delhi University for motivating me and Dr. C.P. Gupta, Reader Shri Ram College of Commerce, Delhi University for his intellectually stimulating discussions with me.

I owe a deep sense of gratitude to Unversity Grants Commission for their generous help in financing the study. I am very much thankful to Dr. Basudeb Sen for writing an encouraging foreword to this work.

I pay my gratitude to my father in law, Shri J.B. Jain and my mother in law Smt. Shimla Jain as their blessings enabled me to complete the work. I place on record my indebtedness to my parents Shri G.P. Gupta and Smt. Sneh Lata Gupta for providing me moral support during the study.

Lastly, I owe a special word of appreciation for my husband Dr. Naveen Jain, my children Ayush & Geetika and all other members of my family for their patient endurance during the course of the study.

Nidhi Jain

List of Tables

1

Introduction

FINANCIAL FLOWS

The term financial flow is rather broad and includes within its ambit private flows, official flows, debt flows, non-debt flows, bilateral flows, multilateral flows. Infact, all the entries that appear in the capital account of the balance of payments of a country represents financial flows. Accordingly financial flow includes direct foreign investment, portfolio investment, external commercial borrowing, grants, assistance from IMF, World Bank etc., NRI deposits, export credits, commercial bank lending etc.

Several definitions of financial flows are given in literature. OECD defines financial flows as " financial flows include portfolio investment and direct investment". The term portfolio investment, here, refers to bilateral portfolio investment by non-banks and banks resident in the donor country, in particular, syndicated and non-syndicated bank lending, the purchase of equity where no direct investment is made, the purchase of bonds issues by developing countries and the purchase of real estate. The amount of bank lending excludes any transactions by banks for which the amounts have been entered under direct investment, guaranteed export credits, or the unguaranteed portion of guaranteed export credits. Direct investment, according to

OECD definition, refers to the change in the net worth of the subsidiary to the parent company as shown in the book of the latter. When a subsidiary's capital is held by several parent companies, the investment is allocated pro-rata according to the percentage of the combined equity capital held by each investment in a developing country through a non-operational subsidiary company in a third country (e.g. the Cayman Islands) is reported as being made by the developed country in which the parent company is located.

Salomon Brothers define financial flows as – "Financial flows include borrowings, total portfolio investment and direct foreign investment". In this definition, borrowings are bonds, private placements, medium term notes, certificates of deposits (CD's), commercial paper, trade financing (both imports and exports), leasing facilities and term bank lending. And, total portfolio investment, as per this definition, is country funds, investments in equity, depository receipts and direct investment in stock markets. The direct foreign investment, here, refers to cash inflows from privatisation and debt conversion swaps for equity investment.

Another definition as given by IFR defines financial flows as – "Financial flows include international borrowings". International borrowings, as per this definition, is each country's international banking loans and bonds, whether public or private, which occurred during the period. Borrowers are listed by country of origin, even where transaction is raised by an international financing subsidiary based offshore.

We may broadly classify the international financial flows as private flows and official development flows. Private financial flows are those that take place through commercial banks, saving institutions, insurance companies, pension funds, international security houses and other financial institutions. In addition to institutional arrangements, commercial suppliers and manufacturers also provide export credit. Foreign direct investment and foreign portfolio investment also constitute other forms of private financial flows.

International movement of capital and surpluses may also come from official sources. Official sources can be subdivided into two categories - first government and government agencies forming direct channel of capital flows and second international organisations such as World Bank and other multilateral development banks called multilateral lenders. Official flows range from grants and highly concessional loans on humanitarian grounds to loans on nearly commercial terms. Loans and grants made on concessional financial terms from official sources with the objective of promoting economic development and welfare is popularly called ODA or Official Development Assistance. ODA may be divided into bilateral assistance/flows and multilateral assistance/flows. Direct flows between Development Assistance Committee (DAC) government and the governments or government agencies of the developing countries are termed as bilateral assistance/flows. Assistance from international organisations such as World Bank, Asian Development Bank and other multilateral development institutions is termed as multilateral assistance flows.

The private flows can be further subdivided into two categories private debt flows e.g. commercial borrowing, trade credit etc. and private non-debt flows viz. foreign direct investment and foreign portfolio investment.

In the light of the growing importance of private, non-debt financial flows vis-à-vis other flows[1] this book looks broadly at financial flows that are (i) private, and (ii) non-debt flows. Thus, in this book the term financial flow refers to foreign direct investment and foreign portfolio investment. ODA, IMF, bilateral, multilateral assistance are official, hence not considered. Likewise, commercial borrowing, NRI deposits, trade credits represent debt flows and hence are not considered. Grants are not considered as they are official flows. External commercial borrowing (ECB) represents debt and hence is not considered.

Though the present study looks at private, non-debt financial flows viz. foreign direct investment (FDI) and foreign portfolio investment (FPI) the focus is on FPI. This is because FDI has different characteristics and implications as compared to FPI. FDI flows, by their nature, tend to be 'long term' in that they are driven by positive, longer-term sentiment and, therefore, more likely to be 'stable' compared with 'short-term' portfolio flows. In addition, to the extent that FDI entails physical investment in plant and equipment it is difficult to reverse.[2] Moreover, FDI is not intermediated through the domestic banking system and hence there is no accompanying expansion in domestic credit (Calvo, Leiderman & Reinhart (1994)).

World Bank (1996) observes that although many of the impacts of FPI can be similar to FDI, portfolio investment can have a much greater effect on domestic capital markets and interest rates. Whereas FDI raises issues of real sector investment regimes, portfolio flows raise issues of financial and capital market regimes and their management. Portfolio investment touches more on issues of disclosure, accounting and auditing than does direct investment.

Beckerman and Das (1998) opine that direct foreign investment and direct portfolio investment induce different types and degrees of macroeconomic perturbation direct foreign investment brought into an economy to finance the full amount of a simultaneous capital equipment import ought to have no effect on money supply. A capital inflow of this kind is self-sterilising since the transaction affects neither the money nor foreign-exchange supplies, and so, in itself generates no monetary perturbation. In contrast, portfolio investment, when used to purchase equities in the secondary market or to repay domestic debt, induces exchange-rate appreciation, generates money expansion and increases equity values. On balance, however, the latter kind of capital flow is likely to present the largest problem for macroeconomic policy. Since nature and impact of FDI is different from nature and impact of FPI, the study focuses on FPI.

Foreign portfolio investments in India have taken place through the route of GDR's, off-shore funds and FII. Monthly data on GDR and off-shore funds has not been complied by RBI or any other source for the first few years and was not available. So, the book has got focussed at some places on FII Investment for which monthly data was available from the date such flows began in India viz. January 1993.

INDIAN FINANCIAL SYSTEM

Conceptually, the term Indian financial system is rather broad and includes within its ambit banks viz. commercial banks, co-operative banks; development financial institutions viz. IDBI, IFCI, ICICI; insurance companies viz. LIC, GIC; investment trusts viz. UTI, money market viz. treasury bills market, call money market, commercial bills market; capital market viz. stock exchanges, new issues market. Infact, the Indian financial system includes the complex of institutions and mechanism which affects the generation of savings and affects its transfer to those who will invest. It is made up of all those channels through which savings become available for industrial investment. It is a set of complex and closely intermixed financial institutions, financial markets, instruments, services, practices and procedures.

The present study focusses on two segments of the Indian financial system viz. the banking sector and the capital market. This is because banks are directly or indirectly intermediating a large proportion of private flows (World Bank, 1997) and because a growing proportion of flows to developing countries is being channelled through their capital markets in the form of portfolio equity capital [World Bank (1997)]. Since the banking system and the capital market are playing a leading role in allocating private financial flows, the present study looks at the impact of financial flows on banking system and capital market. In addition, the study also looks at the impact of financial flows on macroeconomy because country experience with financial flows reveals that it has led to inflation, real exchange rate appreciation, widening of current account deficit etc. and BIS (1996) holds that high inflation can lead to financial fragility[3] and an unsustainable exchange rate can increase the risk of financial fragility[4]. It further holds that macroeconomic instabilities and high inflation have frequently been a cause of poor performance of banking sector. Thus, because high inflation, unsustainable exchange rate have important implications for robustness of financial system, the book also looks into the impact of financial flows on macroeconomy. Thus, this book highlights the impact of financial flows on banking sector, capital market and macroeconomy.

THE STUDY

The main objective of the present study is to ascertain the restructuring that is needed in Indian financial system in response to international financial flows. For this purpose an attempt is made to specifically determine the following:

i) Whether the Indian economy has got overheated as a result of financial flow to India.

ii) What has been impact of financial flows on equity price movement, volatility of share prices and share returns?

iii) Whether there has been a lending boom in India during the period when there has been a surge of financial flow to India?

iv) Whether an increase in lending activity by banks has exacerbated macroeconomic vulnerability and financial sector vulnerability in India?

v) What restructuring should be undertaken in Indian financial system in response to financial flows i.e. to attract and sustain these flows and to minimise the risks posed by international financial flows.

To empirically ascertain the impact of financial flows (particularly FII flows) on financial system (viz. capital market, banking sector and macroeconomy), the following null hypothesis have been formulated:

1. Financial flows have had no impact on economic growth in India.
2. Financial flows have had no impact on inflation in India.
3. Financial flows have had no impact on current account deficit in India.
4. Financial flows have had no impact on real exchange rate in India.
5. Financial flows have not led to macroeconomic overheating in India.

6. Financial flows have had no impact on money supply in India.
7. Financial flows have had no impact on volatility of share prices in India.
8. Financial flows have had no impact on volatility of share returns in India.
9. Financial flows have had no impact on bank lending as a percentage of GDP in India.
10. Financial flows have had no impact on consumption as a percentage of GDP in India.
11. Financial flows have had no impact on investment as a percentage of GDP in India.

In the present study a number of variables have been studied depending on the objective. For example, to ascertain whether Indian economy has got overheated or not, four variables have been studied viz. economic growth, inflation, current account deficit and real exchange rate[5]. These four variables have been chosen as symptoms of overheating.

To analyse the impact on the money supply consequent to financial flows, the behaviour of money supply as represented by M_3 (Broad money), has been examined.

Further, the impact of financial flow on equity price movement was studied by examining the behaviour of BSE Sensitive Index (base 1978-79 = 100). The Reserve Bank All India Index number of ordinary share prices (Base 1980-81 = 100) was the variable whose behaviour was studied to ascertain volatility of share prices and share return.

To ascertain whether India has experienced a lending boom during financial-flow episode, the variable studied is - Bank Lending as a percentage of GDP. Since data on bank lending to the private sector was not available from

RBI or its publications, the study used Bank Credit to Commercial Sector (including RBI credit to commercial sector and other banks' credit to commercial sector) as a proxy variable for bank lending to the private sector. This lending was expressed as a percentage of GDP at factor cost at current prices. And to ascertain whether an increase in lending activity by banks has exacerbated macroeconomic vulnerability, two variables were studied - consumption and investment. Macroeconomic vulnerability has been associated with overconsumption and underinvestment. To ascertain over/under consumption, total consumption (public plus private) has been expressed as a percentage of GDP at factor cost at current prices. Similarly, Gross Domestic Capital formation (GDCF)(by households, private corporate sector and public sector) adjusted for errors and omissions has been taken into account to ascertain over/under investment for India. GDCF was expressed as percentage of GDP at factor cost at current prices to measure over/under investment in India.

Finally, to ascertain whether an increase in lending activity by banks has exacerbated financial sector vulnerability four parameters were studied in respect of all scheduled commercial banks in India - capitalisation, level of provisions, non-performing assets and profitability position. Financial sector vulnerability being inversely related to capitalisation ratio, provisions and contingencies, profitability ratio and directly related to NPA levels. These parameters have been measured thus:

i) Capitalisation: is measured as the stock of capital plus reserves and surplus relative to the stock of bank assets.
ii) Level of provisions: Provisions and contingencies have been expressed as percent to total assets.
iii) NPA level: Gross and Net NPA's have been

examined as percent to Advances and as percent to total assets.

iv) Profitability: has been examined in terms of gross profit/loss as percent to total assets; net profit/loss as percent to total assets and net interest income (spread) as percent to total assets.

A time period of fourteen years - from 1985 to 1999 - has been chosen to do hypothesis testing on the variables selected for the study. 1985 has been chosen as the initial year since the process of liberalisation in India began in 1985 with the Rajiv Gandhi Government at the helm of affairs. This time period has been classified into two categories for hypothesis testing:

i) Period from 1985 to 1992 (when calender years are considered) or 1985-86 to 1991-92 (when financial years are considered). This period represents the pre-financial flow period, more particularly, pre-FII-flow period, and

ii) Period from 1993 till 1999 (when calender years are considered or 1992-93 onwards (when financial years are considered). This period represents during-financial flow period or during FII-flow period.

The period 1992 has been taken as break-point since FII flows to India began from January 1, 1993.

The above period of fourteen years has been shortened at both sides in some cases depending upon availability of data.

The same time period has been considered to calculate coefficient of correlation and coefficient of variation. Where relationship with FII investment is worked out the period of study is 1993 onwards till 1999 since FII's began operating in India since January 1993 only.

For ascertaining financial sector vulnerability the period studied is 1992-93 onwards since comparable data was not available for pre-flow period.

To determine whether there has been a significant difference in the variables studied in the financial flow period as compared to pre-financial flow period, two tests were used viz. t-test for independent samples and Levene's test - the former was used to test for equality of means while the latter was used to test for equality of variances. Hypothesis testing was done at 95% level of confidence and two-tail significance levels were considered.

To measure the volatility of share prices, share return and financial flows, coefficient of variation was chosen as a measure of volatility rather than standard deviation because it being a relative measure, permits comparability amongst variables which standard deviation does not. And, the correlation coefficient was employed to study whether two variables are related or not, e.g., FII investment and BSE index, FII investment and money supply etc.Excel computer package was also used during the study.

The data on macroeconomic variables and banking variables has been obtained from secondary sources. RBI publications viz. Report on Currency and Finance(various issues), Handbook of Statistics on Indian Economy, Report on Trend and Progress of banking in India(various issues), Statistical Tables relating to Banks in India(various issues), RBI Bulletin(various issues) being the data source on all macro-economic and banking variables except real exchange rate. Data on nominal exchange rate and CPI (India and US) has been obtained from International Financial Statistics

(International Monetary Fund). Data on FII investment on a monthly basis has been obtained from SEBI.

CONCLUSION

The book focusses on private non-debt financial flows to India and it studies these flows from 1990 to 1999. It also analyses the impact of financial flows on Indian financial system (i.e. macroeconomy, capital market and banking sector). Finally, the book attempts to enumerate the policies that India needs to adopt to attract and sustain these flows and to tackle the risks posed by these flows

NOTES

1. The private non-debt flows to developing countries were 17.3 billion US dollars during 1983-90. By the end of 1997 this figure rose to 152.9 billion US dollars - an increase of almost nine times. In contrast, private debt flows to developing countries were 17.7 billion US dollars during 1983-90. By the end of 1997, this figure rose to 103.2 billion US dollars - an increase of about six times.

   Even the capital inflow profile of India has undergone a major shift in composition from debt creating capital inflows in favour of non-debt creating foreign investment flows. On a net basis, the sum of two major long term debt creating flows, namely external assistance and commercial borrowing, have declined from an average of $4.5 billion per annum during 1990-92 to $2.28 billion in 1994-95. In contrast total foreign investment flows, direct and portfolio, rose sharply from $0.16 billion in 1991-92 to $4.9 billion in 1994-95.
2. The events surrounding Mexican crisis help support this view. Even as portfolio flows to Latin America fell from a net inflow of $61 billion during 1994 to approximately zero in 1995, substantial net inflows of FDI continued, actually increasing from $24 billion to $25 billion. The experience during Asian crisis provides additional evidence in support of this view. In the face of a massive turnaround of bank lending flows of $73 billion to the affected Asian countries and a notable decline in portfolio flows of $8.5 billion, FDI flows declined by a relatively modest $2.4 billion during 1997.

3. Low inflation can help in avoiding financial fragility. In an environment of high inflation bank lending becomes riskier and development of longer-term securities markets is inhibited. By producing high inflation gains from non-remunerated liabilities, high inflation can encourage new financial institutions to enter an already saturated market. Moreover, financial institutions tend to concentrate on short-term transactions, preferring treasury operations over loans. The quality of financial sector assets thus suffers because credit assessment skills atrophied. This was evident during earlier episodes of hyper inflation in Argentina and Brazil.
4. A sustainable exchange rate can reduce the risk of financial crisis. The longer an unrealistic exchange rate is maintained the greater will be the chance that finance flows to the wrong sector and the higher will be the subsequent costs of dislocation. This will be especially true if a reversal of short-term capital flows forces a large and sudden adjustment. Indeed, several financial crisis in Latin America have been triggered by very abrupt exchange rate changes.
5. In accordance with the World Bank (1997) study, these four variables have been chosen. These variables have been measured thus:(i) Economic Growth— Economic growth has been measured in terms of GDP at factor cost at current prices;(ii) Inflation—Percentage variation in wholesale prices index for all commodities with base 1981-82 = 100 has been taken as a measure of inflation. The average of weeks wholesale price index has been taken into account for all commodities; the basic advantage of this measure of inflation is its high frequency availability that enables continuous monitoring for policy decisions. It is more broad based in that it covers all commodities. (iii) Current account deficit (CAD)-CAD as reported in balance of payments has been expressed as a percentage of GDP at factor cost at current prices; and, (iv) Real Exchange Rate-This has been computed by adjusting nominal exchange rate (end of the period) for inflation differential on the basis of CPI (1990 = 100).

2

International Financial Flows

International financial flows refer to all those flows that appear in the capital account of balance of payments. These flows are not a new phenomenon—this is evident in an IMF study (1997) on international capital movements which traces capital flows to emerging markets since the gold standard era (which lasted from 1870 to 1914) upto the 1990's. Obstfeld and Taylor (1997) provide a view of such flows in a sample of twelve countries since 1870. The extent of global financial flows since 1870 as exhibited in Table 2.1 provides clear evidence of the fact that international financial flows are not a new phenomenon but have existed since a long time.

Bayoumi (1989) and Taylor (1996) also provide statistical evidence on high capital mobility in the late 1800s and early 1900s.

INTERNATIONAL FINANCIAL FLOWS - PRE 1990 EXPERIENCE

Capital was highly mobile in the gold standard era (1870-1914). Financial flows during this period were evident between a set of major capital exporting countries (the United Kingdom and to a lesser extent France and Germany) and a set of emerging markets.[1] When measured relative to GDP, private capital flows of this period were quite

TABLE 2.1

Extent of Global Financial Flow Since 1870 (Mean Absolute Value of Current Account, 12 Countries, Selected Periods, Percent of GDP)

	ARG	*AUS*	*CAN*	*DNK*	*FRA*	*DEU*	*ITA*	*JPN*	*NOR*	*SWE*	*GBR*	*USA*	*All*
1870-1889	18.7	8.2	7.0	1.9	2.4	1.7	1.2	0.6	1.6	3.2	4.6	0.7	3.7
1890-1913	6.2	4.1	7.0	2.9	1.3	1.5	1.8	2.4	4.2	2.3	4.6	1.0	3.3
1914-1918	2.7	3.4	3.6	5.1	–	–	11.6	6.8	3.8	6.5	3.1	4.1	(5.1)
1919-1926	4.9	4.2	2.5	1.2	2.8	2.4	4.2	2.1	4.9	2.0	2.7	1.7	3.1
1927-1931	3.7	5.9	2.7	0.7	1.4	2.0	1.5	0.6	2.0	1.8	1.9	0.7	2.1
1932-1939	1.6	1.7	2.6	0.8	1.0	0.6	0.7	1.0	1.1	1.5	1.1	0.4	1.2
1940-1946	4.8	3.5	3.3	2.3	–	–	3.4	1.0	4.9	2.0	7.2	1.1	(3.2)
1947-1959	2.3	3.4	2.3	1.4	1.5	2.0	1.4	1.3	3.1	1.1	1.2	0.6	1.8
1960-1973	1.0	2.3	1.2	1.9	0.6	1.0	2.1	1.0	2.4	0.7	0.8	0.5	1.3
1974-1989	1.9	3.6	1.7	3.2	0.8	2.1	1.3	1.8	5.2	1.5	1.5	1.4	2.2
1989-1996	2.0	4.5	4.0	1.8	0.7	2.7	1.6	2.1	2.9	2.0	2.6	1.2	2.3

Notes: Annual Data. Parentheses denote average some countries missing.

Source: Obstfeld .M. and Taylor, A.M. (1997), "The Great Depression as Watershed" International Capital Mobility over the Long Run, NBER working paper 5960.

large. The main capital exporter, United Kingdom, for example, saw annual capital outflows averaging almost 5% of GDP over 1880-1914, with levels at times reaching 7% and even 9% in the years before World War I. Among capital importers, similarly, Australia saw annual inflows averaging 9.5% of GDP between 1881 and 1890 [IMF (1997)].

Between 1919 and 1930, global financial flows were highly mobile. During this period United States was a major capital exporting country; United Kingdom's lending during this period was focussed on its colonies. The financial flows during this period were procyclical and made the system far less stable and more prone to crisis [IMF (1997)].

In these periods (1870-1914) and the 1920's divergent macroeconomic developments in capital-exporting and capital-importing countries often generated a boom - bust pattern of financial flows that was sometimes accentuated by crisis in capital-importing countries. Both these were periods when financial flows were highly mobile and both these periods ended by major economic or political events (i.e. World War I and the great depression respectively).

Due to the disruption associated with the great depression and World War II there was a marked downturn in financial flows to emerging market[2] economies during 1930-1950. Similarly, between 1950 and 1972 financial flows to emerging markets were marginal as many countries maintained capital controls during this period[3].Official financial flows and foreign direct investment dominated the limited flows of financial resources between mature and emerging market economies during 1950 and 1972.

In contrast to the limited flows in the 1950s and 1960's, the period since 1973 has witnessed net private financial flows to emerging markets amounting to nearly US $1.32 trillion. Nonetheless the pattern of flows has been highly uneven, with an initial surge of inflows in the 1973-82 period ($163 billion), followed by a collapse of the flows during the rest of the 80's ($103 billion), and then renewed surge in 1990's. The financial flows that took place between the first oil crisis of 1973 and 1982 were closely associated with the recycling of oil revenues Bank loans were the principal instruments for intermediating these flows, and balance of payments data suggest that such loans (including trade credits) accounted for 57% of total flows.

The emergence of debt servicing difficulties in many heavily indebted emerging market countries in mid-1982 brought to an abrupt halt the inflow of private capital. Net private financial inflows fell from a peak of nearly $49 billion in 1981 and $19 billion in 1982 to only $9 billion inflow in 1983 and a $5 billion outflow in 1984.[4] Net private inflows to all emerging markets recovered modestly in the 1986 to 1989 period (averaging roughly $20 billion a year).[5]

INTERNATIONAL FINANCIAL FLOWS IN THE 1990'S: DIFFERENT FROM EARLIER FLOWS

The 1990's has seen a resurgence of international financial flows to developing countries in Asia and Latin America. The financial flows of the 1990's are substantial - both in absolute amount and relative to GDP. The present study focuses on the international financial flows of the 1990's. A number of studies conducted in 1990s to study the international financial flows of the 1990s pointed out the departure of international financial flows of 1990's from the earlier flows. Most of these flows are private in nature - they are flowing from private hands to private hands. The share of official flows (aids, grants, ODA) in total flows has declined.

Even in private flows, the share of debt (viz. commercial bank lending) has declined and non-debt (FDI and FPI) has surged [Cherunilam and Thomas (1996)]. There is a shift from debt to equity financing and from bank to non-bank sources [Gooptu and Ahmed (1993)]. The flows are not equally distributed. 73% of foreign investment went to just 12 countries, the top five country destinations being China, Mexico, Indonesia, Malaysia and Brazil [World Bank, Global Development Finance (1997)]. Bulk of financial flows - 70% have gone to Asia and Latin America [Hernandez and Rudolph (1995)].

Another distinguishing feature of international financial flows of the 1990's is the rapidly rising share of portfolio flows in total flows. Portfolio flows (in the form of bonds, equities, GDR, direct purchase on securities markets) have recently been the fastest growing form of external finance for developing countries accounting for one-fifth of all financial flows to developing countries [Gooptu and Ahmed (1993)].

The investor base and range of instruments of international financial flows have widened in 1990s and recipients of financial flows have also changed. Whereas in 1970's, capital flowed mainly to sovereign and parastatal borrowers, in 1990's, capital is flowing to private sector in recipient countries [Gooptu (1996)] [Reisen (1996)].

Thus, the nature and composition of financial flows has changed in the 1990's. Financial flows in 1990's have not been pulled by deficit running government budgets and public enterprises but essentially by private investors and private firms. Private flows outpace official flows in the 1990's, share of aid in financial flows has declined in 1990's, commercial bank loans—an important flow in 1970's - has disappeared since debt crisis of 1980's; the share of debt in private financial flows has declined and the share of non-debt (FDI and FPI) has increased; there is a spurt in inflow of portfolio investment.[6]

FACTORS STMULATING INTERNATIONAL FINANCIAL FLOWS IN THE 1990'S

The international financial flows of the 1990's (their size and composition) have been influenced by a number of factors. A number of empirical studies have sought to identify the key factors driving these flows in the 1990s. These studies have typically divided the factors influencing financial flows in the 1990's into so-called push and pull factors. Push factors are the factors in the global economy and pull factors refer to factors in the emerging markets. The studies have identified the push factor as global interest rates and pull factor as improvements in countries economic fundamentals and seek to establish whether the flows are driven by cyclical factors (at the international level) or structural factor (at the country level). The debate is on whether the surge in private financial flows to developing countries since the 1990's is essentially a temporary phenomenon, driven in large part by cyclical factors in the international economy, or the result of longer-term structural changes, which would suggest that private capital flows will be sustained.

As private capital flows to developing countries began to surge in early 1990's, coinciding with declining global interest rates, it was generally assumed that these flows are driven primarily by cyclical conditions in industrial countries. This assumption was supported by Calvo, Leiderman and Reinhart (1993) and Fernandez-Arias (1994).

Chuhan, Claessens and Mamingi (1993), on the other hand, found that improvements in country's economic fundamentals (-the country credit rating, secondary bond price, the price-earnings ratio in domestic stock markets, and the black market premium-) were as important as cyclical factors in attracting portfolio flows to Latin America. Domestic factors, moreover, were three to four times more important in explaining financial flows in Asia. Schadler et al. (1993) reaffirmed the importance of the 'pull' factors by observing that the timing of the relevant external (push) factors did not coincide with the surge of private financial flows in each recipient country. Moreover, the persistence and intensity of the inflows has varied across recipient countries. There has been a geographical variation in the distribution of these flows with over 80% of the private financial flows between 1989-94 going to a score of countries. This suggests the important role of domestic factors in determining the size and composition of private financial flows to developing countries.

The prevailing view in the early 1990's was that cyclical factors - downturn in industrial countries and the associated decline in global interest rates - in the international environment were the driving force of private financial flows to emerging markets. The persistence of these flows inspite of global interest rate increases in 1994 and the Mexican peso crisis in 1995 and South East Asian crisis in 1997, suggests that they are being driven by factors other than international cyclical factors [World Bank (1997)]. More recent work-suggests that there are structural forces at work. More specifically, World Bank (1997) found that US interest rates played an important role in driving portfolio flows during 1990-93. Since 1993, however, the relative role of international interest rates has declined and country specific factors have become more important in Latin America and East Asia. Country-specific factors have become particularly important in East Asia. Global interest rates are not significant in explaining FDI flows which are more sensitive to country's macroeconomic fundamentals.

The factors driving international financial flows to developing countries in the 1990's may be listed as :

i) cyclical downturn in global interest rates.

ii) higher long-term expected rates of return in developing countries as a result of policy reforms and improved credit worthiness.

iii) the opportunities that developing countries provide for risk diversification because of low correlation between returns in developing and industrial countries.

The first factor provided the initial impetus for financial flows to developing countries in the 1990's. The latter two factors reflect the structural forces that are at work in driving these flows to developing countries. Although, these forces have always motivated investors, international financial flows have gained momentum in the 1990's as a result of internal and external financial deregulation in both industrial and developing countries and major advances in information technology, communications and financial instruments [World Bank (1997)].

SURGE IN PRIVATE FLOWS IN 1990S

As a result of these changes, developing countries have seen a strong surge in private financial flows. FDI has responded most vigorously to the improving economic environment in developing countries. The driving force for FDI has been the sustained improvement in domestic economic fundamentals. The driving force behind the portfolio flows of the 1990's has been institutional investors including mutual funds, insurance companies, pension funds and more recently hedge funds. The growing role of institutional investors in the 1990's and their desire both to increase overall return on their portfolio and to diversify the risks associated with these portfolios has led to increased portfolio flows to developing countries in the 1990s. The advances in information technologies have allowed international investors to manage the risks associated with internationally diversified portfolios more easily. The management of interest rate, exchange rate and more recently credit risks associated with these portfolios has also been facilitated by the emergence of a variety of new derivative products. These developments have thus created incentives for international investor, especially institutional investors, to deal in an increasingly broad range of instruments issued by private borrowers in emerging markets.

US $404.9 billion has been official development finance to developing countries during 1990-97 whereas US $1192.8 billion has been private flows to developing countries.[7] This reveals that private flows have surged in 1990's , are more important as compared to official flows.

Even in private flows, non-debt flows are more important as compared to debt flows (see Table 2.2).

TABLE 2.2

Total Private Flows to Developing Countries

(US $ Billions)

	1990	*1991*	*1992*	*1993*	*1994*	*1995*	*1996*	*1997*
Debt Flows	15.0	13.5	33.8	44.0	41.1	55.1	82.2	103.2
Non-Debt Flows	26.9	40.1	56.3	110.6	119.5	134.0	164.8	152.9
FDI	23.7	32.9	45.3	65.6	86.9	101.5	119.0	120.4
FPI	3.2	7.2	11.0	45.0	32.6	32.5	45.8	32.5
Total Private Flows	41.9	53.6	90.1	154.6	160.6	189.1	246.9	256.0

Source: World Bank, Global Development Finance, 1998, Analysis and Summary Tables (Washington DC, 1998), p. 3.

Thus, US $387.9 billion have been private debt flows (commercial bank loans, bonds etc.) to developing countries during 1990-97 while private non-debt flows amounted to US $805.1 billion i.e. 32% of private flows to developing countries are debt flows while 68% of private flows to developing countries have been non-debt flows.

In private non-debt financial flows, US $595.3 billion has been FDI flow to developing countries during 1990-97 while US $209.8 billion has been portfolio equity flows to developing countries. Though a major amount has flowed to developing countries in the form of FDI, yet portfolio equity flows exhibit a rapid increase - there is a tenfold increase in portfolio equity flows whereas FDI recorded a five-fold increase between 1990 and 1997

FINANCIAL FLOWS TO EMERGING MARKET ECONOMIES: 1991-2000

Trends in financial flows to emerging market economies reveals that the bulk of such flows are private in nature. Total private capital flow into emerging markets from 1991-1998 was US $1196.4 billions as compared to US $172.1 billion official flow (see table 2.3). Private flows, have been almost seven times the flow on official account during 1991-98. A pick up in net private capital flows to emerging market economies is projected in the years 1999 and 2000 with such flows expected to rise to US $66.7 billion in 1999 and 145.4 billion US $ in 2000 from 64.3 billion in 1998. Net private capital flow during 1999 and 2000 is projected to be around nineteen times the net official flow to emerging market economies.[8] It can also be observed that sharp rise in portfolio flows accounted for bulk of private flows to emerging market economies till 1994. Since 1995, however, bulk of private capital flow is due to net direct investment.

An analysis of geographical distribution of these flows during 1991-98 (see Table 2.4) reflects that the western hemisphere has received the largest proportion 33.9% and Asia has secured the next largest chunk at 31%. By contrast,

TABLE 2.3

Emerging Market Economies: Net Capital Flows[1]

(U.S.$ Billions)

	1991	1992	1993	1994	1995	1996	1997	1998	1999[8]	2000[8]
Total										
Net private capital flows[2]	123.8	119.3	181.9	152.6	193.3	212.1	149.1	64.3	66.7	145.4
Net direct investment	31.3	35.5	56.8	82.7	97.0	115.9	142.7	131.0	116.7	123.3
Net portfolio investment	36.9	51.1	113.6	105.6	41.2	80.8	66.8	36.7	8.0	44.2
Other net investment	55.6	32.7	11.5	–35.8	55.0	15.4	–60.4	–103.4	–58.0	–22.1
Netofficial flows	36.5	22.3	20.1	1.8	26.1	–0.8	24.4	41.7	8.0	2.9
Change in reserves[3]	–61.5	–51.9	–75.9	–66.7	–120.2	–109.1	–61.2	–34.7	–22.6	–75.1
Memorandum										
Current account[4]	–85.1	–75.6	–116.0	–72.0	–91.0	–91.8	–87.1	–59.2	–39.4	–58.7
Africa										
Net private capital flows[2]	8.9	6.9	8.7	4.8	6.8	7.6	16.3	10.3	11.9	16.8
Net direct investment	2.0	1.7	1.9	3.4	4.2	5.5	7.6	6.8	8.0	8.3
Net portfolio investment	–1.5	–0.6	1.0	0.8	1.5	–0.2	2.9	3.5	1.0	2.1
Other net investment	8.4	5.8	5.8	0.7	1.2	2.3	5.8	–	2.9	6.4
Net official flows	7.8	10.5	7.8	14.0	10.8	3.7	–4.5	1.5	0.2	1.1
Change in reserves[3]	–2.5	0.8	0.8	–4.7	–1.7	–7.4	–12.3	2.9	–1.0	–4.6
Memorandum										

	1991	1992	1993	1994	1995	1996	1997	1998	1999[8]	2000[8]
Current account[4]	–7.4	–10.4	–11.0	–11.8	–16.4	–5.7	–6.1	–18.1	–19.7	–17.4
Asia[5]										
Crisis countries[6]										
Net private capital flows[2]	26.8	26.6	31.9	32.2	62.5	62.4	–19.7	–45.3	–25.7	–11.1
Net direct investment	6.1	6.3	6.7	6.5	8.7	9.5	12.1	4.9	8.6	8.3
Net portfolio investment	3.4	5.3	16.5	8.3	17.0	20.0	12.6	–6.5	–3.3	5.9
Other net investment	17.3	15.0	8.7	18.4	36.9	32.9	–44.5	–43.6	–30.9	–25.4
Net official flows	4.4	2.0	0.6	0.3	0.7	4.8	25.0	22.7	0.3	0.6
Change in reserves[3]	–8.3	–18.1	–20.6	–6.1	–18.3	–13.6	37.7	–39.1	–25.1	–20.2
Memorandum										
Current account[4]	–25.2	–16.1	–13.5	–23.2	–40.5	–53.4	–27.0	66.6	50.9	31.3
Other Asian emerging markets										
Net private capital flows[2]	7.2	–8.7	25.5	33.2	32.6	38.1	22.8	–9.6	–6.7	14.0
Net direct investment	8.3	8.5	26.3	38.7	41.1	45.6	50.5	45.1	32.2	37.8
Net portfolio investment	–2.0	2.6	4.5	1.1	–6.1	–7.5	–11.8	–8.8	–13.3	–8.3
Other net investment	0.9	–19.7	–5.4	–6.6	–2.4	0.1	–15.8	–45.9	–25.6	–15.5
Net official flows	6.5	8.3	7.9	5.1	3.8	5.3	3.3	5.9	4.1	6.0
Change in reserves[3]	–31.4	–7.6	–17.2	–47.7	–26.2	–42.5	–46.3	–9.7	1.5	–12.6
Memorandum										

Current account[4]	23.7	14.0	–8.5	–17.1	9.4	17.0	37.5	30.5	22.4	14.9
Middle East and Europe[7]										
Net private capital flows[2]	68.6	35.1	33.7	15.4	10.1	6.8	16.7	26.5	25.6	20.5
Net direct investment	1.2	0.9	3.9	3.8	3.7	2.4	3.3	2.9	4.5	5.9
Net portfolio investment	22.3	13.5	21.8	13.6	9.4	4.1	4.3	8.8	8.0	10.4
Other net investment	45.1	20.7	8.0	–2.0	–3.0	0.4	9.1	14.7	13.1	4.2
Net official flows	3.9	–1.3	2.3	–1.3	–1.4	–0.7	–1.0	–2.2	–2.1	–3.2
Change in reserves[3]	–3.3	1.2	–4.8	–3.6	–12.7	–16.2	–20.4	–5.3	–4.9	–5.8
Memorandum										
Current account[4]	–64.2	–26.7	–31.1	–7.2	–5.2	5.4	2.9	–22.7	–19.1	–15.1
Western Hemisphere										
Net private capital flows[2]	24.1	55.9	62.6	47.5	38.3	82.0	87.3	69.0	38.3	82.5
Net direct investment	11.3	13.9	12.0	24.9	26.1	39.3	50.7	54.0	45.6	43.7
Net portfolio investment	14.7	30.3	61.1	60.8	1.7	40.0	39.7	33.0	2.1	23.2
Other net investment	–2.0	11.7	–10.6	–38.2	10.6	2.7	–3.1	–18.1	–9.4	15.7
Net official flows	2.7	–1.7	0.6	–4.1	–20.6	–13.7	–7.8	1.6	2.6	–3.2
Change in reserves[3]	–17.4	–22.6	–21.3	4.2	–25.5	–28.3	–14.6	17.7	20.5	–18.0
Memorandum										
Current account[4]	–16.9	–34.5	–45.7	–50.9	–35.9	–38.9	–65.1	–89.9	–60.7	–61.7

	1991	1992	1993	1994	1995	1996	1997	1998	1999[8]	2000[8]
Countries in transition										
Net private capital flows[2]	–11.7	3.5	19.6	18.5	42.9	15.1	25.7	13.6	23.3	22.6
Net direct investment	2.4	4.2	6.0	5.4	13.4	13.5	18.5	17.4	17.8	19.2
Net portfolio investment	–	0.1	8.8	21.0	17.8	24.4	19.0	6.7	13.6	10.9
Other net investment	–14.1	–0.7	4.8	–8.0	11.7	–22.8	–11.9	–10.6	–8.1	–7.6
Net official flows	11.1	4.5	0.9	–12.2	–8.5	–0.2	9.3	12.2	2.9	1.6
Change in reserves[3]	1.3	–5.6	–12.8	–8.7	–35.8	–1.0	–5.3	–1.2	–13.5	–13.9
Memorandum										
Current account[4]	4.8	–1.7	–6.3	3.9	–2.4	–16.2	–29.3	–25.6	–13.2	–10.7

1. Net capital flows comprise net direct investment, net porfolio investment, and other long-and short-term net investment flows, including official and private borrowing. Emerging markets include developing countries, countries in transition, Korea, Singapore, Taiwan Province of China, and Israel. No data for Hong Kong SAR are available.
2. Because of data limitations, "other net investment" may include some official flows.
3. A minus sign indicates an increase.
4. The difference between the current account and the sum of net private capital flows, net official flows, and change in reserves is the capital account and errors and omissions.
5. Includes Korea, Singapore, and Taiwan Proviance of China. No data for Hong Kong SAR are available.
6. Indonesia, Korea, Malaysia, the Philippines, and Thailand.
7. Includes Israel.
8. IMF Staff projections

Source: IMF, World Economic Outlook, May 1999, p. 40-41.

only 8.9% of the flows have gone to Africa, around 10.5% to countries in transition and 15.4% to Middle East and Europe. This uneven geographical distribution has also been pointed out in the IMF projections. Accordingly for the years 1999 and 2000, the western hemisphere will attract 53.92% of total net capital flows. Countries in transition will receive next largest chunk i.e. 22.61% of total net capital flow. Middle East and Europe will attract 18.30% of total capital flow while Africa will receive 13.45% of total capital flow. In contrast, flows to Asia are projected to decline substantially amounting to outflows to the tune of US $18.5 billion i.e. Asia is expected to experience outflow amounting to 8.29% of total capital flow to emerging market economies in the years 1999 and 2000.

TABLE 2.4

Distribution of Net Capital Flows

(US $ billions)

Region	*Private Flow*	*Official Flow*	*Total Flow*
Africa	70.3	51.6	121.9
Asia			
Crisis Countries[1]	178.4	60.5	238.9
Other Asia	141.1	46.1	187.2
Middle East & Europe	212.9	-1.7	211.2
Western Hemisphere	466.7	-1.8	464.9
Countries in transition	127.2	17.1	144.3
Total	1196.6	171.8	1368.4

[1] Indonesia, Korea, Malaysia, Phillipines and Thailand

Table 2.3 reflects the drop in net capital flows to emerging market economies in 1994, 1997 and 1998. This drop has been mostly associated with the unfolding of the Mexican crisis and a rise in US interest rates in 1994 and with the South-East Asian crisis during 1997 and 1998. The most affected region being Western Hemisphere in 1994 and

East Asia in 1997, 1998. During 1997 total private capital flows to all regions (viz. Africa, Middle East and Europe, Western Hemisphere and Countries in Transition) increased except for Asia where such flows fell from US $100.5 billions in 1996 to US $3.1 billion in 1997. In 1998, except for Middle East and Europe all other emerging market economies experienced decline in net private capital flows. In Middle East & Europe net private capital flows increased to US $26.5 billion in 1998 from US $16.7 billion in 1997.However, the net private capital flows are expected to pick up in 1999 in Africa, Asia and countries in transition and decline in Middle East & Europe and Western Hemisphere. The 1999 trend is likely to continue into the year 2000 for all countries except Western Hemisphere (where such flows are projected to increase in the year 2000 from US $38.3 billion in 1999 to US $82.5 billioin in 2000) and countries in transition (where net private capital flows are expected to decline to US $22.6 billion in the year 2000 from US $23.3 billion in the year 1999).

ISSUES/CONCERNS RAISED BY INTERNATIONAL FINANCIAL FLOWS OF THE 1990S

Financial flows that are large relative to GDP carry with them certain macroeconomic risks. Some of the risks that a surge in financial flows produces are an appreciation of real exchange rate, an inflationary expansion of domestic money and an unsustainable current account deficit. A sudden and large outflow can, inter alia, produce an exchange rate crisis.

The key short-run macroeconomic concern associated with a surge in financial flows is that of an excessive expansion of aggregate demand - that is, macroeconomic overheating. [World Bank (1997)]. This outcome can be produced through the following transmission mechanism:

- If a country maintains an officially determined exchange rate, the commitment to defend the parity causes the central bank to intervene in the foreign exchange market to purchase the foreign exchange generated by the financial flow. To do so, the central bank creates high-powered domestic money.
- This expansion of the monetary base creates a corresponding expansion in broader measures of the money supply, domestic interest rates and raising domestic asset prices.
- This action in turn triggers an expansion of aggregate demand. If the economy possesses excess capacity, the short-run implications may be to increase domestic economic activity and cause the current account of the balance of payments to deteriorate. Eventually, however (and perhaps rather quickly if domestic excess capacity is limited), excess capacity will be absorbed and the expansion in demand will trigger an acceleration in domestic inflation.
- If the exchange rate peg is maintained, rising domestic prices will cause the real exchange rate to appreciate, abetting the current account deterioration associated with the expansion in aggregate demand.

Thus, by expanding the monetary base, non-FDI capital inflows can lead to an increase in aggregate demand, thus generating inflationary pressures. If the nominal exchange rate is fixed, domestic inflation raises the relative price of non-traded goods and the real exchange rate appreciates. Excess aggregate demand and real exchange rate appreciation would tend to widen the current account deficit of the balance of payments. Inflation and a deteriorating current account position could send adverse signals to long-term external investors about the government's ability to maintain macroeconomic stability (Asian Development Outlook, 1995 and 1996).

Foreign investment may lead to an increase in the volatility of domestic asset prices and returns. This is because with financial openness, domestic capital markets are exposed to new external financial shocks (or these shocks may be transmitted more quickly across borders), such as changes in global interest rates, spillover effects from foreign stock markets and investor herding. Some of these external shocks, particularly changes in global interest rates and certain stock market spillover effects, make asset prices and returns more volatile by affecting fundamentals of an emerging market. But other shocks, such as investor herding and pure contagion effects may change investment in a country even though its fundamentals are unaffected. These shocks are often the result of foreign portfolio investors having little access to information, worsening information asymmetries. Perversely, the improvements in liquidity may make emerging markets more susceptible to external financial shocks, since better liquidity reduces transaction costs and makes it easier for foreign investors to open and liquidate positions [World Bank (1997)].

Information asymmetries may also increase volatility through interaction effects between domestic and foreign investors e.g. a defensive reaction by local investors to the sale of domestic securities by foreign investors, who in turn are responding to events overseas, may magnify the impact of foreign stock market spillover effects on the domestic market. Since local investors generally do not know why foreign investors are changing their holdings, they may react to such changes even though the fundamentals of the domestic market have not changed.

Similarly, information asymmetries could result in foreign investors magnifying the impact of behaviour of domestic agents [World Bank (1997)].

Thus, financial flows may affect fundamental volatility and excess volatility[9] of asset prices and returns. Increased susceptibility to fluctuation in global interest rates and foreign stock markets increases fundamental volatility of asset prices whereas excess volatility of asset prices may increase due to:

i) increased susceptibility to herding behaviour by international investors and cross-country contagion, and

ii) interaction effects between domestic and foreign investors because of incomplete or asymmetric information that magnifies fluctuations.

A surge in financial flows may increase bank lending. While an expansion in lending is generally beneficial, a very rapid expansion in lending can result in a loosening of credit conditions. Under these circumstances of extreme liquidity due to rapid capital inflows, the search for investments may lead banks to extend credit to less profitable ventures or to less credit worthy borrowers. The history of banking crisis in industrial and developing countries alike has shown that certain types of lending particularly real estate finance, lending backed by shares, consumer credit, and loans to bank insiders or related parties - have been more important sources of risk than others.

A surge in bank lending may exacerbate macroeconomic vulnerability. [World Bank (1997)]. This is because a surge in bank lending will be associated with a deterioration in bank's portfolio where banks are poorly managed and supervised. Such poorly managed and supervised banks tend to invest in highly profitable although risky activities. For example, poorly regulated banks may finance consumption booms and speculative activities, such as a boom in construction and real estate, that increase macroeconomic vulnerability. Thus, in countries where credit institutions are not well regulated and supervised and where there are poorly enforced penalties for misallocating credit and mismanaging balance sheets, capital inflows will create further opportunities for banks to expand lending and to expose the financial system to large potential losses. In pursuing a policy of non sterilisation in such weak systems, the authorities run the risk of later having to provide liquidity to, or to recapitalise banks that become illiquid or insolvent as a result of poor management. Moreover, in the event of a reversal of capital flows, weak banks would especially become vulnerable. Owing to poor credit ratings, weaker financial institutions would be unable to access interbank or capital markets and would need public support to remain viable. The history of bank crises, including recent crises in some industrial countries clearly demonstrates how high the public costs can be of such rescue operations.

In countries where the banking system is sound and efficient and where there are effective regulatory and supervisory controls, capital flows are less likely to create additional risks to the financial system. In these countries, banks have the ability when extending loans to anticipate, at least to some extent, the effect of capital flows on their borrowers ability to pay. This ability allows banks to price their loans accordingly, to accumulate reserves against potential loan losses and to reduce the concentration of their loan portfolios to sectors that are more sensitive to capital flows.

If financial flows take place when banking system is weak they could result in banking crisis. Thus, **financial**

flows may lead to lending boom and this lending boom may exacerbate financial sector vulnerabilities if banks are weak i.e. they have a poorly diversified portfolio and lack adequate provisioning [World Bank (1997)].

A rapid growth in bank lending can lead to misallocation of resources, financial distress and banking crisis, especially when conditions in banks are weak, banks are poorly managed, supervised and regulated.

In addition to the increased credit risk generated by the expansion of banks balance sheets, financial flows generate a number of risks in the banking sector of recipient countries. Banks frequently assume market risks - exchange rate, interest rate, equity price risks - that cannot be fully hedged. For example, there are frequent instances where banks, as major foreign borrowers, carry a significant foreign exchange exposure[10] and where banks are exposed to volatility in equity prices by holding sizable equity portfolios.

A sudden and large outflow can, inter alia produce a liquidity problem brought on by the need to refinance a large volume of short-term external debt and difficulties in the banking system caused by the increase in domestic interest rates.

Thus international financial flows of the 1990s raise a number of concerns for the recipient countries. One, a surge in financial flows may overheat the economy. Second, it may increase volatility of asset prices and returns. Third, it may lead to a lending boom which can exacerbate macroeconomic and financial sector vulnerability.

CONCLUSION

International financial flows are not a new phenomenon. The book focuses on the international financial flows of the 1990's as these flows show a marked departure from the earlier flows. The push and full factors are stimulators for these flows in the 1990's. Further, it is observed that developing countries have seen a strong surge in private financial flows in 1990's and that international financial flows of the 1990's may overheat the economy, increase volatility of asset prices and returns and lead to a lending boom which may exacerbate macroeconomic and financial sector vulnerability

NOTES

1. There were two major capital importing country groups. One group, consisting of countries in North America, Latin America (viz. Argentina, Brazil and Mexico) and Oceania (Australia) received capital primarily from the United Kingdom and used it in large part for development finance. The other group consisting of countries in Eastern and Central Europe, Scandinavia, the Middle East, and Africa, was provided finance mainly by France and Germany, often of a non-developmental nature to cover fiscal gaps.
2. The term emerging markets is used to describe the group of countries comprising developing countries, countries in transition and advanced economies of HongKong, China, Israel, Republic of Korea, Singapore and Taiwan Province of China. This is a broader interpretation than is used in many other contexts [IMF (1997)].
3. The purpose of controls was to retain domestic capital within a country or to prohibit foreign capital from entering. Fears of inflation (due to loss of control of money supply), as well as changes in currency value also spurred tight regulation.
4. This abrupt slowdown in lending and in some cases reversals of capital transfers, were even more dramatic for heavily indebted emerging markets in the Western hemisphere, which together saw net private inflows decline from a peak of $46 billion in 1981 and $16 billion in 1982, and then reverse, to outflow of $9 billion and $2 billion in 1983 and 1984, respectively.
5. The Western Hemisphere, however, experienced virtually no net private inflow during that four years period.
6. Portfolio equity flows to developing countries were absent prior

to 1982. The average annual portfolio flows to developing countries, which was $1.3 billion during 1983-90 shot upto $46.9 billion in 1993.

7. World Bank, Global Development Finance 1998, p. 3.
8. US $212.1 billion private flow as compared to US $10.9 billion official flow during the year 1999 and 2000.
9. Excess volatility in asset prices is volatility not due to changes in fundamentals.
10. The gross foreign liabilities of commercial banks have expanded rapidly in many capital importing countries. In Malaysia, foreign liabilities as percentage of GDP increased from 7% to 19% between 1991 and 1993, in Indonesia, it increased from 2% of GDP in 1989 to 6% in the following year. For Mexico it increased from 8% in 1991 to 13% in 1994 and in Thailand, it increased from 4% in 1988 to 20% in 1994.

3

Financial Flows to India

Historically, financial flows to India have been low, discouraged by a tight regulatory regime as well as a highly distorted economy. Prior to 1991, financial flows to India predominantly consisted of external assistance, commercial borrowing and non-resident Indian deposits (Table 3.1). During the 1990's, foreign investments have increased quite dramatically from US $103 million in 1990-91 to US $4,993 million in 1997-98 - an increase of almost 48 times. It has, however dropped in 1998-99 to US $ 2412 million. The importance of external assistance, however, has declined steadily during the 1990s (Table 3.1). Total external assistance declined from US $ 2210 million in 1990-91 to US $820 million in 1998-99. Commercial borrowings, too, have been on the decline since 1990-91 to 1992-93. At the end of 1998-99, however, commercial borrowings stood at US $ 4362 million and were higher as compared to US $2248 million in 1990-91. NRI deposits have also been on the decline - declining from US $1536 million in 1990-91 to US $1125 million in 1997-98. It has however picked up in 1998-99 (see table 3.1). Thus, during 1990-91 to 1998-99, we find that whereas external assistance has declined, however, commercial borrowing NRI deposits and foreign investment has increased during this period. Moreover, though commercial borrowings have recorded an increase during the 1990's, the most rapid increase has

TABLE 3.1

Capital A/c

(US $ million)

	1986-87	1987-88	1988-89	1989-90	1990-91	1991-92	1992-93	1993-94	1994-95	1995-96	1996-97	1997-98	1998 99
Capital Account	4,512	5,047	8,064	6,977	7,188	3,777	2,936	9,695	9,156	4,678	11,287	10,984	8,260
A) Foreign investment	195	434	357	410	103	133	557	4,235	4,807	4,604	5,838	4,993	2,412
B) Externalassistance, net	1,414	2,271	2,216	1,856	2,210	3,037	1,859	1,901	1,526	883	1,109	899	820
C) Commercial Borrowings, net	1,966	976	1,894	1,777	2,248	1,456	–358	607	1,030	1,275	2,848	3,999	4,362
D) Rupee Debt Service	0	0	0	0	–1,193	–1,240	–878	–1053	–983	–952	–727	–767	- 802
E) NRI Deposits, net	1,290	1,419	2,510	2,403	1,536	290	2001	1205	172	1103	3350	1125	1742
F) Other capital	–353	–53	1,087	531	2,284	101	–245	2,800	2604	–2235	–1131	735	-274
Memorandum items													
Current account	–4,560	–4,852	–7,997	–6,841	–9680	–1178	–3526	–1158	–3369	–5899	–4494	–6473	-4038
Overall balance	–47	195	68	136	–2492	2599	–590	8537	5787	–1221	6793	4511	4222
Change in reserves (Increase-,Decrease +)	573	737	1001	740	1278	–3385	–698	–8724	–4644	2936	–5818	–3893	-393

Source: Handbook of Statistics on Indian Economy, Reserve Bank of India, December,1998, 1999.

been in foreign investment, which has increased 25 times as compared to commercial borrowings, which have increased around two-fold (see table 3.1).

The main reasons for the rapid increase in foreign investments in India in the 1990's have been external factors and internal factors. External factors have encouraged foreign investment flows to developing countries and include both cyclical and structural factors. Cyclical factors include depressed global demand for capital and low anticipated rates of return for most assets in industrial countries due to their slow and uneven recovery. Structural factors include the growing importance of professional investment managers in allocating savings, the increasingly global availability of information, and the introduction of instruments to hedge against different sort of risks. These factors have promoted the diversification of international portfolios. Dynamic growth performance and prospects, an investor friendly environment and high domestic interest rates relative to international levels - are the internal factors that have attracted foreign investments to developing countries. The large inflows under both foreign direct and portfolio investment into India reflected sound economic fundamentals and a congenial policy environment. Specifically, the following internal factors have been responsible for an increase in foreign investment flows to India in the 1990's.

- Adoption of a market-oriented approach to foreign investment as part of the economic reform program launched in 1991. Till 1991, foreign companies wishing to invest in India were generally restricted to 40% equity participation, subjected to requirements on technology transfer and limited to priority areas. Foreign portfolio investment was channelled almost exclusively into a limited number of public sector bond issues, while foreign equity holdings in Indian companies were not permitted. In 1991, however, approval for direct investment participation upto 51% in priority areas was made automatic, while the criteria for approval were liberalized more generally.

- Liberalization of restrictions on foreign portfolio investment. In February, 1992, it was announced that Indian firms in good standing would be allowed to raise funds through equity and convertible bond issues in Euromarkets and in September 1992, registered FII's were allowed to purchase both equity and debt securities directly on local markets.
- Foreign investors found Indian stocks particularly attractive for risk diversification purposes given the relatively low degree of correlation (around 28%) between the Bombay Stock Exchange Sensex index and the S&P 500 as compared to other major emerging markets. [Collyns Charles (1995)]
- The structural reforms launched in 1991 enhanced the growth prospects of the corporate sector. Particularly relevant were the elimination of industrial licensing restrictions, liberalization of trade regime, and the opening up to the private sector of a number of activities previously reserved for the public sector.
- Portfolio investments into India have responded to both 'pull' factors (internal factors) and 'push factors' (external factors). While the "pull factors" included the strength of economic fundamentals and banking and financial sector reforms leading

> to growing cross border financial integration, the main "push factors" were the continuing slack in certain industrial country markets and swings in asset prices in those countries forcing investors to look for diversification, subdued inflationary conditions in industrial countries prompting investors suffering from "money illusion" to invest in developing countries in search of higher yields, and worldwide access to quality information facilitating investment decisions in global markets.

India has succeeded in attracting a growing share of FDI inflows into developing countries due to progressive relaxation of norms of equity participation and dividend repatriation announced and implemented since 1991, recent restructuring of Foreign Investment Promotion Board (FIPB) and setting up of Foreign Investment Promotion Council for fast approval.

As a result of these factors there has been an increase in foreign investment flows - Portfolio investment and FDI - to India in the 1990's. The total amount of private non-debt flows to developing countries in the 1990's and India's share in such flows is depicted in Table 3.2. Whereas India was receiving 0.3% of total private non-debt flows to developing countries in 1991, by 1997 this figure had increased to 3.5%. Thus, we find that not only have foreign investment flows to India shown a rapid increase in 1990's but that India's share in private non-debt flows to developing countries has also shown an increase in the 1990's.

TABLE 3.2

India's Share in Private Non-Debt Creating Flows to Developing Countries, 1991-97

US ($ billion)

Category	*1991*	*1992*	*1993*	*1994*	*1995*	*1996*	*1997**
Total private non-debt creating	40	56	111	120	133	165	152
(India's Share %)	(0.3)	(1.0)	(3.7)	(4.2)	(3.7)	(3.4)	(3.5)
Foreign Direct Investment	33	45	66	87	101	119	120
(India's Share %)	(0.3)	(1.0)	(0.9)	(1.5)	(2.3)	(2.3)	(2.3)
Portfolio Equity Investment	7	11	45	33	32	46	32
(India's Share %)	(0.3)	(1.0)	(7.9)	(10.2)	(10.1)	(6.3)	(7.8)

* Projected

Source: Report on Currency and Finance, Vol. 1, 1997-98, Reserve Bank of India.

The magnitude of private, non-debt flows to India in the 1990's is depicted in Table 3.3. Private, non-debt flows to India have recorded a 20 times increase during 1990-99. Such flows to India have shot up dramatically from $103 million in 1990-91 to US $5138 million in 1994-95, slightly dropped in 1995-96 to US $4881 million, again rose in 1996-97 to US $6008 million. However, since than such flows have declined (Table 3.3). The decline is mainly due to a decline in portfolio investment flows, which can be attributed partly to turbulence in the Indian foreign exchange market in the second half of 1997-98. Till 1992-93, direct investment was relatively more important than portfolio investment constituting 68% of total flow during this period. Since 1993-94 to 1996-97, portfolio investment was relatively more important than direct investment constituting 67% of total flow during this period. During 1997-98 and 1998-99, direct investments have once again become relatively more important as compared to portfolio investment - 75% of total flow during this period is in the form of direct investment and 25% in the form of portfolio investment (Table 3.3).

TABLE 3.3

Private Non-Debt Financial Inflows to India

Year	*A.Direct Investment*		*B.Potfolio Investment*		*Total (A+B)*	
	Rs.Crore	*($ mn)*	*Rs.Crore*	*($ mn)*	*Rs.Crore*	*($ mn)*
1990-91	174	97	11	6	185	103
1991-92	316	129	10	4	326	133
1992-93	965	315	748	244	1,713	559
1993-94	1838	586	11,188	3,567	13,026	4,153
1994-95	4126	1314	12,007	3,824	16,133	5,138
1995-96	7135	2133	9,192	2,748	16,327	4,881
1996-97	9571	2696	11,758	3,312	21,328	6,008
1997-98	11824	3197	6,696	1,828	18,520	5,025
1998-99	—	2062	—	-61	—	2,001

Source: Handbook of Statistics in Indian Economy, Reserve Bank of India, December, 1998.

A category-wise breakdown of direct investment flows into India in the 1990's and portfolio investment flows into India in the 1990's is presented in Table 3.4. Much of the private, non-debt flows into India during 1990-99 are accounted for by portfolio investment. Out of the total financial flow to India of about US $28,897 million during 1990-99, US $15,472 million or 54% was on account of portfolio investment. Further, portfolio flows have increased at a faster rate as compared to direct investment in India. Portfolio investment rose from $6 million in 1990-91 to 1828 million in 1997-98 recording three hundred times increase. Direct investment, on the other hand, increased from $97 million in 1990-91 to US$ 3557 million in 1997-98 – an increase of thirty six times.

TABLE 3.4

Private Non-Debt Financial Flows To India: Category-wise Break-up

(US $ million)

	1990-91	*1991-92*	*1992-93*	*1993-94*	*1994-95*	*1995-96*	*1996-97*	*1997-98*	*1998-99*
A. Direct Investment	97	129	315	586	1314	2144	2821	3557	2462
a) Government (SIA/FIPS)	–	66	222	280	701	1249	1922	2754	1821
b) RBI	–	–	42	89	171	169	135	202	179
c) NRI	–	63	51	217	442	715	639	241	62
d) Acquisition of Shares*	–	–	–	–	–	11	125	360	400
B. Portfolio Investment	6	4	244	3567	3824	2748	3312	1828	–61
(i) GDRs	–	–	240	1520	2082	683	1366	645	270
(ii) FII's	–	-	1	1665	1503	2009	1926	979	-390
(iii) Offshore funds & others	6	4	3	382	239	56	20	204	59
Total (A+B)	103	133	559	4153	5138	4892	6133	5385	2401

* Relates to acquisition of shares of Indian companies by non-residents under Section 29 of FERA, data on such acquisition have been included as part of FDI since January 1996.

Source: RBI Bulletin, July 1999, Pg. S 726

Portfolio investment flows in India have come in various forms such as issuance of Global Depository Receipts (GDRs) by Indian Corporates, investment by foreign institutional investors in equity and debt instruments (both corporate and government securities) and through floating of off-shore funds. In portfolio investment flows to India during 1990-99, FII's have occupied predominant place, closely followed by GDR issues and off-shore funds represent a very small percentage of total flow of portfolio investment. Specifically, within portoflio investment flows to India during 1990-99, FII's had a share of 50%, GDR's 44% and off-shore funds 6% — US $ 7693 million, US $6,806 million and US $973 million being the inflow on account of FII's, GDR issues and off-shore funds respectively (Table 3.4 given earlier).

Portfolio investment flows to India witnessed a dip in 1995-96. This dip occurred due to a fall in portfolio flows to emerging markets following monetary tightening in industrial countries particularly the USA and the fall-out of the Mexican crisis of December 1994. Further, portfolio investment flows to India declined substantially during 1997-98 and 1998-99. The decline in portfolio flows from 1997-98 onwards is mainly on account of lower offerings of GDR issues and sharp decrease in investment by FII's. The amount raised under GDR's fell due to pessimistic sentiments prevailing in domestic stock-exchanges. The slackening of investments by FII's was mainly on account of currency turmoil in South East Asia — contagion effect. The decline in portfolio investment since 1997-98 is a consequence of both - enhanced emerging market risk-perception, and the depressed condition of the domestic capital market.

FII INVESTMENT FLOWS TO INDIA IN 1990'S - TRENDS

Portfolio investment by FII's began in 1992-93. It surged in 1993-94 to US $1.67 billion and was maintained in 1994-95 at US $1.50 billion (Table 3.4). These flows, however, slackened in the first part of 1995-96 in the wake of the December 1994 Mexican crisis. From December 1995 there was a resurgence of portfolio investment by FII's. The rapid growth in FII investment continued during April-December 1996. Portfolio investment by FII's in 1996-97 at US $ 1.93 billion was only marginally lower than US $2.0 billion in 1995-96 . It is, however, significantly lower in 1997-98 having fallen to US $979 million. This partly reflects transitory contagion effect of the currency turmoil in some of the countries of South East Asia. The trend of decline in flows of FII intensified in 1998-99 with an outflow of US $390 million in 1998-99 .

The trend in monthly net investments by FII's in India are shown in Table 3.5. The table reveals that for the first time since FII's began investing in Indian securities market in January 1993 monthly net investment by them became negative in November 1997. However, the net outflow of FII investment, which started in November 1997, was reversed in February 1998. During each of the first seven months in the financial year 1998-99 except April, July, and September net FII investment was negative. Since November 1999, however, net FII investment into India has turned positive.

A look at net FII investment into equity market and debt market reveals that FII's have played a more active role in the equity market in India as compared to debt market.[1] In 1997-98, 89.8% of FII investment was in equity market and 10.2% was in 100% debt. In 1998-99, 84.2% of FII investment was in equity market and 15.8% in 100% debt. The amount actually invested in equity and debt segment is given in Table 3.6.

While net FII investment in equity was positive in six months during 1998, that in debt was negative in all months except February and March 1998. Since January 1999, however, net investment by FII's in equity have largely been positive, except during August-October 1999 when

TABLE 3.5

Net Investments* by FII'S in Indian Capital Market

(Rs. crore)

Year	Apr.	May	June	July	Aug.	Sept.	Oct.	Nov.	Dec.	Jan.	Feb.	Mar.	Total
1992-93	—	—	—	—	—	—	—	—	—	0.56	0.29	3.42	4.27
1993-94	4.71	41.39	95.95	148.54	298.67	166.76	195.27	1,087.27	565.30	1,233.60	787.13	820.01	5,444.58
1994-95	525.39	882.00	816.37	328.23	424.65	422.94	544.30	61.88	26.16	232.32	293.10	199.26	4,776.59
1995-96	186.58	203.03	360.37	647.88	548.19	410.18	320.98	191.45	412.59	739.48	1,621.48	1,092.65	6,735.01
1996-97	1,471.34	1,033.13	1,046.29	879.93	150.09	373.24	404.36	402.91	423.36	343.24	424.98	491.20	7,444.07
1997-98	625.66	870.09	1,405.18	996.00	501.43	581.63	651.11	–279.93	–182.90	–373.40	618.71	559.36	5,972.96
1998-99	167.75	-559.49	-897.49	104.67	-410.23	95.03	-566.90	43.42	306.96	360.34	349.47	199.91	-806.56
1999-2000	825.25	1528.25	456.70	159.19	14.09								

* Both by way of debt and equity.

Source : Handbook of Statistics on Indian Economy, RBI, Dec. 1998, 1999.

there was net FII outflow. The net investment of FII's in debt became negative from June-September 1999 apart from February 1999.

TABLE 3.6

Net FII Investment

(US $ million)

	Month	*Equity*	*Debt*	*Total*
1997	March	189.6	8.1	197.6
	April	140.1	23.3	163.4
	May	199.7	13.3	213.0
	June	368.4	45.7	414.1
	July	274.2	7.1	281.3
	Auguest	149.8	(8.8)	141.0
	September	173.2	(8.5)	164.7
	October	174.9	97.0	271.8
	November	(110.6)	(37.1)	(147.8)
	December	(134.2)	(13.4)	(147.5)
	Total for 1997 (March-Dec.)	1620.1	126.6	1746.7
1998	January	(76.6)	(0.6)	(77.3)
	February	188.9	1.3	190.2
	March	114.8	68.3	183.2
	April	(8.4)	(16.4)	(24.8)
	May	(124.3)	(94.1)	(218.4)
	June	(190.5)	(7.5)	(198.0)
	July	22.2	(2.5)	19.7
	August	(90.1)	(16.8)	(106.9)
	September	45.2	(12.0)	33.2
	October	(135.4)	(5.9)	(141.4)
	November	12.9	(60.0)	(47.2)
	December	78.1	(28.8)	49.3
	Total for 1998	(163.3)	(174.9)	(338.2)
1999	January	105.0	1.6	106.6

February	79.9	(3.5)	76.4
March	29.0	36.2	65.2
April	208.3	16.3	224.6
May	394.1	10.9	405.0
June	82.0	-61.2	20.8
July	359.9	-11.3	348.6
August	-26.7	-1.5	-28.2
September	-170.1	-0.3	-170.4
October	-164.0	24.5	-139.5
November	277.0	5.9	282.9
December	363.2	9.5	372.7
Total for 1999	1537.6	27.1	1564.7

Source: Economic Survey, 1998-99, p. 58.
Economic Survey, 1999-2000, p. 66.
SEBI.

GDR ISSUES-TRENDS

There has also been an increase in the capital mobilised by Indian companies by GDR issues. Since May 1992, which was when the first GDR issue was made, till March 1999, Indian companies raised US $6.80 billion through GDR issues (Table 3.4). Inflows through the issuance of global depository receipts (GDR's) declined sharply during 1995-96. During this year (1995-96), Indian companies raised $0.68 billion as compared to $2.08 billion raised during 1994-95 (Table 3.4). During 1994-95, there were 29 GDR issues. This crowding of issues resulted in a clear oversupply of Indian paper in the international markets. With the result, prospective companies either deferred or shelved their plans of making GDR issues, fearing the possibility of having to price their issue at a steep discount over the domestic price. There was a revival in GDR floatation in 1996-97. This period also witnessed the entry of banking and financial institutional sector in the GDR issue market.[2] Since 1997-98, there is a decline in the amount mobilised by GDR issues. The amount of inflow on account of GDR issues was lower in 1997-98 as compared to the inflow in 1996-97, but was almost equivalent to the amount of inflow during 1995-96 (Table 3.4). The decline in GDR inflows in on account of pessimistic sentiments prevailing in domestic stock exchanges.[3]

CONCLUSION

There has been a rapid increase in foreign investments in India in 1990. The main reasons for the rapid increase in foreign investment are external and internal factors. India's share in private, non-debt flows to developing countries has shown an increase in 1990's. Much of the private, non-debt flows into India during 1990-99 are accounted for by portfolio investment as compared to direct investment. In portfolio investment flows to India during 1990-99, FII's have occupied a predominant place.

NOTES AND REFERENCES

Notes

1. FII's have been allowed to invest upto 100% of their funds in debt instruments of Indian comapnies through 100% dedicated debt funds, effective January 15, 1997.
2. During August 1996, ICICI floated GDR issue which raised $230 million. And, State Bank of India completed a GDR issue of $370 million in October 1996.
3. Report on Currency and Finance, 1997-98.

Some Studies on Financial Flows and Their Impact on Financial System—A Review

STUDIES ON FINANCIAL FLOWS

The 1990s have witnessed a surge of financial flows to developing countries. To analyse the flows, a number of studies have been attempted to look at the changing nature and composition of financial flows in the 1990s [Gooptu and Ahmed (1993), Gooptu (1996), Cherunilam and Thomas (1996), Singh (1996)]. Numerous attempts have also been made to study the magnitude of the flows to developing countries [Gooptu (1993), IMF: International Capital Markets: Developments and Prospects (various issues), Hernandez and Rudolph (1995), World Bank (1996) and (1997), United Nations (1997)] to emerging markets [Loon and Dijk (1995), IMF (1997), Chen and Khan (1997), IIF (1999)] and to specific regions [Chen (1992), IMF (1995), ADB (1995), Koenig (1996), Tang and Villafuerte (1995)]. Several studies look into the causes for these flows especially portfolio flows [Calvo, Leiderman and Reinhart (1993), Chuhan, Claessens and Mamingi (1993), Fernandez Arias (1994), Taylor.M. and Lucio Sarno (1997), Chuhan Punam et al. (1998), R.N. Aggarwal (1997)]. There have been some attempts to ascertain whether these flows are volatile or not [Turner (1991), Claessens, Dooley and Warner (1995)]. In addition attempts have been made to ascertain whether they pose risks to receipient countries and what policy options are available to recipient countries to deal with the risk of these flows.

Some of the studies on Financial Flows to Regions other than India are reviewed below :

IMF (1997): It examines capital flows to emerging markets from 1870 to 1996. It specifically looks at capital flows to emerging markets in the classical gold standard era which lasted till 1914, in 1973-89 after the first oil shock and at the capital flows to emerging markets in 1990s. The study also throws light on the factors that have stimulated capital flows in the 1990s. The study compares the nature and scale of capital flows to emerging market countries in the past two decades with those experienced in two earlier periods of high capital mobility : the gold standard period (1870-1914) and the 1920s. Next, the factors that influenced the scale, composition and geographic distribution of the flows to emerging market countries since the mid-1970s are examined and the recent attempts at identifying the key developments in both emerging markets and industrial countries as well as the changes responsible for the resurgence of flows in the 1990s, are reviewed. The determinants of balance of payments and banking crisis that often accompany reversals in capital inflows and speculative attacks on exchange rate arrangements have been examined. It is pointed that reversals in capital inflows have been associated with balance of payments and banking crises and it tries to identify a set of macroeconomic and financial indicators that appear to be the main determinants of such events.

IMF (1995) studies various aspects of capital flows in Asia-Pacific Economic Cooperation Council (APEC) region. It focuses on portfolio capital flows to the Developing Country members of APEC i.e. to Korea, Singapore, Taiwan Province of China, other Asian developing countries, Chile, Mexico etc. It analyses the trends and characteristics of portfolio capital flows and describes the composition and geographical distribution of capital flows. The period covered is 1990-93. Since international issuance of bonds and equities by emerging market economies reached unprecedented proportions in 1991-93, the study examines the characteristics of international transactions in bonds and equities. Further, it provides a brief analysis of the investor base as well as presents some indications of the destination of these capital flows at both the macroeconomic and microeconomic level.

World Bank (1996) traces evolution of capital flows to developing countries. It specifically looks at capital flows to East Asia. Both private and public flows to East Asia are studied from 1970-1994. The countries considered include China, Indonesia, Korea, Malaysia, Philippines and Thailand. It analyses commercial bank syndicated loans, FDI, FPI (Bonds, stock) and considers other capital flows e.g. BOT - Build-Operate transfer, BOOT - build-own-operate-transfer and BOO - build-own-operate financing to East Asia from 1970-1994. The study draws on country experiences in East Asia.

Gooptu (1993) provides an overview of the volume and structure of private cross-border capital flows to developing countries, on a global basis. Particular attention is devoted to the examination of trends in the magnitudes of three types of private capital flows to developing countries, namely, (i) external borrowing (medium and long term as well as short term). Borrowing on international markets by developing countries through bond and equity issues, syndicated loans, euro-commercial papers and medium-term note facilities, underwritten note-issuance facilities and other committed and non-underwritten facilities are studied from 1987 to September 1992. (ii) portfolio investment (i.e. country funds investing in equity, ADRs/GDRs and direct investment by entities abroad in LDC stocks and bonds), and (iii) direct foreign investment. In particular, the trends in equity and bond issues in the major developing country stock markets viz. Argentina, Brazil, Chile, Indonesia, Korea, Malaysia, Mexico, Thailand, Venezuela are examined. The study looks at gross portfolio investment flows to Middle East and N. Africa, Europe, Latin America and Caribbean and Asia from 1989 to 1992 and the destination of portfolio investment in Emerging markets (1989-1992). Gross Portfolio Debt Financing Flows to developing countries from 1989 to 1992 are also presented.

Asian Development Bank (1995) discusses different components of external resource flows viz. (i) official multilateral and bilateral sources and (ii) private sources comprising commercial bank loans, FDI and portfolio investment. The factors motivating these flows are discussed. It analyses the changing composition of external capital flows into Asia and into individual DMCs viz. Malaysia, Thailand, Indonesia, Philippines, China, India and Pakistan from 1987 to 1994. The factors underlying the surge in capital inflows (external and internal factors) and the risks they pose are also considered and various policy options and policy stances adopted by DMCs are analysed.

Loon, F.D. and Dijk, M.P. (1995) presents the net long-term resource flows to emerging markets from 1983 to 1994. Grants/loans/ multilateral/bilateral, official nonconcessionary flows, loans are the official flows that are studied. Among the private flows it looks at the trend in bonds flow, commercial banks, other private flows, foreign direct investment and portfolio equity. It also looks at capital flows (both private flows and official creditor flows) to regions viz. Latin America, Asia Pacific, Central and Eastern Europe and other (including Africa) from 1991 to 1995. The following components of total flow are briefly discussed: FDI, FPI, international bonds, international equity and commercial bank loans. The study notes two important changes in the increasing international capital flows in the 1990s viz. disintermediation effect i.e. securities such as equities and bonds have become more important than bank loans and secondly that source of financing flows in the 1990s has shifted from banks to non-banks through increased portfolio and FDI. The study highlights three disadvantages of capital flows viz. volatility of inflows, their inflationary pressure and their sustainability and suggests the following be adopted - capital controls, central bank intervention, financial derivatives, currency boards. It holds that sound domestic policies are the best way for a country to protect itself against the negative impact of capital inflows.

World Bank (1997) shows that while private investment flows to developing countries continued to grow in 1996, official flows declined. The trends in following financial flows to developing countries (i) official development finance including grants and loans, (ii) total private flows including debt (viz. commercial banks, bonds, others) and FDI and portfolio equity flow are studied from 1990 to 1996. The report held that the flows are not equally distributed among all developing countries - 73% of foreign investment went to just 12 countries, with China receiving 52% of total flows.

Gooptu, S. and Ahmed, M. (1993) look at real aggregate net resource flows (including official grants, net official loans, net private loans, FDI and portfolio equity investment) to developing countries from 1985 to 1992. It holds that there is a shift from debt to equity financing comprising FDI and portfolio investment and from bank to non-bank sources and that portfolio investment flows have recently been the fastest growing form of external finance for developing countries, accounting for one-fifth of all capital flows to developing world. Further, the study holds that these flows are heavily concentrated in a handful of economies (mainly in Latin America). Portfolio equity investment flows (subdivided into country funds, depository receipts and direct equity investment) and Bonds, CPs and CDs flows from 1989 to 1992 are also presented herein.

Pfeffermann, G. (1992) holds that attitudes towards FDI have changed considerably and that during the 1980s many countries have changed their policies to attract FDI. It gives a list of "dos" and "don'ts" that are highly relevant to developing countries such as India which are trying to attract larger flows of FDI. The "dos" and "don'ts" are discussed under following headings - screening investment proposals, investment incentives, transfer of dividends and remittances and investment promotion.

United Nations (1997) notes that the most striking development of 90s - the rapid and steady recovery of long-term financial flows to developing countries - can be almost entirely attributed to the growth in private capital flows. It looks at aggregate net resource flows to developing countries from 1986 to 1995, the data source being World Debt Tables of World Bank. It examines the trend in portfolio equity investment, FDI, private loans and bonds, official loans and official grants. Further it analyses the share of developing economies in the ESCAP region in the aggregate net resource flows to developing countries from 1990 to 1995. It finds that the shares of long-term debt and grants have been declining while the shares of FDI and portfolio flows have both been growing. Further it points that portfolio flows to ESCAP member countries have been confined to economies with functioning equity markets; they are concentrated in five countries viz. India, Malaysia, Philippines, Republic of Korea and Vietnam where they exceed one fifth of total resource flows. In Indonesia, Pakistan and Thailand the portfolio flows exceed 10% of total resource flows. ESCAP developing economies include (i) least developed countries, (ii) East and North East Asia, (iii) South East Asia, (iv) South and South West Asia, (v) North and Central Asia and (vi) Pacific island economies. The following four flows to these countries are analyzed during 1985-89 and 1990-94 (i) Net flow of public and private long-term debt (excluding IMF), (ii) FDI, (iii) Portfolio equity flows, (iv) Grants (excluding technical cooperation). In addition, it specifically looks at international equity and bond issues of selected economies in Asia and Pacific from 1993-1995 (the data source being IMF International Capital Markets) and FDI inflows to ESCAP developing economies from 1984-1995 (the data source being World Investment Report, 1996).

Chen, Z. and Khan, M.S. (1997) examines some of the basic patterns of international capital flows to emerging markets in recent years, including the composition of capital flows, intra-regional flow patterns and the geographical distribution of the flows. A theoretical model that sheds new light on these observed patterns is developed. This model focusses on the cost of financing aspect of capital flows, and shows that the patterns of capital flows are influenced by the combined effects of financial market development and growth potential in the recipient countries.On FDI, portfolio investment and other flows to developing countries in Asia and in Western Hemisphere from 1977 to 1995, it finds two notable features - one is the importance of FDI and the other is rising share of portfolio flows in the 1990s. Further, it has been observed that Western Hemisphere developing countries attracted more portfolio flows relative to FDI than Asian developing countries did; the "medium income countries" experienced more portfolio equity inflows as a percentage of the total capital inflows in recent years than the low income countries did"; and that the "low income countries" relied more heavily on official flows.

Gooptu (1996) provides an overview of recent trends in financial flows to developing countries which highlights the surge of private capital flows to a few developing countries that took place in the 1990s. In addition, it suggests some of the policy issues that one is grappling with in the context of development finance and the fruitful research agenda that emerges from the changing structure of debt and financial flows to developing countries in the 1990s.The study holds that capital flows to developing countries in the 1990s are significantly larger than the 1970s, the investor base and range of investments of private flows are wider now and that the recipients of capital flows within developing countries are also changing. Whereas in 1970s, private capital to developing countries flowed mainly to sovereign and parastatal borrowers, in 1990s the capital is flowing to private sector in recipient countries. The geographical distribution of private capital flows (1990-1994) and the major recipients of private capital flows (1991-94) are also analysed.

Arias, E.F. and Montiel, P.J. (1996) describe the characteristics of the new inflows, analyzing the policy issues they raise, assessing their causes and likely sustainability and evaluating potential policy responses. The desirable policy response is tied to characteristics of the flows themselves as well as to the characteristics of the recipient economy. To identify the characteristics of new inflow episode it looks at annual private capital flows to all developing countries from 1978-81 to 1990-93, to regions (viz. sub-Saharan Africa, East Asia and Pacific, Latin America and Caribbean, Middle East and North Africa, South Asia and Europe and Central Asia) from 1978-81 to 1990-93 and it looks at asset and sectoral composition of long-term private capital inflows from 1978-81 to 1990-93. It finds that the inflows were very large in the early 1990s compared with those in the 1982-89 debt crisis period, but somewhat smaller than in the preceding inflow episode, 1978-81. Secondly, it finds that the surge of inflows has been widespread and especially strong in East Asia and Latin America and that they have recently become important in India and Pakistan as well as in Kenya and Uganda. Thirdly, it holds that there is a shift away from debt instruments in favour of equity instruments both direct and portfolio. Within debt flows, syndicated bank loans are relatively unimportant and that portfolio flows have increased immensely in importance in contrast to entire period of 1978-89.

Reisen, H. (1996) spells out the major reasons why policy makers should be concerned about cyclical inflows, assesses the volatility of different capital-account items (bank lending, FDI and portfolio flow) and compares the recent capital flows to Asia and Latin America for similarities and differences. Specifically, it notes that unlike 1980s, capital flows were not pulled in by deficit running government budgets and public enterprises, but essentially by private investors and private firms. Unlike in the 1980s, when bank lending prevailed in both regions, risk capital has been flowing to both regions as portfolio and direct investment. Another similarity between the two regions is that high share of net flows have gone into foreign exchange reserves. It further states that the nature of FDI in two regions is different, the share and nature of portfolio flows too differ between the two regions and that lending classified as long-term by IMF is important source of capital flow in Asia but negative in Latin America.

Hernandez, L. and Rudolph, H. (1995) studies financial flows, namely, official grants, official loans, private loans, FDI and Portfolio Equity Investment to all developing countries from 1986-93 .It also examines net private long-term flows to all developing countries by region and type of flow from 1988-94. It identifies three outstanding features of the current surge of capital flows to developing countries. First the private capital flows to developing countries accelerated when international interest rates began to fall. Second, the bulk of the capital inflows - 70% - has gone to East Asia and Latin America. Third, in the 1980s syndicated bank lending was the major flow while today FDI and portfolio equity investment play a major role adding upto 68% of total private flows.

Some other studies on certain others aspects of financial flows have also received attention. These are reviewed below :

Taylor, Mark P. and Lucio Sarno (1997) focus on the determinants of the large portfolio flows from the United States to Latin America and Asian countries during 1988-92. Cointegration techniques reveal that both domestic and global factors explain bond and equity flows to developing countries and represent significant long-run determinants of portfolio flows. The study also investigates the dynamics of portfolio flows by estimating seemingly unrelated error - correction models. It holds that global and country-specific factors are equally important in determining the long-run movements in equity flows for both Asian and Latin American countries, while global factors are much more important than domestic factors in explaining the dynamics of bond flows. U.S. interest rates are a particularly important determinant of the short-run dynamics of portfolio, especially bond, flows to developing countries.

Razin, Assaf et al. (1998) highlight some key sources of market failure in the context of international capital flows and provides guidelines for efficient tax structure in the presence of capital market imperfections. The analysis distinguishes three types of international capital flows: foreign portfolio debt investment, foreign portfolio equity investment and foreign direct investment.

Agenor, Pierre-Richard (1998) examines the effects of a fall in world interest rates on capital flows and the real exchange rate in an optimizing framework with imperfect capital markets. The thrust of their analysis is that caution should be exercised before viewing 'autonomous' capital inflows as the main culprit for real exchange rate appreciation and a deterioration of the current account. Ad hoc models in which intertemporal considerations are excluded and in which capital inflows are modelled as having a large direct effect on the demand for non-traded goods and the real exchange rate can be misleading. On the basis of their analysis they conclude that whether a persistent real appreciation is observed depends crucially on the initial level of debt, and on the permanent or temporary nature of the shock.

Cardoso, Eliana and Ilan Goldfain (1998): Using the case of Brazil, the study introduces an empirical measure of capital controls and argues that the government sets capitals taking into account capital flows. It is noted that capital flows and controls are positively correlated in simple OLS regressions where foreign interest rates and contagion effects appear as the main determinants of capital flows of Brazil. It finds that capital controls are effective in the short run but have no lasting effect. VAR impulse responses provide evidence that controls do indeed reduce flows and change their composition away from equity and debt, for about six months. The casuality runs in both directions, capital controls react to capital flows within two months.

Chuhan Punam et al. (1998) investigate the factors motivating the large capital flows to a number of developing countries in recent years. They use monthly US capital flows to nine Latin American and nine Asian countries to analyze the behaviour of bond and equity flows. Employing a panel data approach, they find that although global factors - the drop in US interest rates and the slowdown in US industrial production - are important in explaining capital inflows, country specific developments are at least as important, especially for Asia. They also find that equity flows are more sensitive than bond flows to global factors, but that bond flows are generally more sensitive to a country's credit rating and secondary market debt price.

Gruben, William, C. and Darryl Mcleod (1998) examines the contributions that capital inflows may or may not make to growth in developing countries, as expressed by percentage changes in the gross domestic products of seven Latin American countries and of eleven other developing countries - most of which are Asian. There appears to be an important relation between various categories of capital flows and overall GDP growth for the sample of 18 countries examined here. The study points that the statistical relation between capital flows and subsequent growth is stronger in Latin America than among the Asian countries - where domestic savings play a more significant role in the economy. However, the relation between capital flows and subsequent growth seems not to have changed much in the 1990s. In

Latin America, essentially , growth leads to additional capital inflows whereas the relation between capital flows and growth is weaker outside Latin America. Further, the study finds that when and where capital inflows do affect growth, FDI tends to have the most pronounced positive impact on it. The correlation between FDI and growth has clear policy implications for privatization initiatives and foreign ownership restrictions. It is noted that though the sample of portfolio equity flows is much smaller, they also have a smaller but positive correlation with economic growth generally. Despite the complications that volatile capital flows create for macroeconomic and exchange rate policies, the study suggests overall positive correlation between growth and capital flows. However it may not be proper to apply lessons from Mexico's experience to other countries or to draw conclusions about the welfare impacts of capital flows from Mexico's experience alone.

Fernandez-Arias, Eduard (1996) studies the determinants and sustainability of the widespread private capital inflows to middle income countries after 1989. This pull/push issue has been addressed by developing a structural model of international portfolio allocation in which the importance of country creditworthiness is made explicit and its determinants analysed. It points that sustainability of capital inflows is vulnerable to external factors even when accompanied by improved country creditworthiness, but that soft landing is possible. An analytical model focussing on country risk is developed and used empirically. It is argued that the observed improvement in country creditworthiness is mostly due to the decline in international interest rates and that therefore its importance as a proximate cause does not support the "pull" interpretation. The study suggests that all things considered, in most countries, the key answer that emerges is `push'.

Claessens, S., Dooley, M.P. and Warner, A. (1995) observe that a distinction is often made between short-term and long-term capital flows: the former are deemed unstable hot money and the latter are deemed stable cold money. They seek to determine whether the label of the flow can be identified when only time series statistics on persistence are given. Using time-series analysis of balance of payments data for five industrial and five developing countries, they find that in most cases the labels "short-term" and "long-term" do not provide any information about the time-series properties of the flow. In particular, long-term flows are often as volatile as short-term flows and the time it takes for an unexpected shock to a flow to die out is similar across flows. Long-term flows are also at least as unpredictable as short-term flows, and knowledge of the type of flow does not improve the ability to forecast the aggregate capital account. The study holds that an attempt to reduce capital account volatility by administratively limiting short-term inflows is unlikely to be effective because there is little evidence that these flows really are more volatile than other flows.

Some of the important Studies On Financial Flows To India are listed below :

Gopinath, T. (1997) surveys the foreign investment policy since India's independence and examines the trends of foreign investment flows (which have grown substantially since 1992) in terms of number of approvals as well as the actual inflows, including country and industry-wise details of foreign investment during the period. The analysis is based essentially on the data on the FDI. A brief analysis of country and industry wise portfolio investment flows is presented to the extent such details were available. With a view to understand the factors influencing the prospective inflows, the factors analysed are: market size (measured in terms of GDP or personal disposable income), health of the host country's economy (measured in terms of forex reserves and annual average rate of inflation), risk factors [viz. gross fiscal deficit (GFD) and debt service ratio (DSR)]. The study postulates a positive relationship between forex reserves and inflow of foreign investment, a direct and positive relationship between market size variable and flow of foreign investment. A negative relationship is hypothesised between rate of inflation and flow of foreign investment and between GFD and DSR and flow of foreign investment. The data period considered is 1980-81 to 1994-95. Hypothesis is tested with the help of OLS method. The study found that signs of all independent variables are in agreement with those postulated in hypothesis. The results indicate that economic fundamentals are as important as the policies themselves in regard to attracting foreign investment.

Mani Sunil and Nandakumar Parameswar (1993) evaluates the relative importance of private loans (commercial loans) vis-à-vis FDI, as a course of external capital to India. These are viewed in the context of such flows to developing countries as a whole, trends in which, the paper points out, do not hold out much promise for India. Specifically, the study looks at official and private flows to India from 1970 to 1989. The private flows in a narrow sense consist of commercial loans, suppliers credit and borrowings from the bond market and , in a broad sense consist of essentially private flows plus net FDI and other capital investments (viz. portfolio investments). Structure of official and private flows is also analysed from 1970-89. The study notes that much of the financial flow to India in the 1980s has been debt-creating and estimates the share of debt-creating flows in total financial flows to India from 1970-89. The debt-creating flows in total financial flows are estimated by deducting the grant element in both official and private flows and also the FDI and other capital movements. Further, the study analyses, in depth, the size, structure and cost of commercial lending to India against the background of such flows to the developing world as a whole. The growth in FDI in India, the sectors in which it has played an important role are also delineated and the pros and cons of a policy of welcoming FDI are assessed. The study concludes that in the 1990s, the government has placed more emphasis on securing substantial capital flows through FDI. But developments in FDI inflows world-wide do not hold much promise for India.

Gangadhar, V. and Yadagiri, M. (1997) examines and brings out the dimensions and trends of FDI vis-à-vis actual inflows in India. The study finds that during 1991-95, the year 1995 accounted for highest number of foreign collaborations; SIA route dominated in initial years of liberalisation and FIPB route in latter years of liberalization, FDI approvals have increased significantly from 1992; inflows as a percentage of approvals showed a declining trend; the consumer sector has attracted 25.4% of FDI flow while services sector has attracted 21.1%. It is felt that priority should be to basic and capital goods and infrastructural development sectors rather than the consumer goods. Hence it holds that it is not desirable to allow further investment in consumer goods sector by FDI.

Collyns Charles (1995) review the recent experience with capital inflows and assesses their impact on the Indian economy. It looks at the pattern of recent flows, contrasts India's experience with that of other countries that have also recently received large private inflows, and considers the factors underlying the flows. It also examines the impact of resource flows on firms (microeconomic), on the macroeconomic environment, and on the financial system. Finally, it assesses the sustainability of capital flows to

India in the wake of the Mexican crisis. Specifically, it analyses capital account transactions of India from 1985-86 to 1994-95, FDI and FPI into India from 1990-91 to 1994-95, Indian GDR Issues from 1992-93 to 1994-95, Eurobond issues by Indian companies from 1993-94 to August 1994-95, investments by FIIs from January 1993 to March 1995, Direct and Portfolio investment in selected developing countries during 1993-94 and at sectoral distribution of foreign investment 1991-91.

The present study is distinct from these studies in Indian context as it focuses on private non-debt financial flows and it studies these flows from 1990 to 1999.

STUDIES ON IMPACT OF FINANCIAL FLOWS ON FINANCIAL SYSTEM

Impact on macroeconomy is the focus in some of the following studies :

Corbo Vittorio and Hernandez, L. (1994) review the macroeconomic effects of capital flows. They note that capital inflows can increase domestic expenditure, appreciate real exchange rate, and result in a larger trade deficit and acceleration of domestic inflation. According to them, capital inflows, by permitting a relaxation of the liquidity constraint facing recipient countries, may reduce domestic interest rates, and result in an increase in the level of domestic expenditure. Part of the increase in expenditure will go into tradable goods and part into non-tradable goods. The increase in expenditure on tradable goods will increase the size of the trade deficit. An increase in the demand for non-tradable goods will result - independently of the exchange rate regime - in an increase in the relative price of non-tradable goods, i.e., an appreciation of real exchange rate. The real appreciation will occur either through an appreciation of the nominal exchange rate (under a floating exchange rate system), or through an increase in the nominal price of the non-tradable good (in a fixed or pre-announced exchange rate system). They further hold that the same sort of process will be set in motion by an increase in short-term borrowing, an increase in official capital, or an increase in direct foreign investment. However, the latter two types of capital flows are much less reversible and therefore the real appreciation will be much less volatile the study holds. Another side effect of capital inflows as mentioned in the study is inflation i.e. in a fixed or predetermined exchange rate system, the monetization of large capital inflows will have an inflationary effect through the price of the non-tradable goods. The study holds that governments in developing countries should be concerned about these impacts of capital flows on macroeconomy because the appreciation of the real exchange rate can put in jeopardy the success of the recently implemented trade liberalization reforms and because an increase in domestic inflation can erode the credibility of the undergoing price stabilization programs. A too sudden increase in the current account deficit over GDP ratio, especially if due to domestic consumption boom, could raise the country's risk premium as well as restrict its future access to international capital markets. For a sample of four Latin American countries (Argentina, Chile, Columbia and Mexico) and five East Asian countries (Indonesia, Korea, Malaysia, Philippines and Thailand), it examines impact of capital flow on average inflation, real effective exchange rate, reserve money, investment, national saving and current account deficit from 1986 to 1992. The analysis revealed that all the countries have been successful in avoiding a permanent and significant increase in inflation. In fact, in Argentina and Mexico, inflation has been decreasing for the past three to four years, while in other seven countries inflation has remained fairly stable. Malaysia showed the lowest inflation rate among all countries in the sample. Secondly, the study found that Chile, Indonesia and Malaysia avoided a significant real exchange rate appreciation (Malaysia showed a real depreciation) and Argentina, Korea, Mexico and Philippines showed a strong appreciation of the real exchange rate. Thailand, the study found, lay in between these two groups. Thirdly, it found that the countries that have received the largest capital inflows are not those that have experienced the largest real exchange rate appreciation.

Aggarwal, R.N. (1997) studies the impact of flow of foreign portfolio investment on several macroeconomic parameters using trend and ratio methods. Trend growth rates have been estimated for inflation rate, real exchange rate, growth of economic activity and foreign exchange reserves for a sample of 5 countries viz. India, Korea, Malaysia, Indonesia and Thailand. The study found that inflation rate showed a rising trend in all the sample countries; exchange rate has depreciated in India, Indonesia and Malaysia while it has appreciated slightly in Korea and Thailand. Index of economic activity show an upward trend in all the countries considered in the sample. The period covered by the analysis is 1986 to 1993. For the Indian case study monthly data has been used for the period January 1993 to December 1994.

Collyns Charles (1995) reports that surge in financial flows has led to rapid increase in domestic liquidity, an accumulation of international reserves as the RBI intervened to avoid an exchange rate appreciation, rising inflation and an appreciation of the real exchange rate. The period covered by the analysis is 1991/92 to 1994/95. Specifically, it found that reserve money increased by 25%, inflation rose from 7% in March 1993 to about 12% in March 1994, and the real effective exchange rate appreciated by about 4%. In 1994/95, it however found that money growth dampened, inflation came down towards the end of the year and the real effective exchange rate also depreciated (as the U.S. dollar weakened against third countries). The study further held that so far the capital inflows have not had a marked impact on the current account of the balance of payments. The current account deficit, it found, contracted from 2% of GDP in 1992/93 to virtual balance in 1993/94, and a small deficit (about 1/2 or 1% of GDP) was recorded in 1994/95. It felt that the CAD is likely to widen in coming years.

Beckerman and Das (1998) indicates/reveals that capital inflow generates monetary expansion, real effective currency appreciation, reduces nominal and real interest rate and encourages economic activity particularly capital formation. It further holds that different capital inflow modalities induce different type and degree of macroeconomic perturbation. DFI, it says, has no effect on money or foreign-exchange supply whereas portfolio investment induces exchange rate appreciation, generates money expansion, and increases equity values and it is the latter kind of capital flow that is likely to present the largest problem for macroeconomic policy. The period covered by the study is 1993-1995. The study observed that capital inflows generated little direct capital formation during 1993 and 1994, gross international reserves rose from U.S.$ 9.8 billion in March 1993 to U.S. $ 25.2 billion in March 1995; broad money supply grew from March 31 to November 1994 by 13.6% as compared to 10.8% in corresponding period of 1993. The study specified that the principal source of inflationary pressure during 1993 and 1994 was the growth in primary liquidity resulting from growth in net foreign exchange assets of the Reserve Bank. This, it held, resulted in turn from (a) capital inflows in combination with (b) the policy choice to forestall nominal exchange rate appreciation. Finally the study noted that during 1993 and 1994, capital inflows mainly took the form of portfolio investment for the stock market and corporate issues whose proceeds were used to retire expensive debt. In general, then, these capital inflows were not the kind that generated more or less simultaneous imports. In effect, what this meant was that capital inflows were not in Keyne's terminology "transferred" to India by means of accompanying imports. Instead of becoming physical capital, they simply became generalized aggregate demand thus explaining the persistence of inflation.

Pohit, S. (1993) analyzes whether a causal relationship can be identified between total capital inflows and domestic savings and domestic investment in India. However, it uses current account balance as a proxy for capital inflow. By running causality tests between current account on one hand and domestic savings, investment and fiscal balance of the public sector on the other hand, it found that current account and hence capital inflow reflects increased consumption.

Calvo, G.A., Leiderman, L. and Reinhart, C.M. (1994) observe that capital inflows are associated with inflation, real exchange rate appreciation and a deterioration in the current account (of the balance of payments). It finds that a substantial fraction of the inflows has been chanelled to reserves in Latin America (reserves increasing by about $ 52 billion in 1990-92). Further it found that for Latin America as a whole, 45% of the inflows went into reserve accumulation, and the remainder financed wider current account deficits. For Asia, during 1989-92, it found that the proportion of capital inflows chanelled into reserve accumulation was 62% and that there was a sharp building up in international reserves both in Latin America and Asia. The study found that the capital inflows led to real exchange rate appreciation in Latin America (except Brazil) but in Asia such an appreciation was not the norm because in Asia such flows financed investment, concided with a contraction in fiscal expenditure and because monetary policy in Asia was successful in limiting expansion in credit and monetary aggregate.

Schadler, S., Carkovic, M., Benett, A. and Kahn, R. (1993) review the experiences of six countries viz. Chile, Columbia, Egypt, Mexico, Spain and Thailand. It found that in these countries not all of the feared effects of inflows materialized. Typically, money growth was little affected and inflation did not rise. In Egypt and Columbia it fell over a short inflow period; in Mexico and Chile an initial acceleration in prices was reversed. Further it found that real effective exchange rates rose significantly - by more than 10% - in each country except Thailand. Also, it found that in each country, official reserves rose, in terms of both U.S.-dollars and months of imports. The study held that surges in capital inflows should ease domestic money market conditions and lower domestic interest rates and found that in Chile, Columbia, Mexico and Spain real interest rates dropped after the surge in inflows. In Egypt, it found that the large initial increase in real interest rates was not reversed while in Thailand the real interest rates were quite stable. The study felt that the stability of money growth could be viewed as evidence that these country's relatively aggressive sterilization was successful in insulating the economy - particularly money growth and the current account from the inflows.

Calvo, G.A., Leiderman, L. and Reinhart, C.M. (1996) observe that large capital inflows can have less desirable macroeconomic effects including rapid monetary expansion, inflationary pressures, real exchange rate appreciation, and widening current account deficits. Based on a sample of 4 Asian countries (viz. Indonesia, Malaysia, Philippines and Thailand) and 5 Latin American countries (viz. Argentina, Brazil, Chile, Columbia and Mexico), the study finds that a substantial portion of the surge in capital inflows has been channeled to accumulation of foreign exchange reserves. From 1990 to 1994, the share going to reserves has been 59% in Asia and 35% in Latin America. Secondly, it finds that in most countries the capital inflows have been associated with widening current account deficits. Thirdly, it finds that there has been a rise in private consumption spending particularly in Argentina, Brazil, Columbia and Mexico. Fourthly, it finds that in almost all of the countries examined money supply grew rapidly both in nominal and real terms. Lastly, the study found that in most Latin American countries, capital inflows have been associated with a marked real exchange rate appreciation whereas in Asia such an appreciation is only evident in the Philippines; for the remaining Asian countries the real exchange rate remained stable through the inflow period. This difference in real exchange rate appreciation can be explained in terms of differences in composition of aggregate demand in the two regions and the difference in behaviour of public sector consumption.

World Bank (1997) observes that a key short-run macroeconomic consequence of capital inflows is an excessive expansion of aggregate demand i.e. macroeconomic overheating. It evaluates whether twenty developing countries (including India) actually experienced macroeconomic overheating. A broad finding of the study is that countries have generally succeeded in avoiding overheating. It found that majority of countries managed to reduce inflation during the period of capital inflow and where there was an increase it was relatively modest. This favourable outcome it found was achieved despite an acceleration in GDP growth in most of these countries. Specifically, it found that 13 of the countries in the sample reduced their inflation rates during their inflow episodes, and five of the 13 saw large decelerations. As for real exchange rate, the study found that the surge in capital inflows also did not result in an appreciation of the real exchange rate - only 12 countries in the sample registered real appreciation. In the 5 East Asian countries, it found that four had large real depreciation while one kept its real exchange rate approximately stable. By contrast, the six of the seven Latin American countries in the sample, the study found registered real appreciation, and in most cases the magnitude was substantial. Moreover, it found that for most of the countries affected, the mechanism generating real appreciation was clearly not an acceleration of inflation because 12 countries that registered a real appreciation, 10 did so with reduced domestic inflation. Further, in respect of current account deficit, the study found that current account deficit widened in most countries in the post surge period. Only in 3 (out of 20) countries the CAD fell during the inflow period and that there were substantial differences in the magnitude of increases in CAD. The study further found that real exchange rate and current account outcomes have been associated, even if only weakly, with each other (the simple cross-country correlation between real appreciation and increases in CAD being 0.60). The study also found that there were substantial differences in the composition of absorption. For some countries, notably Chile and East Asian countries, it found that a widening in the current deficit was primarily reflected in an increase in investment. This orientation towards investment, the study pointed out, was associated in these countries with faster economic growth. In contrast, the composition of absorption was more skewed towards consumption in Argentina, Columbia, Hungary, Mexico, Peru and Poland. This pattern of absorption was strongly correlated with the degree of real exchange rate appreciation

In particular, the study revealed that an increase in consumption to GDP ratio is associated with real appreciation, the simple cross-country correlation being 0.74. The study felt that the differences in the composition of absorption and the appreciation of the real exchange rate between these two groups of countries have been largely due to fiscal policy. In sum, the study found that developing countries have been able to date (upto 1994-1995) to counter most of the symptoms of overheating.

Asian Development Outlook (1995 & 1996) analyzes DMC experiences. It found the China, Indonesia, Malaysia, Sri Lanka and Thailand observed acceleration in the rate of growth of GDP while in India, Pakistan and Philippines there was a lagged response in output. Further it found that there was a significant increase in the investment, GDP ratio during the capital inflow phase in China, Indonesia, Malaysia, Philippines and Thailand. The South Asian economies particularly India and Pakistan, the study found, were unable to push up the investment rates despite substantial inflows in 1993 and 1994; instead these flows contributed to a sharp increase in foreign exchange reserves. Domestic savings as a proportion of GDP increased in following countries according to this study - India, Indonesia, Malaysia, Pakistan, Sri Lanka and Thailand. In India, Pakistan and Sri Lanka the increase in domestic savings was largely due to a decline in private consumption as a proportion of GDP. Further, the study pointed out that most of the economies experienced a significant widening of external current account deficit during the capital inflows phase mainly because of a sharp rise in domestic investment in relation to national savings. In India, the study observed, CAD remained low in both 1993 and 1994 largely because of sluggish private and public investment in conjunction with rising domestic savings.

Impact of Financial Flow on Capital Market

Some of the studies that examine impact on capital market are:

Rajan Goyal (1995) tests the impact of opening up of the capital market on stock return volatility. The Autoregressive Conditional Heteroskedasticity (ARCH) model is used to calculate share return volatility. The study found that the globalisation of the Indian capital market has not added to stock market volatility. The focus of the study is on examining the nature and trends in the stock return volatility and assessing the role of 'carry-forward system' in causing variations in the volatility levels. The study analyses the trends in daily and in monthly volatility estimates of stock market returns along with an analysis of stock returns volatility trends during pre- and the post-carry forward ban period.

BIS (1996) tested whether the presence of foreign investors in emerging market equities in the 1990s has made these markets volatile. Based on a sample of seventeen countries (including India), the study found that the presence of foreign investors in emerging market equities in the 1990s has not necessarily made these markets volatile. The study found that in all but two of the countries (viz. India and Columbia) price volatility was lower in the 1991-95 period than in 1986-90 period. The study used standard deviation of month-on-month changes as a measure of volatility.

Bekaert G. and Harvey, C.R. (1995) analyzes the volatility of returns in emerging equity markets. It seeks to ascertain why volatility is so different across emerging equity markets and traces the influence of world factors and local factors on market volatility. In addition, it investigates whether capital market liberalization policies affect volatility. Analysis is based on a sample of 20 countries . The statistics used include the average (annualized) arithmetic return, annualized standard deviation and the first order correlation. It considers total returns: dividends and capital gains. The study found first that emerging market returns are characterized by high volatility as compared to developed countries. Secondly, it held that in fully integrated markets volatility is strongly influenced by world factors while in segmented capital markets, volatility is more likely influenced by local factors. Thirdly, the study found that more open economies (in terms of world trade) have significantly lower volatilities, markets with a few very large stocks have lower volatility, a larger number of companies decreases volatility, a lower credit rating is associated with higher volatility, larger equity market (in terms of market capitalization to GDP) implies lower volatility. Fourthly, the study found that capital market liberalizations significantly decrease volatility in emerging markets. Of the 17 countries, where there was a liberalization within the sample, only 4 showed evidence of increased volatility (Pakistan, Columbia, Venezuela and Turkey). In most countries the study found that volatility decreases. Particularly, dramatic decreases were found in 5 countries viz. Taiwan, Mexico, Portugal, Argentina and Brazil.

Kim, E.H. and Singal, V. (1993) study the impact of opening up of markets on stock returns, volatility of stock returns and on stock price volatility. Further, it seeks to determine whether change in stock price volatility is due to volatility of portfolio flows, exposure to foreign stock markets or changes in domestic macroeconomic factors. The study is based on a sample of 20 countries . The study finds that stock returns increase immediately after market opening. At the same time, volatility of stock prices falls after about a one-year lag and that stock markets, on the average, become less volatile after opening to foreign equity flows. Further the study finds that volatility of stock returns is not influenced by price swings in foreign stock markets and volatility of capital flows in and out of that economy. The study finds a positive correlation between volatility of industrial production and stock price volatility. The study indicates that domestic investors earn higher stock returns, but without stock market volatility.

Samal, K.C. (1997) studies the influence of FIIs on equity price movement in India particularly in Mumbai stock exchange and the influence of FIIs on equity market development. Analyzing yearly data from 1992-93 to 1995-96 as well as quarterly data from January 1993 to December 1994 and from January-March 1995 to October-December 1996 on Mumbai Stock Exchange Sensitive Index and net FII investment in India, he finds positive correlation between the two (r = 0.39, 0.53 and 0.33 respectively). The study finds that FIIs have not helped in equity market development in India and that equity market development depends on economic growth of a nation and not on portfolio investment by FIIs. The study finally holds that to develop equity market, it is necessary to encourage small domestic investors to participate in it and counter the tendency of the FIIs to destabilise the emerging equity market.

Pal, P. (1998) discusses the impact of FIIs on the primary market. It finds that the P/E ratio of the Sensex has shown a steep decline over the years (it averaged a modest 13.5 in November 1997 from a high of 54 in June 1994) implying that the so-called reduction in the cost of capital did not occur in practice for India. Further, it reveals that since 1993-94, there has not been any significant rise in the new issue, both on BSE as well as in the country. The study concludes that FII investment has not led to significant rise in activities of the domestic primary market. In fact, it has declined and become more subdued in recent years. The substitution of retail investors by the FIIs has taken its toll on the primary market. Further, the study holds that the dominance of FIIs and the uncertainty over the political stability of the country has resulted in an increase in the volatility of share prices. The study finds a steep rise in volatility around 1992 in India. IFC global index is used to calculate volatility in the study and volatility is observed from 1981 to 1995. This increased volatility has ensured that retail investors stay out of the market. The study notes that there are allegations of price rigging and money laundering against FIIs. The study finds that the entry of FIIs into the Indian stock market has failed to invigorate it and the supposed linkage that increased stock market liquidity will attract more domestic savers into the market has not worked in India. On the other hand there are reasons to believe that too much FII involvement has actually scared small savers away from the market.

RBI Annual Report (1995-96) analyzes movements in BSE sensitive index and lagged net investment by FIIs from February 1993 to February 1996. It finds that the two are significantly correlated with r = 0.49.

ISID (1999) analyzes whether FII operations have influenced the trading pattern on Indian stock exchanges. Instead of confining to a comparison of the movement of share price index and net investments by FIIs, it examines pattern of investment by five US-based India specific funds. The results suggest the resemblance between FII investment profile and trading pattern at the BSE. The study feels that the growing emphasis on computer software, consumer durable goods and pharmaceutical sectors in the Indian stock markets seems to have much to do with FIIs preferences for these sectors. The study holds that the implication that can be drawn from the similarity in FII's investment profile and trading pattern at BSE is that the Indian investors, since they perceive FIIs to trade on the basis of well-researched strategies, have started following the FIIs like a 'herd' and in the process accentuated the selective process introduced by the FIIs. The study observed that many mutual funds have recently floated specific funds for the sectors favoured by FIIs. In such a situation, it held that sudden withdrawal of FIIs or change of strategy by them can cause a devastating effect on the domestic stock market through demonstration effect. The study concluded that the entry of FIIs has not resulted in greater depth in Indian stock market instead it has led to focussing on certain sectors. The study opined that growing concentration of trading in a few sectors would reduce the stability base of the stock markets and held that the expectation that foreign investments would reduce the volatility which results from thinness of the markets by adding liquidity to local markets has been belied.

IMF (1995) examines the effects that capital inflows can have on securities market in recipient countries. According to it, portfolio capital inflows may affect the efficiency with which domestic financial assets are priced. The presence of foreign investors can also increase stock price volatility by magnifying price fluctuations in the local market. Apart from having an impact on market efficiency and market volatility, inflows may also lead to greater integration of securities markets, allowing shocks in one country to be transferred to other countries. Accordingly the study undertakes market efficiency tests, daily market index return volatility and extreme price movement analysis and volatility spillover analysis. In respect of impact of capital flows on market volatility the study seeks to ascertain whether stock price volatility has increased in absolute terms in emerging markets? Has this volatility increased in emerging stock markets relative to return volatility in United States? And has the probability of large declines in stock prices increased? The study based on a sample of 4 countries, viz. Hong Kong, Korea, Thailand and Mexico, finds that absolute volatility of stock returns has shown little evidence of increasing during periods of increased portfolio flows, the exception being Hong Kong in the period when portfolio flows were very volatile. In Mexico and Korea, absolute price volatility (measured by standard deviation of daily return) actually declined. The decline in volatility, the study holds, might be due in part to an increase in liquidity associated with the inflow of capital.

Folkerts-Landau, David & others (1995) holds that capital flows may lead to greater integration of capital markets and expose the smaller and less liquid stock markets to spillovers of turbulence from industrial country securities market. With respect to impact of capital flows on equity price volatility in these countries it finds that volatility in emerging markets, as measured by the standard deviation of stock returns remains very high by industrial country standards. For the period January 1992 to July 1994, daily stock return in these emerging markets were twice as variable as stock return in United States. The study notes that one fundamental reason for high price volatility in many APEC developing countries is a lack of information and emphasises that when information is uncertain and disclosure is inadequate, unsubstantiated rumours cause volatility. It suggests that differences in the availability and quality of information and the speed with which it is disseminated can affect the impact of sudden changes in portfolio flows on both price and volume volatility, especially in relatively small and illiquid equity markets. Further, the study opines that the effect that portfolio flows can have on emerging stock market depends importantly on the size of the flow relative to the size of the market and the capacity of the market to quickly process and absorb foreign orders and transactions. The study measures portfolio flow versus trading volume for four countries from October 1993 to February 1994. It finds that in Korea and Thai stock markets portfolio flows were small relative to trading volumes but were significant in Hong Kong and Mexico. The study held that the differences in the size of portfolio flows relative to trading volume may explain why the recent surge in inflows affected individual markets differently. The study found that some of the APEC developing countries have recently established derivatives market and opines that derivative products, because they are highly leveraged, can also facilitate speculation, which can lead to stock market volatility and more extreme price movements. It felt that availability of derivative instruments and program trading in Hong Kong may also explain why the Hong Kong market experienced the greatest increase in both absolute and relative volatility and a relatively high increase in volatility spillover effects when portfolio flows became very volatile.

World Bank (1997) holds that foreign portfolio investments increase price-earnings ratios and depth and liquidity of the domestic capital market which, in turn, reduces the cost of capital for domestic firms. Moreover, it opines that foreign participation may have important spillover effects on emerging markets in the form of improved accounting and disclosure practices and human capital. It finds that an increase in both market capitalization and trading volume has been associated with an increase in foreign portfolio flows. It feels that there is correlation between the two and not causation and that it is difficult to disentangle the causal effect of international integration. It studies the domestic trading activity/GDP (%) in selected emerging markets (including India) during pre-episode period and 1994. It finds an increase in domestic trading activity as a percentage of GDP in all emerging markets except India where the ratio fell from 9.33% to 7.06% in

1994. New listings, however, it found were higher in India during the inflow episode as compared to pre-episode phase. Moreover, the study points out that financial integration may lead to an increase in volatility of domestic asset prices and returns, volatility may originate from both domestic and international sources, as well as result from changes in country fundamentals or market inefficiencies. It suggests that volatility tends to decline as emerging markets become less prone to fundamental shocks through improved economic policies and diversification. But excess volatility resulting from information asymmetries and other market imperfections including foreign investor herding and pure contagion can be tackled through reforms and improvements in attributes of capital markets themselves. It finds that market development is strongly associated with lower volatility (r = - 0.60).

Collyns Charles (1995) observes that the impact of foreign capital flows on Indian financial markets has been more qualitative than quantitative. It points out that total FII investment on Indian stock exchanges is considerably less than 5% of market capitalization and that FII transactions have not exceeded 10% of market turnover in any single month. It further observes that the introduction of foreign investment in Indian equity has not added significantly to market liquidity or to volatility of stock prices. Price volatility, it finds, has declined since mid-1992 compared with the previous two and a half years. The study further observes that the presence of FIIs in Indian markets has probably contributed to a process that was already under way - the growing role of the wholesale capital market and the evolution of the institutions and financial structures to support it. FIIs have given additional momentum to efforts to improve market efficiency and transparency, including overhaul, settlement and transfer systems, introducing screen-based trading, tightening regulatory safeguards and introducing new financial instruments such as derivatives for better risk management. The study explores whether the emergence of an offshore market in Indian equity - the GDR market - has had a significant impact on domestic market in the underlying shares, as has occurred elsewhere and reports that to date links between offshore market for Indian GDRs and iocal markets have been limited. GDR prices of Indian companies, it finds, have tended to be more volatile than the prices of those companies on the Bombay Stock Exchange and an upward movement of prices on the Bombay Stock Exchange has tended to be associated with an increase in GDR price relative to Bombay stock exchange price and vice versa.

Beckerman and Das (1998) note that India's equities market responded vigorously to the unprecedented inflow of funds and that price earnings ratio and market capitalization rose sharply over 1993 and 1994.

Financial Flows and the Banking System

Some of the studies on impact on banking system are reviewed below:

Corbo, V. and Hernandez, L. (1994) note that capital inflow will increase the volume of funds being intermediated through the domestic capital markets, and therefore, will cause an expansion in the volume of domestic financial assets and liabilities. It holds that the larger amount of funds being intermediated may exacerbate moral hazard problems, and result in a financial bubble that could eventually lead to a financial crisis in countries where there is weak supervision of financial system. The study, however, does not empirically test the impact of capital flows on the banking system for the sample of four Latin American countries and five East Asian countries.

BIS (1996) holds that the periods of high rates of credit

expansion have preceded many banking crisis in developing countries, both in 1980s and more recently. Specifically, it measures bank credit to the private sector as a percentage of GDP for a sample of 17 countries including India for the year 1980 and 1994. It finds that the rate of credit expansion in a number of Asian countries, particulary Hong Kong, Taiwan, Malaysia and Thailand, was unusually rapid in 1994 as compared to 1980. For India, it noted that there was a marginal increase in bank credit to private sector as a percentage of GDP. The ratio for India increased from 22.2% in 1980 to 24.1% in 1994. The study held that it is important to bring rates of credit expansion to more sustainable levels to maintain stable and healthy banking systems. The study further measured non-performing loans as a percentage of total loans for the years 1990, 1994 and 1995. In India, it found that the percentage dropped from 23.6% in 1994 to 19.5% in 1995. The following countries, however, have shown an increase in NPA as a percentage of total loans - Taiwan, Indonesia, Brazil, Columbia and Mexico. The increase was most significant in Mexico where it increased from 2.3% in 1990 to 19.1% in 1995.

Folkerts-Landau, David and others (1995) observe that capital inflows have led to an expansion of bank balance sheets in several APEC developing countries because a significant portion of these captial inflows either entered the recipient countries directly through, or ultimately were deposited in, the banking system of the recipient country. It studies the impact of capital inflows on domestic credit in selected APEC countries (viz. Indonesia, Korea, Malaysia, Philippines, Taiwan Province of China and Thailand) from 1985 to 1993. It finds that capital inflows have not had great potential for altering the level of domestic credit in Korea, Taiwan Province of China and Philippines and enumerates the reasons for the same. It holds that countries that have experienced the greatest net capital inflows (viz.

Thailand, Indonesia and Malaysia) have also experienced rapid expansions in the commercial bank sectors. An analysis of bank balance sheets by it reveals (i) that the period of high net capital inflows coincided with an increase in liabilities of the banking sector, often driven by foreign borrowing, (ii) that these sources of funds allowed banks to expand their balance sheets despite a reduction in funding from the central bank and the government, and (iii) that these funds were allocated mostly to domestic lending, with some increase in private sector securities investment. The study further notes that banking problems in many countries have most often been the result of bad credit decisions and inept management of credit risk, including overexposure to certain types of risk, Large and relatively volatile capital flows, the study feels, can contribute to problems especially when bank balance sheets are badly structured, by causing large swings in bank liquidity that result in alternating periods of credit expansion and contraction. The study observes that when the banking sector is a conduit for capital inflows two major areas of concern are the ability of the banking system to assess price and manage risk and the adequacy of the supervisory and regulatory framework to prevent and contain systemic risk, particularly in the presence of safety nets and the problems of moral hazard. The study does not relate to India's experience in this regard.

IMF (1995) studies the impact that capital inflows have had on banking systems by examining elements of consolidated balance sheets in a sample of 10 countries (viz. Chile, Indonesia, Korea, Malaysia, Mexico, Philippines, Sri Lanka, Taiwan Province of China, Thailand and Turkey) from 1985 to 1994. It finds that the ratio of commercial bank assets to GDP (which is a measure of size of country's banking system) has been affected in countries that have received high capital inflows. It also finds that periods of aggressive sterilization have been associated with very low growth in bank assets, and the relaxation of sterilization coincided with rapid bank asset expansions. In addition to affecting the size of the commercial banking system in recipient countries, the study found that capital inflows have also changed the composition of bank balance sheets - banks in recipient countries relied more heavily on foreign capital and used these funds to expand domestic lending and securities investment. The study also found that countries with the largest capital inflows experienced the greatest expansion in non-government deposits in the commercial banking system. In the case of Malaysia, Mexico and Thailand, the study found that there was an increase in foreign currency denominated liabilities as a share of GDP during periods of capital inflows. Funds so obtained were directed mostly towards domestic, rather than foreign investments. Domestic lending to private sector was found to increase in Indonesia, Mexico and Thailand with the onset of high capital inflows - the increase being much more than the increase in foreign liabilities. The study concludes that a rapid expansion in bank balance sheets implies the possibility that credit risk exposures and market risk exposures have increased sharply. The study does nto cover Indian experience.

World Bank (1997) looks at how the banking system has been affected by capital inflows. It draws on the experience of a wide range of country episodes during the 1980s and the 1990s. The study, however, does not cover Indian experience. From a review of country experiences the study found (i) countries that received substantial capital inflows as part of the process of financial integration typically experienced lending booms as was evident from bank lending to the private sector as a share of GDP, (ii) countries that had the largest lending booms typically saw a significant increase in macroeconomic vulnerability, measured by a widening of current account deficit, above what would be expected on the basis of size of the inflows; a consumption boom relatively larger than what would be expected given the size of the inflows; and a lower level of investment than would be expected given the size of the inflows. It found that every one of these country episodes with symptoms of increased macroeconomic vulnerability ended in a banking crisis; (iii) lending booms are associated with increase in financial sector vulnerability, despite the fact that booms tend to improve bank profitability and hence offer the opportunity for the banking sector to strengthen its resistance to shocks. In the majority of country episodes, the study found that banks showed a deteriorating shock absorption capacity during the lending boom period. Only in three of the country episodes (Chile, Columbia and Malaysia during 1990s), the study found that banks consistently improved their resilience to shocks as measured by improved liquidity, higher capitalization rates and loan loss provisions, lower stock of non performing assets and reduced exposure to foreign exchange risk. The study also found that countries that did not improve conditions in the banking sectors during inflow period, but rather allowed bank lending to increase without addressing underlying weaknesses, generally experienced a banking crisis later on; (iv) all of the countries in which lending booms were associated with an increase in financial sector vulnerability and in which macroeconomic vulnerability increased or remained constant, experienced banking crisis. Furthermore, it found that countries that improved their macroeconomic stance - such as Indonesia, the Philippines and Thailand - managed to avoid or at least delay banking crisis despite some worsening in banking sector vulnerability.

CONCLUSION

A review of the above studies reveals that no study till

date has studied private non-debt financial flows to India, its impact on macroeconomy, capital market and banking system in India and the restructuring that is needed in the light of the risks posed by such flows and to attract and sustain such flows. It is this void that the present study attempts to fill.

Impact of Financial Flow on Indian Financial System: Analysis of Data

Financial flows can have an impact on the financial system of the recipient country. For instance, a surge in financial flows may overheat the economy; it may increase volatility of asset price and returns and it may lead to a lending boom which may exacerbate macroeconomic and financial sector vulnerability. In this chapter an attempt is made to find out whether this chain of logic has actually worked for India. The aim is to complement text book explanations and prescriptions with analysis of actual experience in India and to draw policy implications for India.

To ascertain the impact of the financial flows on the Indian financial system the chapter is organised in three sections. Section I looks into the impact these flows have had on the macroeconomy, section II focuses on impact of financial flows on capital market and in section III an attempt is made to study the impact of financial flows on banking sector.

SECTION I

FINANCIAL FLOW AND MACROECONOMY

An attempt has been made herein to determine whether:

1. Foreign exchange reserves have increased in India as a consequence of financial flow to India.
2. RBI has intervened in the foreign exchange market to prevent nominal appreciation of currency.
3. Money supply has increased consequent to financial flow in India.
4. There is any relationship between FII investment and money supply in India.
5. Increase in money supply, if any, has led to inflation in India in the 1990s.
6. There is any relationship between FII investment and inflation.
7. Real exchange rate has appreciated in India as a consequence of financial flows to India in 1990s.
8. Current account deficit (CAD) has widened due to financial flows to India in 1990s.
9. Appreciation of real exchange rate has led to widening of CAD in India.
10. Indian economy got overheated as a consequence of financial flow to India.

FINANCIAL FLOW AND INCREASE IN RESERVES

An examination of India's Balance of Payments (Table 5.1) since 1990-91 reveals that a significant portion of financial flows in India have been channeled to reserves in India. This is evident from the increase in reserves in all years from 1992-93[1] except 1995-96 when the international reserves decreased. A small proportion of the total capital flow (=

16.27%) was channeled to reserves in 1992-93[2], the rest of the total financial flow was used to finance current account deficit.

TABLE 5.1

India: Balance of Payments

(Rs. Crores)

Year	*Current A/c*[1]	*Capital Account plus Errors and Omissions*[1]	*Change in reserves*[2]
1990-91	-17,368.5	15,075.4	2,293.1
1991-92	- 2,237.3	11,588.6	-9351.3
1992-93	-12,763.5	15,244.1	-2,480.6
1993-94	- 3,635.8	31,022.2	-27,366.4
1994-95	-10,582.6	25,157.1	-14,574.5
1995-96	-19,606.7	9,809.0	9,797.7
1996-97	-15,839.1	36,598.0	-20,758.9
1997-98	-24,555.0	38,922.6	-14,367.6

1 A minus sign indicates a deficit in the pertinent account
2 A minus sign indicates an increase
Source: Report on Currency & Finance — various issues.

In 1993-94, out of the Rs. 31,002.2 crore total capital flow, 88.27% was accumulated as reserves and the remaining i.e. 11.73% was used to meet current account deficit. In 1994-95, of the Rs.25,157.1 crore total capital flow to India, Rs. 14,574.5 or 57.93% was accumulated as reserves and 42.07% was used to finance current account deficit. In 1995-96, given the growth in current account deficit and a distinct decline in capital flows, the reserves recorded a decrease of Rs. 9,797.7 crore in sharp contrast to the surpluses since 1991- 92. A sharp increase in imports in the face of a moderation in capital flows reversed the position of increase in reserves in 1995-96. In 1996-97, out of the total capital flow of Rs. 36,598 crore, 56.72% was accumulated as reserves and the rest (i.e. 43.28%) was used to meet the current account deficit. During 1997-98, a smaller proportion of the total flow on capital account viz. 36.91% was accumulated as reserves. This was due to widening of the current account deficit during 1997-98.

Financial flow to India in the form of FII investment began in 1992-93 and till 1997-98 they had increased foreign exchange reserves by Rs. 69,750.3 crore (Table 5.1). During the period 1992-93 to 1997-98, 44.5% of the inflows have been channeled to reserves, while the remainder has financed wider current account deficits in India[3] (Table 5.1).

Thus, there has been a sharp build up in the international reserves in India during the inflow period. This is highly desirable since the recent crisis in South-East Asia has brought into sharper focus the need to maintain high levels of reserves to counter the increased volatility in short-term capital inflows. To forestall the threat of a serious decline in reserves, inflows and outflows need to be carefully monitored and calibrated at all times.

FINANCIAL FLOWS AND RBI'S INTERVENTION IN FOREIGN EXCHANGE MARKET

The surge of financial flow (in the absence of any widening of current account deficit) created excess supply condition in the foreign exchange market. The RBI consequently intervened in the foreign exchange market to prevent nominal exchange rate from appreciating[4]. Thus, financial flow have necessitated RBI intervention in the foreign exchange market with a view to prevent undue exchange rate appreciation and maintain external competitiveness.

During 1993-94, RBI purchased foreign currency from the market because of conditions of excess supply created by financial flows. Such purchases were US$ 13,940 million during 1993-94. RBI purchases of foreign exchange during 1994-95 were US$ 10,304 million (US$ 8.7 billion were purchased during April-October 1994 and US$ 1.7 billion purchases were made during November 1994 till March 1995). During April 1995 till December 1995, RBI, however sold foreign exchange. Net sales of US$ 348 million were made in second, third and fourth quarters of 1996-97, an improvement in supply position in foreign exchange market following the institution of a series of policy measures during the second half of 1995-96 enabled gross purchases by RBI from the market amounting to US$ 2063 million.

The resurgence of capital inflows in the absence of any widening of current account deficit necessitated intervention purchases of US$ 7801 million by RBI in 1996- 97.

Large financial flows in the face of weak demand necessitated intervention purchases of the order of US$ 7208 million during April-September 1997. This phase was followed by a period October-December 1997 of relatively dull supply condition strewed with disparate exchange rate expectation, till active demand control measures by the RBI in mid-January 1998 restored normalcy in the market.

During October-December 1997, there was net intervention sales of US$ 3896 million by RBI. Since mid-January, 1998 the direction of net intervention changed and excess supply in foreign exchange market resulted in net purchase by the RBI of US$ 3869 million.

Since financial flow to India in the form of FII's began in 1992-93 till 1997-98, RBI has actively intervened in foreign exchange market. In response to an increase in foreign-exchange reserves consequent to the financial flow, RBI has been purchasing foreign exchange from 1993-94 till 1997-98 except for April

1995-December 1995 and October 1997 - December 1997 when it sold foreign exchange.

FINANCIAL FLOW AND MONEY SUPPLY

The arrival of financial flow together with cental bank intervention resulted in substantial upward pressure on the money supply. Table 5.2 depicts the money supply position in India in the pre-flow period (1985-86 to 1991-92) and flow period (1992-93 to 1997-98).

An attempt was made to determine whether money supply (M_3) has increased consequent to financial flow (particularly FII flow). For this purpose, hypothesis testing was done. The following null and alternate hypothesis were formulated:

> H_0 = Money supply has not increased consequent to FII flow.
>
> H_1 = Money supply has increased consequent to FII flow.

TABLE 5.2

Money Supply in India

	Year	*Broad Money (M_3) (Rs. Crore)*	*Percentage Variation*
Pre-FII flow period			
	1985-86	1,19,394	16.0%
	1986-87	1,41,632	18.6%
	1987-88	1,64,275	16.0%
	1988-89	1,93,493	17.8%
	1989-90	2,30,950	19.4%
	1990-91	2,65,828	15.1%
	1991-92	3,17,049	19.3%

FII Flow period			
	1992-93	3,66,825	15.7%
	1993-94	4,34,407	18.4%
	1994-95	5,31,426	22.3%
	1995-96	6,04,007	13.7%
	1996-97	7,01,848	16.2%
	1997-98	8,25,389	17.6%

Source: Handbook of Statistics on Indian Economy, RBI, December 1998.

To test the above hypothesis, monthly data on money supply (M_3) was considered for the period under study, i.e. 1985-98. This data on M_3 was bifurcated into two categories:

1. Pre FII flow period data on M_3 - this included monthly data on M_3 from January 1985 to December 1992.
2. FII flow period data on M_3 - this included monthly data on M_3 from January 1993 to December 1997.

t-test for independent samples was employed to ascertain whether money supply has significantly increased during FII flow period. *The analysis indicated that 2-tail significance is 0.000. Since this value is less than 0.05, null hypothesis is rejected at 95% level of confidence and we conclude that there is significant difference in money supply in the two periods under study (1985-92 as compared to 1992-97). The money supply, in fact, has significantly increased in the FII flow period (i.e. 1993-97) as compared to 1985-92 (since the mean during 1985-92 was found to be 2,09,661.44 as compared to Rs. 5,69,267.48 for 1993-97).*

Thus, money supply in India has significantly increased during 1993-97 - the period of FII flow into India as compared to the period when there was no FII flow (1985-92).

GRAPH 5.1

M3 (Monthly Data) 1985-98

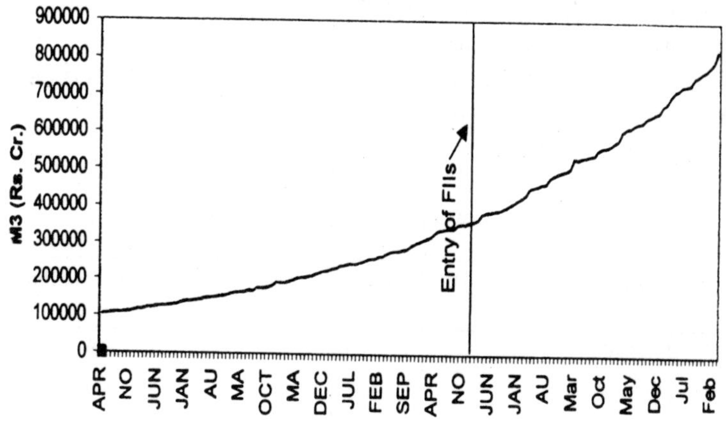

Money supply (M_3) has increased at a faster rate since the entry of FII's in India is also apparent from Graph 5.1which shows monthly data on M_3 from 1985-98.

Money supply has significantly increased during FII flow period (i.e. 1993 onwards) as compared to pre-FII flow period under study.

To further ascertain whether there is any relationship between FII investment and money supply, correlation coefficient was calculated between net FII investment (Rs. crore) and percentage variation in M_3 based on monthly data from January 1993 onwards. *It was found that there is very weak correlation between FII investment and percentage variation in M_3 with $r = 0.110053$. The percentage variation in M_3 seems to be correlated with some factor other than FII investment[5].*

MONEY SUPPLY AND INFLATION

In addition to the above, an attempt was made to ascertain whether an increase in money supply (on account of financial flow) has led to inflation in India or not. Table 5.3 depicts the position of inflation in India from 1984-85 to 1997-98. Percentage variation in Wholesale Price Index is used as a measure of inflation in India.

TABLE 5.3

India: Inflation (Measured by % Variatioin in WPI)

Year	*WPI (Average of week) 1981-82 = 100*	*% age variation*
1984-85	120.1	6.5
1985-86	125.4	4.4
1986-87	132.7	5.8
1987-88	143.6	8.2
1988-89	154.3	7.5
1989-90	165.7	7.4
1990-91	182.7	10.3
1991-92	207.8	13.7
1992-93	228.7	10.1
1993-94	247.8	8.4
1994-95	274.7	10.9
1995-96	295.8	7.7
1996-97	314.6	6.4
1997-98	329.7	4.8

Source: RBI Handbook of Statistics on Indian Economy, December 1998.

With a view to ascertaining whether an increase in money supply has been associated with inflation or not, correlation coefficient between percentage variation in money supply (M_3) and percentage variation in WPI was calculated based on monthly data from 1988[6] to 1998. It was found that r = -0.16664 i.e. the percentage variation in money supply and inflation are negatively correlated. *An increase in money supply has not increased inflation in India during the period considered. Rather, inflation in India has declined despite increase in money supply. Also, we find that no significant relation exists between money supply and inflation since r is very small. Hence it may be concluded that inflation has declined because of higher stock of foodgrains, slack in export demand and sluggish industrial growth. In general, because of subdued demand in the economy inflation has declined during flow period.*[7]

FINANCIAL FLOW AND INFLATION

The study made an attempt to ascertain whether financial flow to India (in the form of FII investment) has led to inflation in India or not. For this purpose hypothesis testing was done. The following null and alternate hypothesis were formulated:

H_0 - FII flow to India has not led to inflation.

H_1 - FII flow to India has led to inflation.

To test the above hypothesis, monthly data on wholesale price index was considered from April 1988 to January 1999 and from this percentage variation in WPI was calculated. This was used as a measure of inflation. The monthly data was bifurcated into two categories:

I. Pre-FII flow period data on inflation - this covered monthly data on inflation from May 1988 to December 1992.

II. During FII flow period - this included monthly data on inflation from January 1993 to January 1999.

t-test for independent samples for equality of means was employed to ascertain whether FII flows have increased inflation in India or not. The analysis indicated that 2-tail significance is 0.084. At 95% level of confidence since this value is greater than 0.05, null hypothesis is accepted and we conclude that there is no significant difference in inflation during the periods studied. Though there is no significant difference in inflation after FII flows, yet the analysis indicates that average inflation has marginally dropped in the FII inflow period (it was 0.0059) as compared to pre-FII inflow period (when it was 0.0078).

FII flow to India has not led to inflation in India. This finding is contrary to theoretical prediction that financial flow may lead to inflation[8].

Further an attempt was made to determine whether there is any relationship between FII flow and inflation. For this purpose correlation coefficient was calculated between FII investment (Rs. crore) and percentage variation in WPI based on monthly data from January 1993 to January 1999. It was found that the two are negatively correlated. An increase in FII flow has led to a decline in percentage variation in WPI (i.e. inflation). There is in fact no significant relationship between FII investment and percentage variation in WPI since r = -0.159. *Inflation in India has been more strongly correlated to factors other than FII flow.*

FII FLOW AND REAL EXCHANGE RATE IN INDIA

An attempt was made to ascertain whether FII flow has led to appreciation of real exchange rate in India.

The position of Real effective exchange rate in India from 1984-85 to 1997-98 is depicted in Table 5.4.

TABLE 5.4

Real Effective Exchange Rate (REER) Base (1985 = 100)

Year weights	*Export-based variation*	*%age weights*	*Trade-based variation*	*%age of*
1984-85	100.44	-3.9	100.86	-3.2
1985-86	97.85	-2.6	98.27	-2.6
1986-87	90.12	-7.9	90.24	-8.2
1987-88	85.39	-5.2	85.36	-5.4
1988-89	80.26	-6.0	80.41	-5.8
1989-90	77.34	-3.6	78.44	-2.4
1990-91	73.33	-5.2	75.58	-3.6
1991-92	61.36	-16.3	64.20	-15.1
1992-93*	61.74	0.6	65.92	2.7
1992-93@	54.42	—	57.08	—
1993-94@	59.09	8.6	61.59	7.9
1994-95@	62.04	5.0	64.75	5.1
1995-96@	59.57	-4.0	62.17	-4.0
1996-97@	60.74	2.0	63.43	2.0
1997-98@	63.68	4.8	66.92	5.5

* For the period April 92 - February 1993.

@ Based on FEDAI indicative rates.

Note:

1) 36 country bilateral weights.
2) Depreciations are shown with (-) sign.
3) Indices from 1984-85 to 1992-93 are based on official exchange rate.

Source: Report on Currency and Finance, Volume 2, 1997-98.

The following hypotheses were formulated to ascertain whether FII flow to India has appreciated real exchange rate or not:

H_0 - FII flow has had no impact on real exchange rate in India.

H_1 - FII flow has had an impact on real exchange rate in India.

The entire period of study was bifurcated into two groups:

Group 1: Pre-FII flow period - This covered the period January 1985 to December 1992.

Group 2: During-FII-flow period - This covered the period from January 1993 to March 1999.

Independent samples test i.e. t-test for equality of means was used to ascertain whether there is any significant difference in Real effective exchange rate during pre-FII flow period and during FII flow period. The analysis revealed that significance (2-tail) is 0.00 which is less than 0.05. Hence we reject null hypothesis at 95% level of confidence and conclude that there is a significant difference in REER both trade-based and export-based during FII flow period as compared to pre-FII flow period. The average trade-based REER has declined from 80.78 during pre-FII flow period to 62.67 during FII flow period. Similarly, the average export-based REER during pre-FII flow period was 79.51 and the average export based REER during FII-flow period was 60.77. *Thus, we find that real exchange rate in India has depreciated during FII flow period*[9]. *This is in contrast to the theoretical production that FII flow may appreciate real exchange rate.* It seems that the real exchange rate has depreciated rather than appreciating because inflation has not increased in India and theory holds that rising domestic prices, if exchange rate peg is maintained causes real exchange rate to appreciate.

FINANCIAL FLOW AND CURRENT ACCOUNT DEFICIT (CAD)

An attempt was made to ascertain whether financial flow

to India in the form of FII investment has led to widening of current account deficit or not. For this purpose, the study tried to ascertain whether there is any significant difference in current account deficit during-FII inflow period as compared to pre-FII inflow period. The following hypotheses have been formulated for the above purpose:

H_0 - FII flow has had no impact on current account deficit in India.

H_1 - FII flow has had an impact on current account deficit in India.

If FII flow has had no impact on current account deficit in India then there should no significant difference between current account deficit in pre-FII-flow period [i.e. 1985 quarter one (Q_1) - 1992 quarter four (Q_4)] and during FII flow period [i.e. 1993 Q_1 - 1999 Q_1].

Taking quarterly data on CAD from 1985 to 1999 and employing independent sample test viz. t-test for equality of means, we find that significance (2-tailed) is 0.0547 which is greater than 0.05. Hence at 95% confidence level, we accept null hypothesis that FII flow has had no impact on current account deficit in India. *There is no significant difference in the current account deficit in the two periods.*

GRAPH 5.2

Current Account Deficit (Rs. Cr.)

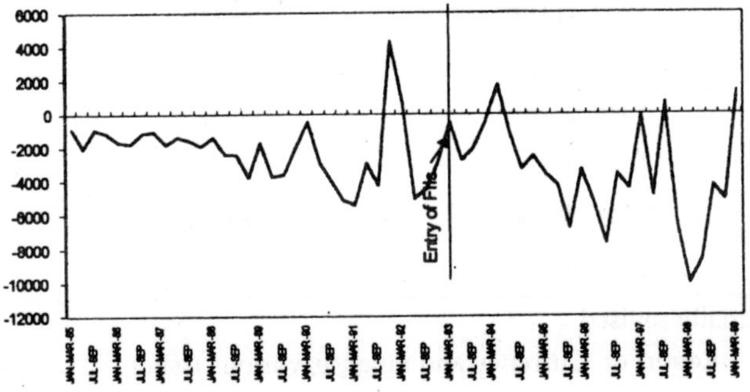

Levene's test for Equality of Variances indicates that significance (0.0193) is less than 0.05. Hence at 95% confidence interval, we reject null hypothesis and conclude that there is significant difference in the variability of current account deficit in two periods. The CAD has shown greater fluctuation/variability in the period 1993 onwards (Graph 5.2). *Thus, since the entry of FII's in January 1993 in India, the variability of current account deficit has increased.*

The position of current account deficit in India since 1984-85 is depicted in Table 5.5.

TABLE 5.5

India: Current Account Deficit

(Rs. crore)

Year	*Current Account Deficit*
1984-85	-2852.4
1985-86	-5955.8
1986-87	-5830.0
1987-88	-6292.6
1988-89	-11580.1
1989-90	-11388.6
1990-91	-17368.5
1991-92	-2237.3
1992-93	-12763.5
1993-94 (PR)	-3635.8
1994-95 (PR)	-10582.6
1995-96 (PR)	-19606.7
1996-97 (PR)	-15839.1
1997-98 (PR)	-20884.6
1998-99	-16787.6

PR : Partially revised

Source: Report on Currency and Finance, various issues.

Further, hypotheses testing was done on current account deficit as a percentage of GDP to ascertain whether financial flow to India in the form of FII investment has had an impact on CAD as a percentage of GDP. The methodology was same as for CAD except that here instead of quarterly data annual data was used. The current account deficit as a percentage of GDP in India is depicted in Table-5.6.

TABLE 5.6

Current Account Deficit as a Percentage of GDP

(Rs. crore)

Year	*CAD*	*GDP at factor cost at current prices*	*CAD as a % of GDP*
1985-86	5955.8	2,33,799	2.5474%
1986-87	5830.0	2,60,030	2.2420%
1987-88	6292.6	2,94,851	2.1342%
1988-89	11580.1	3,52,706	3.2832%
1989-90	11388.6	4,08,662	2.7868%
1990-91	17368.5	4,77,814	3.6350%
1991-92	2237.3	5,52,768	0.4047%
1992-93	12763.5	6,30,772	2.0235%
1993-94	3635.8	7,32,874	0.4961%
1994-95	10582.6	8,68,019	1.2192%
1995-96	19606.7	10,06,286	1.9484%
1996-97	15839.1	11,49,215	1.3783%

Taking annual data on CAD as percentage of GDP from 1985-86 to 1996-97and employing independent sample test viz. t-test for equality of means, we find significance (2-tailed) is 0.0813 which is greater than 0.05. Hence at 95% confidence level, *we accept null hypothesis that there is no significant difference in current account deficit as a percentage of GDP in the pre-FII-flow period (1985-86 to 1991-92) and FII flow period (1992-93 to 1996-97). Thus, FII flows to India since January 1993 have had no impact on current account deficit as a percentage of GDP. The current account deficit as a percentage of GDP has, infact, not widened in India during FII flow period since average CAD (as a percentage of GDP) during pre-FII-flow period was found to be 2.4333% while for FII-flow-period was 1.4130%.*

RELATION BETWEEN REAL EXCHANGE RATE AND CAD

If real exchange rate appreciates current account deficit widens. To test whether this chain of logic held for India, the real exchange rate was calculated. Obtaining nominal exchange rate, US CPI and India's CPI from International Financial Statistics the real exchange rate was calculated on an annual basis from calender year 1985 to 1997 by the formula:

$$\text{Real Exchange rate} = \frac{\text{Nominal exchange rate X Consumer Price (U.S.)}}{\text{Consumer price (Home country)}}$$

The real exchange rate in India, thus obtained is presented in Table 5.7.

Thus in India, we find that real exchange rate has depreciated during FII flow period (Graph 5.3), [since average Real Exchange Rate Index for 1985-92 was 97.82 while the same for 1993-97 was 136.789 - the rise in the index denoting depreciation of rupee] and current account deficit as a percentage of GDP has also narrowed [the average CAD as a percentage of GDP for 1985-86 to 1991-92 was 2.43% while for 1992-93 to 1996-97 was 1.41% - the fall in the percentage denoted that CAD as a percentage of GDP has narrowed in India during FII flow period.

TABLE 5.7

India: Real Exchange Rate (1985-1997) Base (1990 = 100)

Year	*Real Exchange Rate*	*Real Exchange Rate Index (Base: 1990 = 100)*
1985	15.00716	83.036
1986	15.16440	83.906
1987	14.18100	78.465
1988	15.65839	86.640
1989	17.61026	97.440
1990	18.07300	100.000
1991	23.63391	130.769
1992	22.10432	122.306
1993	25.63241	141.827
1994	23.85048	131.967
1995	24.93610	137.974
1996	24.06027	133.128
1997	25.13020	139.048

Note: A rise in the index denotes depreciation of rupee.

GRAPH 5.3

Real Exchange Rate Index (1990: 100) (Quarterly Data 1986-98)

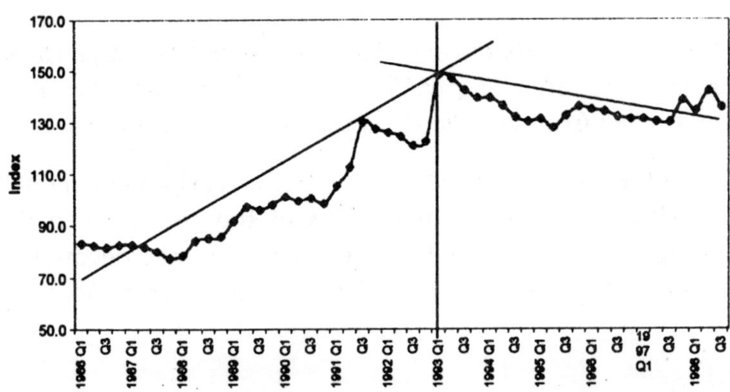

FINANCIAL FLOW AND MACROECONOMIC OVERHEATING

An attempt was made to ascertain whether the Inian economy got overheated as a consequence of financial flow or not. To see whether the Indian economy actually experienced macroeconomic overheating, the study, following World Bank (1997), examined the behaviour of four variables during the period when India received large FII flows and during immeidately preceding period of equal length. The four variables examined are: aceleration of economic growth, large current account deficits, accelerating inflation and an appreciation of the real exchange rate.

The behaviour of these four variables during FII inflow and pre-FII inflow period is depicted in table 5.8.

Thus, we find that India experienced faster growth but no other variable (inflation, CAD, real exchange rate) experienced the outcome associated with overheating. In fact, inflation declined, current account deficit (as a percentage of GDP) narrowed down, real exchange rate depreciated during inflow period. India has, thus, avoided the overt symptoms of overheating, except for acceleration of economic growth. Substantial acceleration of inflation - the factor most directly indicative of overheating - has been completely absent in India. Though India has experienced sharp acceleration of growth, this could be because of a factor other than financial flow viz. a change in policy regime.

Our results are consistent with World Bank (1997) results, which found that most of the countries in the sample had avoided the symptoms of macroeconomic overheating, except for pressures on the current account.

TABLE 5.8

Macroeconomic Performance During Inflow Period

	Average Annual GDP(Rs. crore)	*Average annual inflation (%age variation in WPI)*	*Average annual current account deficit (as a % of GDP*	*Average annual real effective exchange rate*		*Average Annual Real Exchange Rate*
				Trade-based	*Export-based*	
Pre inflow period 107.43(c)	(1986-92)	4,17,360.200*	8.8121	2.4488	79.0383	77.9667
Inflow period (1992-98)	8,77,433,200**	8.0169	1.4131	62.4900	59.6000	136.78(d)
Change (percent) from immediately preceding period of equal length	110.23%	-9.02%	-42.29%	-20.94%(a)	-23.56%(a)	27.33%(e)

* From 1987-88 to 1991-92.

** From 1992-93 to 1996-97.

a) A minus sign indicates depreciation.

c) Based on calender years (1988-92) Base (1990 = 100).

d) Based on calender years (1993-97) (1990 = 100 Base).

e) A rise in index denotes depreciation of rupee.

SECTION II

FINANCIAL FLOW AND CAPITAL MARKET

In the present study, an attempt has been made to determine whether:

i) FIIs have influenced equity price movement in India or not.

ii) Share price volatility has increased in India consequent to entry of FIIs, and

iii) Share returns volatility has increased in India consequent to entry of FIIs[10].

FII INVESTMENT AND EQUITY PRICE MOVEMENT

To ascertain whether FII investment has increased equity prices and their withdrawal depressed equity prices coefficient of correlation has been calculated between net FII investment and BSE Index from 1991-92 to 1997-98. The data on BSE Index and FII investment is summarised in Table 5.9

TABLE 5.9

BSE Index and FII Investment

Year	*BSE Index (Base : 1978-79)*	*FII Investment ($ m.)*
1991-92	1868.08	0
1992-93	2895.67	1
1993-94	2898.69	1665
1994-95	3974.91	1503
1995-96	3288.68	2009
1996-97	3469.24	1926
1997-98	3812.68	979
1998-99	—	-390

Source: Report on Currency and Finance, RBI (various issues) RBI Bulletin (March 1999-July 1999).

Analysis reveals that net FII investment and share price movement is positively correlated with coefficient of correlation between Net FII investment and BSE index from 1991-92 to 1997-98 amounting to 0.599318. The correlation coefficient between net FII investment and BSE index from 1991-92 to 1997-98 with lag [FII = (-1)] was found to be 0.780449. The results indicate that lagged net FII investment in India has significantly affected BSE sensex positively.

During the period November 1997 to September 1998 when FII investment into India was largely negative (excepting March 1998) the relationship of FII investment to BSE sensitive index was found. The co-efficient of correlation was used to study the relationship between the two. Movement of BSE sensitive index and lagged net FII investment from November 1997 to September 1998 was found to be highly correlated with r = 0.575549. The net FII investment without lag and BSE index during this period were found to have a lower degree of correlation with r = 0.268558.

Huge investment by FIIs have become a crucial factor influencing movement of share prices in India's equity market. Share prices in India are now influened, among othe factors, by the inflow of portfolio capital in the form of FII investment. This is because of the relatively small size of India's market capitalisation and the low level of floating stocks. It is also apparent from our analysis that net FII investment affects equity price movement with a lag.

FII INVESTMENT AND SHARE PRICE VOLATILITY

Based on Reserve Bank All India Index Number of Ordinary Share Prices (Base 1980-81) share price volatility was calculated. Following Reserve Bank and World Bank (1997) coefficient of variation was used to measure the volatility of share prices.[11] Table 5.10 exhibits the share price volatility for each year from 1985-98.

It is interesting to note that the volatility of share prices has not increased since 1993 (Graph 5.4), the year in which FII's entered the Indian capital market.

TABLE 5.10

Share Price Volatility (1985-98)

Year	*Std. Deviation*	*Average*	*Coeff. Of Variation (%)*
1985	31.42	242.70	12.946
1986	12.92	238.35	5.421
1987	10.50	213.49	4.919
1988	35.28	224.57	15.714
1989	25.10	340.79	7.367
1990	90.80	471.28	19.267
1991	126.29	636.31	19.848
1992	203.74	1163.30	17.514
1993	106.82	955.65	11.179
1994	157.44	1516.78	10.380
1995	123.63	1273.75	9.706
1996	124.03	1161.02	10.683
1997	62.92	1071.92	5.870
1998	77.87	976.20	7.977

Thus, volatility of share prices has not increased when FII's entered the market. It is also interesting to note that volatility marginally increased in 1996. Since then, volatility of share prices has continuously declined. Since 1993 volatility of share prices has continuously declined. Only marginally did volatility increase in 1996.

The analysis revealed results inconsistent to theoretical

GRAPH 5.4

Volatility in Share Prices (1985-1998)

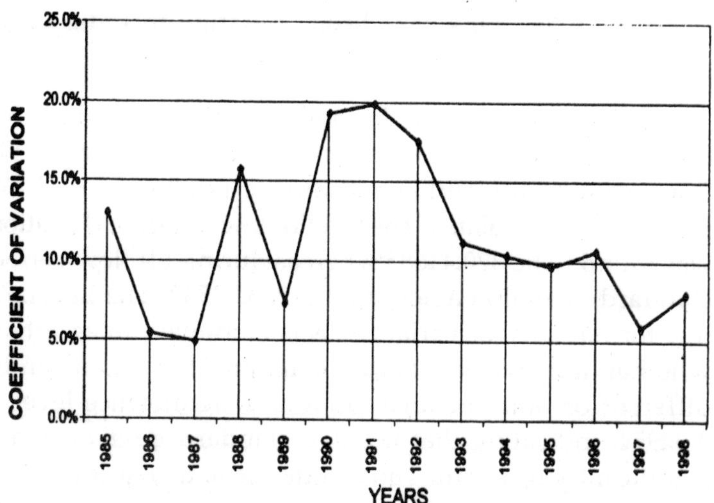

predictions that the presence of foreign investors can increase volatility of domestic asset prices.

To further ascertain whether FII investment has influenced share price volatility in India or not hypothesis testing was done. The following null and alternate hypothesis were formulated for this purpose:

> H_0 = FII flows have had no impact on share price volatility in India.
>
> H_1 = FII flows have had an impact on share price volatility in India.

To test the above hypotheses the period of study 1985-1998 was divided into two parts:

i) Period from 1985 to 1992 - this is the period prior to entry of FII's in India. It is termed as Pre-FII flow period, and

ii) Period from 1993 to 1998 - this is the period when FII's have been operating in India - it is termed as FII flow period.

Taking monthly data for both pre-FII flow period and during FII flow period, the standard deviation for pre-FII flow period (96 months) and during FII flow period (69 months) was calculated. The pre-FII flow standard deviation was found to be 320.44683 whereas during FII flow period standard deviation amounted to 223.77589. The Levene's test for equality of variances was employed to ascertain whether the two standard deviations are significantly different or not. The analysis found significance level = 0.02954, indicating that the two standard deviations are significantly different. The results made us reject the null hypothesis at 95% level of confidence. The results, however, did not show an increase in share price volatility. It indicated a decline in share price volatility because during FII flow standard deviation was smaller as compared to pre-FII standard deviation.

FII investment has not increased share price volatility in India during 1985-98. Share price volatility has in fact declined.[12]

RECONCILING EMPIRICAL RESULTS WITH THE THEORETICAL PREDICTIONS

How can the empirical results that volatility declined be reconciled with the theoretical prediction that volatility may increase? Volatility has declined during inflow period because emerging markets have undertaken economic reform and stabilisation programs, diversified their economy reducing vulnerability to real external shocks and also improved their capital markets. Thus, though theoretical predictions are that price volatility may increase during inflow period, improvement in domestic fundamentals, stabilisation of economic policies and improvements in capital market attributes has led to a decline in overall volatility. World Bank (1997) found that improvement in capital markets have been a significant factor in reducing volatility; that capital market development is strongly associated with lower volatility.

In India too, these factors reducing volatility have been operating. Since 1991-92, the Government introduced policy reforms to stabilise the economy and has been undertaking several steps to improve the capital market. Consequently volatility of share prices in India has declined rather than increased consequent to FII flows.

In the present study an attempt was made to ascertain whether stock price volatility is related to volatility of FII flows. *The correlation coefficient between volatility of FII flows and volatility of share prices reveals that the two are negatively correlated with r = - 0.358.* Table 5.11 reveals the share price volatility and volatility of FII flows from calender year 1993 to 1998.

TABLE 5.11

Share Price Volatility and Volatility of FII Flows

Year	*Coefficient of Variation (%)*	
	FII	*Share price*
1993	148.769%	11.179
1994	61.607%	10.380
1995	51.563%	9.706
1996	48.624%	10.683
1997	115.057%	5.870
1998	433.831%	7.977

Graph 5.5 shows the relation between share price volatility and volatility of FII flows.

GRAPH 5.5

Share Price Volatility and FII's Investment Volatility (1993-98)

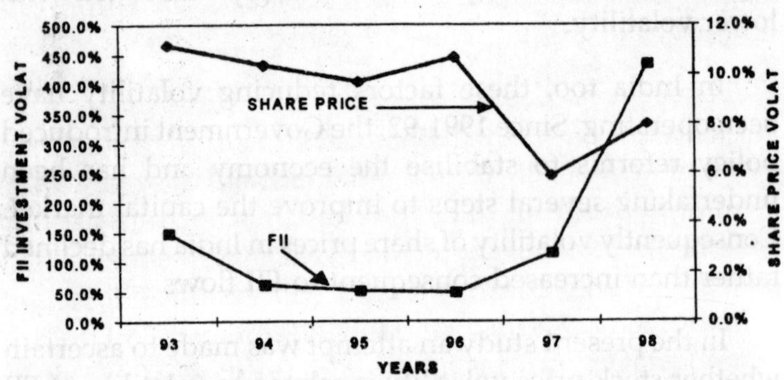

When we run a regression of stock price volatility on FII flow volatility, we find that 12% of volatility in share prices is explained by volatility in FII flows (R-square = 0.1283).

FII INVESTMENT AND SHARE RETURN VOLATILITY

Following Rajan Goyal (1995), share return was defined as:

$R_t = (I_t - I_{t-1})/I_{t-1}$ where

R_t is the share return for period t and

I_t is the share price index for period t.

To calculate the share return, the share price index has been used. Share return is computed on a monthly basis from January 1985 to September 1998. Plotting share return over time (Graph 5.6) we find that share return has not increased upon entry of FIIs in India.

GRAPH 5.6
Share Return (1985-1998)

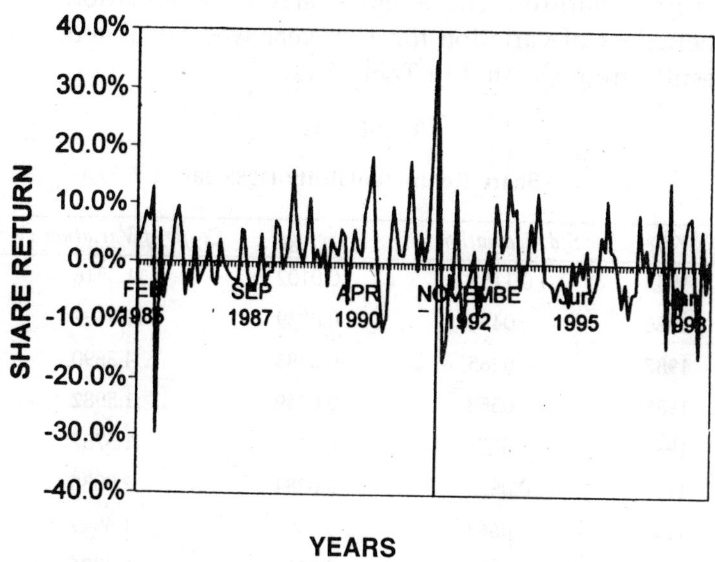

To further ascertain whether there exists any relationship between net FII investment and share return, the correlation coefficient between the two were calculated with lag and without lag based on monthly data. The results are as follows:

> Correlation coefficient between share return and FII investment (without lag) = 0.4812
> Correlation coefficient between share return and FII investment (with lag) [FII = (-1)] = 0.3192

The results indicate that share returns are positively correlated with FII investment. The degree of relationship is low to moderate.

SHARE RETURN VOLATILITY

Co-efficient of variation was used as a measure of share return volatility. The average standard deviation and coefficient of variation for each year was calculated. The results are presented in Table 5.12.

TABLE 5.12

Share Return Volatility (1985-98)

Year	*Std. Deviation*	*Average*	*Coeff. of Variation (%)*
1985	0.1153	0.0102	11.3516
1986	0.0464	-0.0039	11.9497
1987	0.0365	-0.0083	4.3690
1988	0.0558	0.0349	1.5982
1989	0.0379	0.0240	1.5787
1990	0.0825	0.0284	2.9036
1991	0.0663	0.0394	1.6849
1992	0.1578	0.0290	5.4326
1993	0.0684	0.0174	3.9401
1994	0.0581	0.0032	17.9974
1995	0.0293	-0.0305	0.9606
1996	0.0568	-0.0094	6.0754
1997	0.0812	0.0070	11.6670
1998	0.0813	-0.0068	12.0474

Graph 5.7 shows the volatility of share returns from 1985 to 1998. It is interesting to note that share return volatility suddenly increased in 1994. This implies that FII investment temporarily increased share return volatility after a lag.

To further ascertain whether FII investment has influenced share return volatility in India or not hypothesis

GRAPH 5.7

Share Return Volatility (1985-1998)

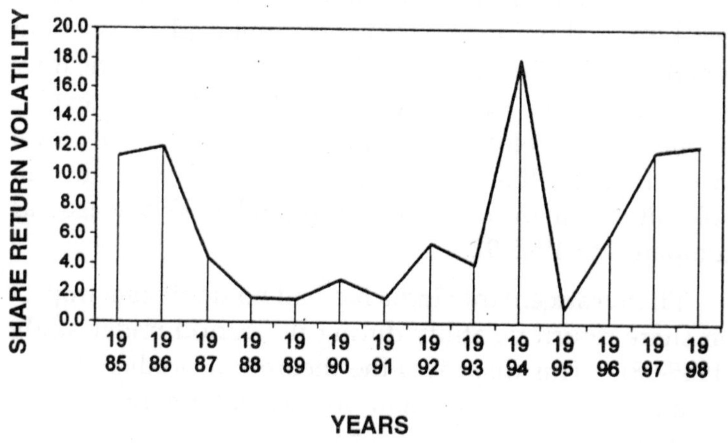

testing was done. The following null and alternate hypothesis were formulated for this purpose.

> H_o = FII flows had no impact on share return volatility in India.
>
> H_1 = FII flows have had an impact on share price volatility in India.

To test the above hypotheses, the period of study 1985-1998 was divided into two parts:

i) Period from 1985 to 1992 - this is the period prior to the entry of FII's in India. It is termed as pre-FII flow period, and
ii) Period from 1993 to 1998 - this is the period when FII's have been operating in India. It is termed as during FII-flow period.

The pre-FII flow period covered 95 months and the during-flow period covered 69 months. The pre-FII flow standard deviation was found to be 0.083 whereas during FII fow standard deviation amounted to 0.065. The Levene's test for equality of variances was employed to ascertain whether the two standard deviations are significantly different or not. The analysis found significance level = 0.4307. We, therefore, accept null hypothesis (at 95% level of confidence) that there is no significant difference in volatility of share return in the period 1993 onwards as compared to 1985-92.

FII investment into India has had no significant impact on share return volatility during the period under study (1985-98).[13] This disproves the theoretical prediction that opening up of markets and consequent financial flows add to volatility of stock returns.

These results in the Indian case are not very surprising since the cumulative net investment by FII's from 1992-93 upto December 1997 has not been more than 1.07% of the market capitalisation during this period.

SHARE RETURN VOLATILITY AND VOLATILITY OF FII FLOWS

The study made an attempt to ascertain whether share return volatility is related to volatility of FII flows. The correlation coefficient between volatility of share return and volatility of FII flows reveals almost no relationships between the two in India since r = 0.2294. Table 5.13 shows the relationship between share return volatility and volatility of FII flows.

That there exists no relationship between share return volatility and volatility of FII flows is also evident from Graph 5.8. Only 5% volatility in share return is explained by volatility of FII flows.

TABLE 5.13

Share Return Volatility and Volatility of FII Flows

Year	*Coefficient of Variation (%)*	
	Share return	*FII*
1993	3.940	148.769
1994	17.997	61.607
1995	0.960	51.563
1996	6.075	48.624
1997	11.667	115.057
1998	12.047	433.831

GRAPH 5.8

Share Return Volatility and FII Volatility

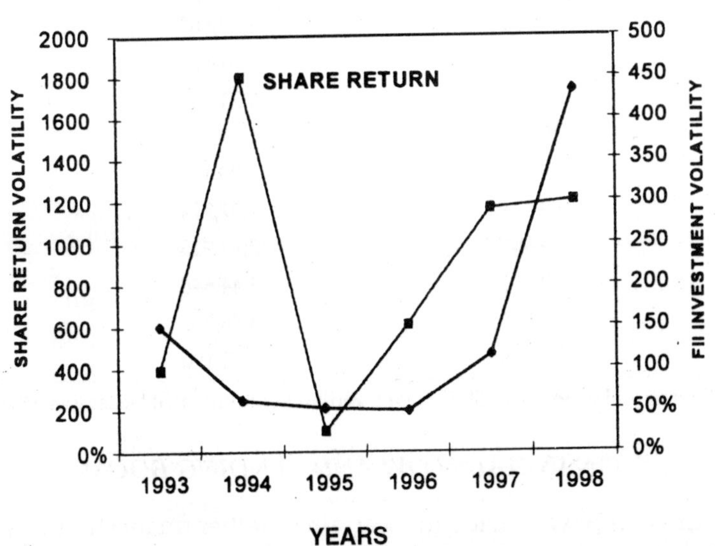

SECTION III

FINANCIAL FLOW AND BANKING SECTOR

An attempt was made to determine whether:

i) India experienced a lending boom alongwith financial flow to India.
ii) Increase in bank lending has exacerbated macroeconomic vulnerability in India, and
iii) Increase in bank lending has exacerbated financial vulnerability in India.

TABLE 5.14

India: Bank Credit (1985-98)

Year	*Bank Credit (Rs. Crore)*
1985-86	82,803
1986-87	94,741
1987-88	1,07,487
1988-89	1,27,882
1989-90	1,51,704
1990-91	1,71,769
1991-92	1,87,993
1992-93	2,20,135
1993-94	2,37,774
1994-95	2,92,723
1995-96	3,44,648
1996-97	3,76,307
1997-98	4,32,190

Source: Handbook of Statistics on Indian Economy, RBI December 1998.

FINANCIAL FLOW AND LENDING BOOM

An attempt was made to ascertain whether financial inflows have financed a rapid expansion in bank lending or not in India. Table 5.14 depicts the amount of credit extended by banks in India in the pre-FII inflow episode (1985-86 to 1991-92) and FII inflow episode (1992-93 to 1997-98).[14]

To ascertain whether India has experienced a lending boom as capital has flowed to India in the form of FII investment, bank lending as a percentage of GDP was calculated. The results are shown in Table 5.15.

TABLE 5.15

Bank Lending (as a %age of GDP)

Year	*Bank lending (Rs. crores)*	*GDP (Rs. crore)*	*Bank Lending as a %age of GDP*
1985-86	82,803	2,33,799	35.4163
1986-87	94,741	2,60,000	36.4346
1987-88	1,07,487	2,94,851	36.4547
1988-89	1,27,882	3,52,706	36.2574
1989-90	1,51,704	4,08,662	37.1221
1990-91	1,71,769	4,77,814	35.9489
1991-92	1,87,993	5,52,768	34.0094
1992-93	2,20,135	6,30,772	34.8993
1993-94	2,37,774	7,32,874	32.4440
1994-95	2,92,723	8,68,019	33.7231
1995-96	3,44,648	10,06,286	34.2495
1996-97	3,76,307	11,49,215	32.7447
1997-98	4,32,190	—	—

India has not experienced rapid credit expansion during periods of strong FII inflows since average bank lending (as a percentage of GDP) during pre-FII inflow period was 35.9491 whereas average bank lending during FII inflow period (1992-93 to 1996-97) was 33.6121.[15] *This figure for India is quite low as compared to figures for Indonesia (48.6%), Malaysia (127.9%), Phillipines (48.4%), Thailand (96%) and South Korea (96.3%).*[16]

Further, hypothesis testing was also done to ascertain

whether there has been a significant increase in bank lending (as a percentage of GDP) during the FII-inflow episode. The following null and alternate hypotheses were formulated for this purpose:

> H_o - There is no difference in bank lending (as a percentage of GDP) during FII inflow episode.
>
> H1 - There is a significant difference in bank lending (as a percentage of GDP) during FII inflow period.

The FII inflow period being the period from 1992-93 onwards and pre-FII inflow period being 1985-86 to 1991-92.

Employing t-test for independent samples, the study found that 2-tail significance (= 0.003) < 0.05. Hence we reject null hypothesis at 95% level of confidence and conclude that there is a significant difference in bank lending as a percentage of GDP in the FII inflow period as compared to pre-FII inflow period. Average annual bank lending as a percentage of GDP has infact declined in the FII-inflow period.

The theoretical prediction that inflows often finance a rapid expansion in bank lending did not hold true in India.[17]

One possible explanation for the absence of lending boom in India during inflow period is that banks in India, under heavy pressure to avoid taking on loans that might turn out non-performing, tended to use the increased liquidity with them primarily to purchase government securities rather than to increase credit availability. Domestic interest rates declined under the pressure of the growing liquidity, which further encouraged the banks to purchase government securities for capital gains. Toward the end of 1994, however, when the capital inflows eased off and interest rates began to rise, commercial banks in India began expanding their loan books and reducing their holdings of government securities.

BANK LENDING AND MACROECONOMIC VULNERABILITY

A surge in financial flow may increase bank lending and exacerbate macroeconomic vulnerability by biasing the increase in aggregate expenditures that would result from an increase in financial flow towards consumption instead of investment. The study made an attempt to find out whether the increase in bank lending consequent to financial flow has exacerbated macroeconomic vulnerability in India by reducing potential investment and financing a consumption boom.

Following World Bank (1997), macroeconomic vulnerability is measured by excess consumption and under-investment.

To ascertain whether there has been an increase in bank lending during FII flow period following null and alternate hypotheses were formulated:

> H_0 - There is no difference in bank lending during FII inflow episode.
>
> H_1 - There is a difference in bank lending during FII inflow period.

The FII inflow period being the period from January 1993 to March 1998 and pre-FII inflow period being April 1990 to December 1992. Considering monthly data and employing t-test for independent samples, the study found that 2-tail significance (= 0.000) < 0.05. Hence we reject null hypothesis at 95% confidence level and conclude that *there is a significant difference in monthly bank lending during*

FII inflow period as compared to pre-FII inflow period. The average monthly lending has infact increased during FII flow period (=30,22,91.9265 Rs. crore) as compared to pre-FII flow period (=1,76,218 Rs. crore).

Next, the study tried to find out whether this increase in bank lending during FII flow period has been associated with over-consumption and under-investment or not.

OVER CONSUMPTION

The position of final consumption expenditure in India from 1985-86 to 1996-97 is given in Table 5.16 below.

TABLE 5.16

Final Consumption Expenditure (at Current Prices)

(Rs. Crore)

Year	*Private*	*Public*	*Total*
1985-86	1,77,758	29,174	2,06,932
1986-87	1,99,998	34,625	2,34,623
1987-88	2,24,061	40,843	2,64,904
1988-89	2,58,993	47,331	3,06,324
1989-90	2,90,072	54,203	3,44,275
1990-91	3,32,364	61,779	3,94,143
1991-92	3,85,150	69,459	4,54,609
1992-93	4,35,317	78,596	5,13,913
1993-94	4,98,927	89,926	5,88,853
1994-95	5,75,335	1,00,498	6,75,833
1995-96	6,49,094	1,15,957	7,65,051
1996-97	7,34,866	1,32,166	8,67,032

Source: Handbook of Statistics on Indian Economy, RBI, December 1998.

To ascertain whether there has been overconsumption in India during FII flow period, total consumption as a percentage of GDP was calculated as is depicted in Table 5.17.

Hypothesis-testing was done to ascertain whether there is a significant difference in consumption (as a percentage of GDP) during FII flow period. For this purpose following hypotheses were formulated:

> H_0 - There is no difference in consumption (as a percentage of GDP) during FII flow period.
> H_1 - There is a difference in consumption (as a percentage of GDP) during FII flow period.

TABLE 5.17

Total Consumption (As a Percentage of GDP)

Year	*Total Consumption (Rs. cr.)*	*GDP (Rs. cr.)*	*Consumption as a % of GDP*
1985-86	2,06,932	2,33,799	88.50%
1986-87	2,34,623	2,60,030	90.23%
1987-88	2,64,904	2,94,851	89.84%
1988-89	3,06,324	3,52,706	86.85%
1989-90	3,44,275	4,08,662	84.24%
1990-91	3,94,143	4,77,814	82.49%
1991-92	4,54,609	5,52,768	82.24%
1992-93	5,13,913	6,30,772	81.47%
1993-94	5,88,853	7,32,874	80.35%
1994-95	6,75,833	8,68,019	77.86%
1995-96	7,65,051	10,06,286	76.03%
1996-97	8,67,032	11,49,215	75.45%

The FII flow period being the period from 1992-93 to 1996-97 and pre-FII flow period being the period from 1985-86 to 1991-92. Considering annual data and employing t-test for independent samples, the study found that 2-tail significance (= 0.0012) < 0.05. Hence we reject null hypothesis at 95% level of confidence and conclude that *there is a significant difference in annual consumption (as a percentage of GDP) during FII inflow period as compared to pre-FII inflow period.*

Further, the FII flow period has not been a period of overconsumption in India as compared to pre-FII flow period since average annual consumption (as a percentage of GDP) during FII flow period (= 78.23%) and during pre-FII flow period (= 86.34%). Similarly, private consumption (as a percentage of GDP) was also found to decline in India during FII flow period (the figure for pre-FII flow period being 73.226% and FII-inflow period being 66.364%).

An increase in bank lending during FII inflow period has been associated with underconsumption [as denoted by decline in consumption (as a percentage of GDP)]

UNDER INVESTMENT

The position of investment (gross domestic capital formation - adjusted) in India from 1985-86 to 1996-97 is depicted below in Table 5.18.

TABLE 5.18

India: Investment (1985-97)

(Rs. Crore)

Year	*Household*	*Private Corporate Sector*	*Public*	*Total*
1	2	3	4	5
1985-86	19,620	14,404	29,417	63,442
1986-87	18,251	15,506	34,142	67,899
1987-88	29,798	12,025	33,059	74,882

1	2	3	4	5
1988-89	41,068	15,978	39,365	96,411
1989-90	45,299	19,330	45,566	1,10,195
1990-91	59,923	23,082	52,151	1,35,156
1991-92	47,220	36,311	56,537	1,40,068
1992-93	59,430	47,463	62,763	1,69,656
1993-94	55,156	47,853	69,523	1,72,532
1994-95	86,510	68,120	86,749	2,41,379
1995-96	1,14,702	1,01,801	88,477	3,04,980
1996-97	1,22,899	1,04,734	94,215	3,21,848

Source: Handbook of Statistics on Indian Economy, RBI, December 1998.

To ascertain whether there has been under investment during FII flow period, total investment (as a percentage of GDP) was calculated as is depicted below.

TABLE 5.19

India: Investment as a Percentage of GDP (1985-97)

Year	*Investment (Rs. crore)*	*GDP (Rs. crore)*	*Inv. as %age of GDP*
1985-86	63,442	2,33,799	27.14%
1986-87	67,899	2,60,030	26.11%
1987-88	74,882	2,94,851	25.40%
1988-89	96,411	3,52,706	27.33%
1989-90	1,10,195	4,08,662	26.96%
1990-91	1,35,156	4,77,814	28.29%
1991-92	1,40,068	5,52,768	25.34%
1992-93	1,69,656	6,30,772	26.90%
1993-94	1,72,532	7,32,874	23.54%
1994-95	2,41,379	8,68,019	27.80%
1995-96	3,04,980	10,06,286	30.31%
1996-97	3,21,848	11,49,215	28.01%

Hypothesis testing was done on the above data to ascertain whether investment (as a percentage of GDP) had changed during FII flow period. The following hypothesis were formulated for this purpose:

> H_0 - There is no difference in investment (as a percentage of GDP) during FII flow period.
>
> H_1 - There is a difference in investment (as a percentage of GDP) during FII flow period.

The FII flow period was the period from 1992-93 to 1996-97 and the period from 1985-86 to 1991-92 was considered pre-FII flow period. Considering annual data, t-test for independent samples was applied. The study found that significance (2-tailed) (= 0.54) > 0.05. Hence, we accept null hypothesis at 95% level of confidence that there is no significant difference in investment (as a percentage of GDP) during FII flow period as compared to pre-FII flow period.

Further, FII flow period has not been a period of under investment since average annual investment as a percentage of GDP during FII inflow period was found to be 27.31% which is greater than the average for pre-FII flow period (= 26.65%). Thus, the study found that an increase in bank lending during FII flow period has not been accompanied by under-investment during this period.

An increase in bank lending during FII-flow period in India has not exacerbated macroeconomic vulnerability.

BANK LENDING AND FINANCIAL SECTOR VULNERABILITY

A surge in financial flow may increase bank lending and exacerbate financial sector vulnerability if the banks are not able to improve their ability to absorb negative shocks arising from greater risk exposure of banks due to increased lending. The study made an attempt to find out whether the increase in bank lending during FII flow period has exacerbated financial sector vulnerability in India. Following World Bank (1997) the study uses the following indicators to assess the financial health, risk exposure and resilience to shocks of Indian banking sector - capitalisation ratio, level of provisions and non-performing assets and profitability indices.[18] The trend behaviour of these variables was studied on the lines adopted by World Bank (1997) to find whether financial sector vulnerability has increased (i.e., shock absorbing capacity of banks has declined) during the period of increase in bank lending. Financial sector vulnerability being inversely related to capitalisation ratio, provisions and contingencies, profitability ratio and directly related to NPA levels.

(i) Capitalisation ratio

Capitalisation ratio is measured as the stock of capital plus reserves and surplus relative to the stock of bank assets. The capitalisation ratios of all scheduled commercial banks in India is presented in Table 5.20.

The table reveals that capitalisation ratios have improved since 1992 in case of Indian banks. In SBI and its associates the capitalisation ratio recorded an increase of 176% between 1992 and 1999. For other banks the increase was as follows: Nationalised banks - 89.4%; other scheduled commercial banks = 167.3%; foreign banks - 157.3% and regional rural banks - 213.9%. All scheduled commercial banks in India have shored up their capitalisation ratio by 122.4% between 1992 and 1999.

The significant improvement in capitalisation ratio of banks in India suggests that financial sector vulnerability has not increased in India during the period of increase in bank lending.

TABLE 5.20

Capitalisation Ratio – All Scheduled Commercial Banks

(%)

	1992	*1993*	*1994*	*1995*	*1996*	*1997*	*1998*	*1999*
SBI & Associates	1.671	1.790	3.3959	3.5552	3.7892	4.8021	5.1711	4.6187
Nationalized Banks	3.122	3.261	5.9596	7.2522	6.6824	6.6624	6.8998	5.9137
Other Scheduled Commercial Banks	2.146	2.523	3.0255	5.0198	7.2213	6.6331	6.5241	5.7373
Foreign Banks	3.650	5.785	7.9386	9.4301	10.5342	11.1803	11.4651	9.3932
RRB's	1.834	1.7676	1.3303	1.3218	2.2248	3.7912	5.4241	5.7570
All scheduled Commercial Banks	2.601	2.8768	5.0253	5.9729	6.0086	6.3728	6.6835	5.7844

Source: Statistical table relating to banks in India, RBI, various issues.

The banking system in India has been successful in building a large cushion in the financial system against the kind of banking calamities hitting East Asian countries. Under-capitalised banks are simply an invitation to banking misbehaviour and a heighted risk of banking collapse. Well capitalised banks are usually better monitored by their shareholders and therefore hold safer portfolios than do poorly capitalised banks.

A better indicator of soundness of viability of banks is the level of capital, and more pragmatically, the level of capital weighted by the associated risks. As per the prudential norms, the commercial banks are required to achieve 9% Capital to Risk-Weighted Assets RAtio (CRAR) by March 31, 2000. This ratio for public sector banks in India stood at 11.2 in 1998-99 and reflects that financial sector vulnerability has not increased in India even in terms of CRAR.

(ii) Level of Provisions

In India, between 1991-92 and 1998-99, Indian banks exhibited a fall in provisions and contingencies (as % to total assets). In case of SBI and its seven associates, provisions and contingencies (as % to total assets) fell by 56.2% and for nationalised banks the same declined by 12.4%. Provisions and contingencies (as % to total assets) declined even in old private banks and foreign banks - the decline being 51.3% for old private banks and 53.4% for foreign banks. Only in case of new private banks there was a rise in level of provisions and contingencies of about 74.4% between 1994-95 and 1998-99. The decline in level of provisioning was most pronounced in India in foreign banks (53.4% as compared to 39.5% for PSBs and 50.7% for private banks). The level of provisions in Indian banks is presented in Table 5.21.

The decline in level of provisions in Indian banks is indicative of increased financial sector vulnerability since an increase in level of provisions strengthens the shock absorbing capacity of banks.

TABLE 5.21

Level of Provisions - All Scheduled Commercial Banks

(Provisions & Contingencies as % to total assets)

	1991–92	*1992–93*	*1993–94*	*1994–95*	*1995–96*	*1996–97*	*1997–98*	*1998–99*
SBI and Seven Associates,	2.54	1.59	1.19	1.41	1.67	1.35	0.98	1.11
19 Nationalised Banks	0.97	2.12	2.70	1.02	1.50	0.85	0.71	0.85
27 Public Sector Banks	1.57	1.92	2.14	1.16	1.56	1.03	0.81	0.95
25 Old Private Banks	1.50	1.00	1.26	1.00	1.04	0.98	1.16	0.73
9 New Private Banks	—	—	—	0.43	0.92	1.24	1.32	0.75
34 Indian Private Banks	1.50	1.00	1.26	0.90	1.02	1.05	1.21	0.74
42 Foreign Banks	3.50	4.74	2.28	2.27	1.77	2.44	2.94	1.63
All Scheduled Commerical Banks	1.71	2.11	2.10	1.22	1.54	1.15	1.02	0.98

Source: Report on Trend & Progress of Banking in India, RBI, various issues.

(iii) Non-performing assets

Public sector banks in India have been in a position to improve the quality of their assets by reducing the stock of non-performing assets. Gross NPAs as % to Gross advances have declined by 31.47% between 1993 and 1999 while net NPA as a % to net advances declined by 24.3% between 1995 and 1999. As a % to total assets, gross NPAs have declined by 43.2% and net NPAs by 22.5%.[19] The position of public sector banks in respect of non-performing assets is depicted in Table 5.22.

TABLE 5.22

Non-performing Assets (NPA) of Public Sector Banks (1993-1999)

(Rs. Crore)

End March	*Gross NPA*	*% to Gross advances*	*% to Total Assets*	*Net NPA*	*% to Net advances*	*% to total Assets*
1993	39,253	23.2	11.8	—	—	—
1994	41,041	24.8	10.8	—	—	—
1995	38,385	19.5	8.7	17,567	10.7	4.0
1996	41,661	18.0	8.2	18,297	8.9	3.6
1997	43,577	17.8	7.8	20,285	9.2	3.6
1998	45,653	16.0	7.0	21,232	8.2	3.3
1999	51,710	15.9	6.7	24,211	8.1	3.1

Source: RBI Bulletin, Report on Trend & Progress of Banking in India, RBI, 1998-99.

Private sector banks in India have, however, increased their financial vulnerability as gross NPAs have increased by 6.68% as a % to total assets and by 22.97% as a % to gross advances between 1996-97 and 1998-99. Net NPAs, too, have increased by 11.8% as % to total assets and by 28.9% as % to net advances over the same period in case of private sector banks in India. The increase in NPAs is due to a significant decline in standard assets.[20] The position of private sector banks in respect of non-performing assets is depicted in Table 5.23.

A similar trend was seen in the case of foreign banks in India. In their case, gross NPAs increased by 62.8% as a % to gross advances and by 38.1% as a % to total assets between 1997 and 1999. Net NPAs, too, have increased by 5.3% as % to net advances. However, as a % to total assets, net NPAs have declined by 11.1% between 1997 and 1999.

The position of foreign banks in India in respect of NPA is depicted in Table 5.24.

TABLE 5.23

Non-performing Assets of Private Sector Banks (1996-97 to 1998-99)

	Gross NPA		*Net NPA*	
	As % to Gross Advances	*As % to Total Assets*	*As % to Net Advances*	*As % to total Assets*
25 old Private Banks				
1996-97	10.71	5.23	6.65	3.11
1997-98	10.92	5.06	6.46	2.84
1998-99	12.96	5.77	8.42	3.57
9 New private Banks				
1996-97	2.63	1.34	1.97	0.95
1997-98	3.51	1.57	2.63	1.12
1998-99	5.67	2.26	4.15	1.62
34 Indian Private Sector Banks				
1996-97	8.49	4.19	5.37	2.54
1997-98	8.67	3.95	5.26	2.29
1998-99	10.44	4.47	6.92	2.84

Source: Report on Trend & Progress of Banking in India, RBI, 1998-99.

The decline in NPA of public sector banks (from 1993 to 1999) is indicative of decline in financial sector vulnerability in their case while the increase in NPA of private sector banks and foreign banks (during 1997-1999) is reflective of an increase in vulnerability in their case. For all scheduled commercial banks in India, gross NPAs to total assets declined from 7% in 1997 to 6.2% in 1999 and net NPAs to net total assets also declined

TABLE 5.24

Non Performing Assets of Foreign Banks in India: 1997 to 1999 (as at end – March)

(Amount in Rs. crore)

		Gros NPA's				Net NPA's		
	Gross Advances	*Gross NPA's*	*% to Gross Advances*	*% to total Assets*	*Net Advances*	*Net NPA's*	*% to Net Advances*	*% to total Assets*
1997	27,525	1,181	4.3	2.1	26,853	516	1.9	0.9
1998	30,972	1,976	6.4	3.0	29,652	666	2.2	1.0
1999	31,433	2,201	7.0	2.9	29,890	607	2.0	0.8

Source: Report on Trend & Progress of Banking in India, RBI, 1998-99

from 3.3% in 1997 to 2.9% in 1998-99 - the declines indicating reduced financial sector vulnerability of scheduled commercial banks in India.

(iv) Profitability ratio

Banks profitability has been examined by observing the behaviour of gross profit/loss as a % to total assets, net profit/loss as % to total assets and net interest income (spread) as % to total assets.

TABLE 5.25

Gross Profit/Loss - All Scheduled Commercial Banks in India

(as % to total assets)

	1991–92	*1992–93*	*1993–94*	*1994–95*	*1995–96*	*1996–97*	*1997–98*	*1998–99*
SBI and Seven Associates,	2.54	1.59	1.19	1.41	1.67	1.35	0.98	1.11
SBI and Seven Associates	2.75	1.82	1.44	1.95	2.10	2.18	2.03	1.63
19 Nationalised Banks	1.27	0.42	0.72	1.12	1.14	1.26	1.33	1.22
27 Public Sector Banks	1.84	0.94	0.99	1.41	1.49	1.60	1.58	1.37
25 Old Private Banks	2.08	1.36	1.82	2.16	2.10	1.89	1.97	1.21
9 New Private Banks	—	—	—	1.07	2.77	2.98	2.86	1.78
34 Indian Private Banks	2.08	1.36	1.82	1.96	2.23	2.18	2.25	1.42
Foreign Banks	5.06	1.86	3.79	3.93	3.35	3.62	3.91	2.53
All Scheduled Commerical Banks	2.08	1.03	1.25	1.64	1.69	1.82	1.84	1.47

Source: Report on Trend & Progress of Banking in India, RBI, various issues.

Banks in India have improved their gross profit as % to total assets between 1992-93 and 1998-99. The gross profit/loss as a % to total assets has increased for all banks between 1992-93 and 1998-99 viz., public sector banks, private banks and foreign banks - the increase being 45.7% in case of public sector banks, 4.4% in case of private banks and 36% in case of foreign banks. The scenario of banks in India in respect of gross profit/loss as % to total assets is depicted in Table 5.25. There was a sharp decline in this ratio in 1992-93 when prudential norms were introduced. Since then there has been a healthy upward trend in this ratio for all scheduled commercial banks viz. public sector banks, private banks and foreign banks.

The gross profit/loss as percentage to total assets has improved by 42.7% for all scheduled commercial banks in India since the onset of FII flows in India implying that financial sector has not become vulnerable during the period of increase in bank lending.

If we look at net profit/loss figures for Indian banks as a percentage to total assets we find that during the period of increase in bank lending (1992-93 onwards) this ratio has improved in all scheduled commercial banks. Net profit/loss as a percentage to total assets increased by 145.4% in case of all scheduled commercial banks during the period of increase in bank lending (1992-93 to 1998-99). The increase in respect of respective banks being: SBI and its associates - 131.8%, Nationalised banks - 121.6%, old private banks - 41.2%, foreign banks - 131.3% during the period 1992-93 to 1998-99. In new private banks net profit/loss as percentage to total assets recorded an increase of 60.9% between 1994-95 and 1998-99.

The financial sector vulnerability as measured by net profit/loss as percentage to total assets reveals that Indian banking system has not increased its vulnerability during the period of increase in bank lending since the profitability position of banks has improved during this period.

The net profit/loss scenario of all scheduled commercial banks in India is depicted in Table 5.26:

TABLE 5.26

Net Profit/Loss - All Scheduled Commercial Banks in India

(as % to total assets)

	1991–92	*1992–93*	*1993–94*	*1994–95*	*1995–96*	*1996–97*	*1997–98*	*1998–99*
SBI and Seven Associates,	2.54	1.59	1.19	1.41	1.67	1.35	0.98	1.11
SBI and Seven Associates	0.21	0.22	0.25	0.54	0.42	0.84	1.06	0.51
19 Nationalised Banks	0.30	–1.71	–1.98	0.10	–0.36	0.41	0.62	0.37
27 Public Sector Banks	0.28	–0.99	–1.15	0.25	–0.07	0.57	0.77	0.42
25 Old Private Banks	0.57	0.34	0.56	1.16	1.06	0.91	0.81	0.48
9 New Private Banks	–	–	–	0.64	1.85	1.73	1.55	1.03
34 Indian Private Banks	0.57	0.34	0.56	1.06	1.21	1.13	1.04	0.68
Foreign Banks	1.57	–2.88	1.51	1.66	1.58	1.19	0.97	0.90
All Scheduled Commerical Banks	0.39	–1.08	–0.85	0.41	0.16	0.67	0.82	0.49

Source: Report on Trend & Progress of Banking in India, RBI, various issues.

Another profitability ratio that the study used to measure financial sector vulnerability during period of increase in bank lending is - net interest income (spread) as percentage to total assets. Since 1992-93 till 1998-99, this ratio has improved for public sector banks but deteriorated in case of private banks and foreign banks. All scheduled commercial banks in India have recorded an increase of 10.8% in this ratio between 1992-93 and 1998-99. During this period SBI and its associates exhibited a fall in asset profitability of 5.3%; the fall in old private banks being 25.8%; in foreign banks asset profitability declined by 2.5%. The net interest income (spread) for all scheduled commercial banks is exhibited in Table 5.27.

The increase in spread during the period of increase in bank lending for all scheduled commercial banks implies that increase in bank lending has not increased financial sector vulnerability.

TABLE 5.27

Net Interest Income (Spread) – All Scheduled Commercial Banks in India

(as % to total assets)

	1991–92	*1992–93*	*1993–94*	*1994–95*	*1995–96*	*1996–97*	*1997–98*	*1998–99*
SBI and Seven Associates	3.80	3.01	2.68	3.26	3.34	3.48	3.14	2.85
19 Nationalised Banks	2.86	2.02	2.17	2.73	2.92	2.97	2.78	2.79
27 Public Sector Banks	3.22	2.39	2.36	2.92	3.08	3.16	2.91	2.81
25 Old Private Banks	4.02	2.91	2.97	3.04	3.14	2.93	2.57	2.61
9 New Private Banks	—	—	—	1.17	2.84	2.88	2.23	1.98
34 Indian Private Banks	4.02	2.91	2.97	2.69	3.08	2.92	2.46	2.09
Foreign Banks	3.92	3.56	4.21	4.24	3.74	4.13	3.93	3.47
All Scheduled Commerical Banks	3.31	2.51	2.54	3.00	3.13	3.22	2.95	2.78

Source: Report on Trend & Progress of Banking in India, RBI, various issues.

An increase in bank lending since 1992-93 in India has not exacerbated financial sector vulnerability in India since three of the four variables used to measure financial sector vulnerability have not deteriorated during this period for all scheduled commercial banks. All scheduled commercial banks have improved their capitalisation ratio, profitability ratio and reduced their NPA as a percentage to total assets. Only in respect of provisions and contingencies we find that all scheduled commercial banks in India have weakened themselves. It seems that because India has meshed financial sector reforms with the surge in financial flows several symptoms of a weakening banking system are not present in India.

CONCLUSION

Financial flows to India have not had an adverse impact on the Indian financial system. The theoretical predictions that financial flows may overheat the economy, it may increase volatility of asset prices and returns and it may lead to a lending boom which may exacerbate macroeconomic and financial sector vulnerability have not proved true for India.

NOTES

1. This was the year when FII's entered the Indian market.
2. The capital inflows under consideration appear in the form of surpluses in the capital account of about Rs. 15,244.1 crore in 1992-93, Rs. 31,002.2 crore in 1993- 94, about Rs. 25,157.1 crore in 1994-95, Rs. 9809 crore in 1995-96, Rs. 36,598 crore and Rs. 38,922.6 crore in 1996-97 and 1997-98 respectively.
3. Calvo, Leiderman and Reinhart (1994) found that 45% of the inflows in Latin America during 1990-92 went into reserve accumulation while in Asia, it found that the proportion of inflow channeled into reserve accumulation was 62% during 1989-92.
4. RBI has been intervening in the light of financial flows to India because exchange rate regine in India is market determined by demand and supply in the foreign exchange market. There is no officially fixed exchange rate of Re. RBI stands ready to intervene to maintain orderly market conditions and to curb excessive speculation. In floating exchange rate, intervention by Central Bank is passive whereas in fixed exchange rate domestic authorities actively intervene.
5. Money supply in India seems to be more closely related to NRI flow.
6. Data for the period 1985 to 1987 was not available for WPI with base 1981-82 = 100.
7. According to Reddy Y.V. (1999) the underlying logic behind the concept of core-inflation could be utilised to explain the so-called current puzzle of low current rate of inflation and relatively high growth in money supply.
8. The finding is however consistent with World Bank (1997) study

which found that thirteen out of twenty countries studied had reduced their inflation rates during their inflow episodes, and five of the thirteen saw large decelerations. Even Corbo.V. & Hernandez L. (1994) found that all the countries studied have been successful in avoiding a permanent and significant increase in inflation.

9. World Bank (1997) found that none of the five East Asian Countries studied experienced a large real appreciation during their inflow periods: four had large real depreciations, while the other kept its real exchange rate approximately stable. Thus our finding is consistent with World Bank (1997). Real appreciation was experienced by six of the seven Latin American countries in the sample studied by World Bank (1997).

10. FIIs are predominant in Portfolio flows to India and monthly data on GDR and off-shore funds was not available for first few years, so study focuses on FIIs.

11. Most of the studies have used standard deviation as a measure of volatility. Instead of standard deviation, which measures absolute volatility the study uses coefficient of variation as a measure of volatility.

12. Most empirical studies have cocluded that asset price volatility did not increase during the current inflow period, e.g. BIS (1996), Bekaert & Harvey (1995), Kim and Singal (1993). Most of these studies found a decline in absolute volatility. However, in a cross- country study of emerging markets, Aziz (1995) reports that Indian stock price volatility has increased since FIIs have been permitted to participate. This conclusion is based on a very broad time comparison: the period 1976 - May 1992 compared with the period June 1992 - February 1994. If one looks at a shorter time span, the opposite seems to be the case: price volatility has declined since mid-1992 compared with the previous two and a half years [Collyns Charles (1995)]. A number of factors, however, may account for this decline other than opening of the market.

13. This finding is in tune with the findings with regard to other markets. IMF (1995) found that absolute volatility of stock market returns did not increase during periods of high and volatile portfolio inflows in Korea, Mexico and Thailand. Bekaert & Harvey (1995) as well observed that volatility of returns remain unchanged or declined in 13 out of their sample of 17 countries after liberalisation of their capital markets. Rajan Goyal (1995) found that globalisation of Indian capital market through FII investment and GDRs have not added significantly to stock

market volatility. Kim and Singal (1993) found an increase in share returns in the mid 1980s for Zimbabwe and in the late 1980s for Greece. In the rest of the sample (18 countries), they found no appreciable change in volatility of returns with time.

14. The data on bank lending to private sector was not available from RBI or any other Indian source and in its absence the study relied on data pertaining to bank lending to commercial sector which includes RBI's credit to commercial sector and commercial bank credit to commercial sector.
15. Examples of rapid credit expansion during periods of strong capital inflows include Mexico, where commercial bank loans to private sector increased from 27% of GDP in 1991 to 47% in 1994. The same ratio increased in Indonesia from 25% in 1988 to 53% in 1994 and in Thailand from 51% to 89% over 1988-94.
16. These figures are for the year 1996 as reported by Institute of International Finance, Merrill Lynch.
17. World Bank (1997) found that in all except two countries (viz. Chile and Venezuela in 1990s) the share of bank lending to GDP was higher in the inflow period than in the years prior to the inflow. For all countries and all episodes taken together, the average lending to GDP ratio during the years prior to the inflow surge was 29.4%. During the inflow periods, the average lending to GDP ratio was 40.9%.
18. Certain other indicators of banks ability to withstand shocks are liquidity of these assets, relative maturity of their assets compared with their liabilities, magnitude of exposure to foreign exchange risk, sectoral risk. Position of Indian banks on these parameters is evaluated later due to non-availability of continuous and consistent data.
19. It is important to consider net NPAs (i.e. net of provisioning) rather than gross NPAs in India because Indian banks are typically hesitant to write off NPAs even when adequate provisions have been made.
20. The share of standard assets to total advances has come down from 91.5% in 1996-97 to 91.3% in 1997-98 and further to 89.6% in 1998-99.

6

Restructuring in Indian Banking Sector in 1990's

Restructuring of banking sector in 1990's was undertaken as part of a comprehensive package of structural reforms Restructuring of banking sector is directed towards making the Indian banking system stronger, more resilient and geared to meet the challenges of globalisation. The present chapter attempts to give an overview of India's attempts to restructure its banking sector in 1990's.

RESTRUCTURING OF BANKS: PHILOSOPHY AND STRATEGY

The major objectives of banking sector reforms, as elaborated by Dr. Rangarajan, Governor RBI, fall under three broad categories viz.

1. Measures aimed at removing the external constraints bearing on the profitability of banks.
2. Measures aimed at improving the financial health of banks by introducing appropriate prudential norms, and
3. Measures aimed at institutional strengthening

including improving the competitiveness of the banking system.

More specifically, the restructuring programme includes measures which would:

(i) bring about suitable modifications in the policy framework within which various components of the financial system operate, such as rationalisation of interest rates, reduction in the levels of resource preemptions and improving the effectiveness of direct credit programmes.

(ii) affect improvement in the financial health and competitive capabilities by means of prescription of prudential norms, recapitalisation of banks, restructuring of weaker banks, allowing freer entry of new banks and generally improving the incentive system under which banks function.

(iii) build financial infrastructure relating to supervision, audit, technology and legal framework and

(iv) upgrade the level of managerial competence and the quality of human resource of banks by reviewing the policies relating to recruitment, training and placement.

There are certain 'commandments' or pre-requisites for restructuring of the banking sector. First and foremost, macroeconomic stabilisation is a must during the restructuring process. Fiscal and external policies must support monetary policy in maintaining the overall macroeconomic balance. Secondly, during the restructuring period, prudential regulation must be introduced and adhered to in order to help safeguard against a financial crisis and prevent the undermining of monetary control, and macroeconomic adjustment. Thirdly, the Government must simultaneously implement wide-ranging reforms in other sectors specially those which require support from the banking system to get the best results.

RESTRUCTURING OF BANKS IN INDIA: SALIENT FEATURES

In conformity with the broad philosohpy and strategy for reform, salient features of the restructuring exercise in India could be analysed under following categories. Restructuring strategy had the following key components:

(A) STRENGTHENING OF CAPITAL

Recapitalisation: A major component of the restructuring programme of public sector banks undertaken by the Government and the RBI involves an aggressive programme to recapitalise them by injecting capital funds. The Government of India made a provision of Rs. 5,700 crore in the Union Budget 1993-94 for recapitalisation of nationalised banks. Recapitalisation of 19 nationalised banks was undertaken on January, 1, 1994.[1]

For further strengthening the capital base of nationalised banks, a sum of Rs. 5,600 crore was provided in the Union Budget 1994-95. The Government of India released an amount Rs. 5,287.12 crore in 1994-95.

In 1995-96, Government released a sum of Rs. 850 crore towards recapitalisation of 6 nationalised banks,[2] with a view to strengthening their capital base for achieving 8% capital to risk weighted assets ratio (CRAR).

During 1996-97, the Government of India contributed a sum of Rs. 1,509 crore towards recapitalisation of six nationalised banks.[3] During 1998-99, the Government extended recapitalisation facility to three public sector banks and provided a sum aggregating Rs. 400 crore[4] as compared with Rs. 2700 crore provided during 1997-98 to three public sector banks. The capital contribution by the government to the nationalised bank upto March 31, 1999 amounted to Rs. 20,446.12 crore.

Public Issue of Shares: SBI accessed the capital market and raised Rs. 2,212 crore in the form of capital and Rs. 1000 crore through bonds.

Oriental Bank of Commerce was the second nationalised bank to access the capital market by raising a sum of Rs. 387.24 crore in October 1994. During 1996-97, Dena Bank entered the capital market and raised Rs. 180 crore in 1996. In December 1996, Bank of Baroda entered the capital market in February 1997 and raised Rs. 675 crore.[5] Further, during 1997-98, three public sector banks, viz., Corporation bank (Rs. 304 crore), State Bank of Travancore (Rs. 90 crore) and State Bank of Bikaner and Jaipur (Rs. 65.94 crore) accessed the capital market to raise their capital. During 1998-99, the Reserve Bank gave approval for two public issue of South India Bank Limited. and UTI Bank Limited.

Issue of Sub-ordinated Debt Instruments for Inclusion in Tier II Capital: Besides raising equity capital, public sector banks were permitted to raise subordinated debt through private placement, for inclusion under Tier II capital for capital adequacy purposes. The amount raised by the banks is given in Table 6.1.

TABLE 6.1

Subordinated Debt Raised by Public Sector Banks 1996-97 to 1998-99

1996-97

Sl. No.	*Name of Bank*	*Amount Permitted*	*Amount Raised*
1.	Punjab National Bank	190	189.98
2.	State Bank of Mysore	70	75.00
3.	State Bank of Travancore	25	N.A.
4.	State Bank of Bikaner and Jaipur	40	N.A.

1997-98

Sl. No.	*Name of Bank*	*Amount Permitted*	*Amount Raised*
1.	Punjab and Sind Bank	100	100
2.	Bank of India	700	Nil
3.	Syndicate Bank	80	60
4.	Dena Bank	200	155

1998-99

S. No.	*Name of Bank*	*Amount Raised*
1.	Catholic Syrian Bank	16.60
2.	United Western Bank Ltd.	70.00
3.	ICICI Bank	68.00
4.	Federal Bank Ltd.	150.00

N.A. Not Available

Source: Report on Trend and Progress of Banking in India, various issues.

Write-off of Capital: The Government is encouraging PSB's to raise capital through public issues. The write -off of accumulated losses against paid-up capital would enable PSB's to have earnings per share at higher level for making public issues. As banks with cumulative losses were not able to set off their losses against their capital, the Banking Companies (Acquisition and Transfer of Undertakings) Acts 1970/1980 were amended in January 1995 enabling Banks to reduce their paid-up capital subject to the stipulation that the paid-up capital cannot be reduced at any time below 25% as on the date of the amendment. The sum provided by the Government of India towards writing down of the capital base of nationalised banks is given in Table 6.2.

The aggregate capital allowed to be written off by nationalised banks till March 31, 1999 Rs. 6,037.18 crore.

TABLE 6.2

Write off of Capital by Public Sector Banks
1995-96 to 1998-99

Year	*Name of Bank*		*Amount (Rs. crore)*
1995-96	1.	Bank of India	1369.92
	2.	Dena Bank	136.29
1996-97	1.	Allahabad Bank	532.00
	2.	Overseas Bank	1,000.00
1997-98	1.	Canara bank	507.10
1998-99	1.	Andhra Bank	243.37
	2.	Bank of Maharashtra	418.18
	3.	Punjab and Sind Bank	462.47
	4.	Syndicate Bank	942.62

Source: Report on Trend and Progress of Banking in India, various issues.

(B) CAPITAL ADEQUACY NORMS IMPOSED ON BANKS

In order to improve the financial health of the banking

system, the Reserve Bank introduced a risk based capital standard for banks in 1992-93. Indian banks with international presence were advised to achieve a capital to risk-weighted assets ratio (CRAR) of 8% by March 31, 1994. Foreign banks operating in India were advised to achieve this norm of 8% by March 31, 1993, and all other banks wee advised to achieve 4% ratio by March 31, 1993 and 8% by March 31, 1996. Indian banks having branches abroad were given one-year extension to achieve the capital adequacy norm of 8% i.e. by March 31, 1995.

All but one public sector bank as on March 31, 1998 met the enhanced minimum capital adequacy ratios. This contrasts with the position in March 1993 when as many as 26 public sector banks had not attained the prescribed minimum CRAR of 8%. Only 4 Indian private sector banks out of 34 were still to meet the target in March 1997. All the new private sector banks as well as foreign banks have fully complied with the minimum ratios.

The Narasimham Committee Report (1998) pointed out the ned for improving capital adequacy, in the light of the significantly high "cost of servicing of the loans."

The Narasimham Committee 1998 recommended that taking into consideration the substantial off-balance sheet exposures of banks the minimum capital to risk assets ratio be increased to 9% by 200 and 10% by 2002 and that capital adequacy requirements, should take into account market risks in addition to the credit risks.

Endorsing this view, The Monetary and Credit Policy statement of October 30, 1998 announced the raising of the minimum capital to risk asset ratio from the existing 8% to 9% by March 31, 2000 and to 10% as early as possible thereafter.

(C) CHANGES IN STATUTORY PRE-EMPTIONS: REDUCTION IN SLR AND CRR

Indian banking system has operated for a long time with a high level reserve requirement both in the form of Cash Reserve Ratio and Statutory Liquidity Ratio. banks were required to maintain 15% CRR on net demand and time liabilities (NDTL) and incremental CRR on net demand and time liabilities (NDTL as on May 3, 1991. Banks were also required to maintain 38.5% SLR on domestic liabilities and 30% on non-resident liabilities. An attempt has been made to bring down the pre-emptions in the from of reserve requirements i.e. to lower both CRR and SLR to boost the profitability of banks.

Apart from removing the incremental CRR since 1991, the average CRR has been brought down. The objective has been to take the CRR to 10% and below

The need for augmenting the lendable resources of banks prompted the reductions in CRR. The reductions of CRR freed cash balance and augmented the lendable resources of the scheduled commercial banks. The total amount released through CRR cuts amounted to Rs. 17,850 crore during the fiscal year 1996-97. These measures have significantly strengthened the liquidity position of the SCBs. The SLR has also been brought down form pre-form peak of an effective rate of 37.5% to 25% in a phased manner and stands at 25% of demand and time liabilities from the fortnight ended October 22, 1997.

(D) INTEREST RATE LIBERALISATION

For long, an administered structure of interest rates that was characterised by detailed prescriptions on the lending as well as the deposit side was in vogue. In recognition of the problems arising from administrative control over interest rates, such as market fragmentation, inefficient allocation of resources and the like several attempts were made to rationalise the level and structure of interest rates in the country.

The rationalisation in the structure of interest rates culminated in the move by RBI, abolishing the minimum lending rate in October 1994 and leaving banks to determine their prime lending rate in October 1994 and leaving banks to determine their prime lending rates while retaining the two concessional rates on lending for small borrowers. On the deposit side, since July 1996, RBI prescribes only a maximum rate for deposits upto one year. Deposit rates have also been freed except for prescription in respect of savings deposit and NRI deposits.

Interest rates in India were further deregulated during 1997-98. The minimum period of maturity of term deposits was reduced form 30 days to 15 days in April 1998 and interest rates on them too have been deregulated. Interest rates on small loans upto Rs. 2 lakhs each, were not to exceed the lending rates that are applicable to the prime borrowers in the category of over Rs. 2 lakh. During 1997-98 and 1998-99, so far the bank rate has been activated to serve as a reference rate as well as an effective signalling mechanism for influencing the direction of interest rate movements in the economy.

Thus, the interest rate regime which was extremely complex has now been rationalised.

(E) PRUDENTIAL ACCOUNTING NORMS RELATING TO INCOME RECOGNITION, ASSET CLASSIFICATION AND PROVISIONING FOR BAD AND DOUBTFUL DEBTS

These have been introduced in a phased manner beginning

1992-93. These norms have been progressively tightened with a view to achieving international best practices.

With regard to income recognition, banks cannot recognise income on non-performing assets (NPAs). Banks have now been given a clear definition of what constitutes NPA. With regard to income recognition in India, income stops accruing when interest or instalment of principal is not paid within 180 days. The international norms is 90 days and the Narasimhan Committee (1998) recommended the introduction of the norm of 90 days in a phased manner by the year 2002.

With regard to asset classification, banks are required to classify assets into four broad groups: (a) standard assets (b) sub-standard assets (c) doubtful assets and (d) loss assets. Earlier there was system of classifying the assets into eight health codes.[6] The length of delinquency in payment is the determining factor for classification on an asset into the above mentioned four categories.

As regards *provisioning,* all loss assets are required to be written off or fully provided for. Hundred percent provisioning is required for unsecured advances in doubtful assets' category and from 20-50% on secured portion depending on the period for which the asset has remained doubtful. 10% provisioning is required for sub-standard assets. With regard to provisioning, till recently, there was no requirement for a general provision on standard assets. The Narasimhan Committee (1998) however recommended a general provision, say, of one percent and suggested that it be introduced in a phased manner.

The internationally accepted prudential regulations have produced sea-change in the functioning of banks. The Reserve Bank reiterates that banks should adhere to the prudential norms on asset classification, income recognition and provisioning and avoid the practice of evergreening.

(F) CREATION OF COMPETITIVE ENVIRONMENT

A more competitive environment has been created. Banks are facing competition from NBFC's on the lending side and from Mutual funds and other similar institutions on the deposit side. banks are also facing competition from within the industry. New Banks are being set up in the private sector since January 1993. There is more liberal policy of permitting branches of foreign banks in India. This has brought in competition for the existing banks, namely public sector, who were so far complacent with themselves. The increasing share in total banking business of the foreign and private banks in the last few years is reflective of their competitive edge and their potential.

The new private banks have commenced business viz. UTI Banks Ltd., Indus Ind Banks Ltd., ICIC Banking Corporation Ltd., Global Trust Bank Ltd., Centurion Bank Ltd., HDFC Bank Ltd., Times Bank Ltd., bank of Punjab Ltd., Development Credit Bank Ltd. and IDBI Bank Ltd. Two more 'in principle' approvals were granted during 1995-96. During the year 1996-97, six new foreign banks opened their branches in India viz. Krung Thai Bank PLC, Oversea-Chinese Banking Corporation, Commercial Bank of Korea, Hanil Bank, Sumitomo Bank and Toronto Dominion Bank. With this total number of foreign banks and their branches in India stood at 42 and 182 respectively.

(G) DIVERSIFICATION IN BANKING

Banks were also allowed to diversity their activities by undertaking non-traditional activities. Banking Regulation Act 1949 was amended in 1983 to permit banks undertake para-banking activities by forming separate capitalised subsidiaries. banks have accordingly set up subsidiaries for undertaking merchant banking and securities related activities, equipment leasing, hire purchase, factoring services, mutual funds, housing finance, venture capital, credit cards business etc. While the sponsor banks are required to monitor the performance of the subsidiaries, they are expected to maintain an arms length relation with their subsidiaries with regard to their business. In 1994, banks were also allowed to undertake departmentally para banking activities such as leasing, hire purchase, factoring etc. Thus, in India now banks undertake para banking activities either through subsidiaries or in-house or both.

A few illustrations of para banking activities in India are listed below. During the year 1996-97, the Bank of Baroda and the Punjab National Bank were granted final approval for setting up, respectively, in the money market of BOB Capital Markets Ltd. (a wholly owned subsidiary to undertake merchant banking, leasing and hire purchase business) and PNB Securities Ltd. (a wholly-owned subsidiary to undertake securities broking business) respectively.

Five Banks, viz., the ABN Amro Bank, ANZ Grindlays Bank, Canara bank, Deutsche Bank and the Bank of Madura Ltd. were given approval during the year 1996-97 for setting up money market mutual fund (MMMF).

During 1997-98 the State Bank of India was accorded final approval for setting up a subsidiary jointly with the SBI Capital Markets Ltd., Associate banks of SBI and Asian Development Bank, viz. SBI Securities Ltd., for undertaking securities broking and trading activities.

Thus, banks in India are undertaking para banking activities through subsidiaries (such as leasing, merchant banking, mutual funds, factoring, housing finance etc.)

and in house in fields such as money market mutual funds, credit cards etc. The reason for bank entering para banking activities include the need for a profit centre, diversification of earnings, maximisation of economies of scale, the desire to have leading positions in all financial services etc.

(H) STRENGTHENING OF THE SUPERVISORY SYSTEM

The system of external supervision of banks has been revamped with the setting up of a separate Board for Financial Supervision (BFS) within the RBI, concentrating exclusively on supervisory issues. The Board ensures compliance with regulations and guidelines in the area of credit management, asset classification, income recognition, capital adequacy, provisioning and treasury operations.

The RBI supervisory strategy comprises both off-site surveillance and on-site inspections. A detailed *off-site surveillance system* has been made operational since 1995 to ascertain the financial condition of banks in between on site examinations, identify banks showing financial deterioration and act as a trigger for supervisory actions over bank. In regard to *on site inspection,* the focus is now on the evaluation of total operations and performance of banks under the CAMELs system i.e. Capital adequacy, asset quality, management, earnings, liquidity and internal control systems. The RBI prepared the supervisory rating model based on CAMELS factors for rating of Indian commercial banks which would identify banks whose conditions warrant special supervisory attention. A supervisory rating model based on CACS factors i.e. capital adequacy, asset quality, compliance and systems has been introduced in respect of foreign banks in India.

The new approach to annual financial inspections has

been adopted from the cycle of inspections commencing July 1997. The main endeavour of this system is to detect problems before they manifest themselves. Thus, the present supervisory system makes a substantial improvement over the earlier system in terms of frequency, coverage and focus as also the tools employed. Nearly one half of the Basle Core Principles for effective Banking Supervision has already been adhered to and the remaining are at different stages of implementation.

(I) REDUCTION IN NPA (IMPROVING THE QUALITY OF BANKS ASSETS

A major task before the Indian Banks is to reduce the ratio of non-performing assets to total assets. based upon the new income recognition norms, it was estimated that in 1992-93, the ratio of non-performing assets to total assets for the banking industry as a whole was around 23.2%. The level of NPA's are showing a decreasing trend. NPAs has come down form 23% in 1992-93 to 17.8% of total advances as of March 1997 and to 16% in 1997-98 (Table 6.3) Gross NPAs as a proportion to total assets.[7] PSB's declined from 11.8% in 1992-93 to 7% in 1997-98. The percentage of Net NPA's[8] to net advances was 9.18% in 1996-97 and declined to 8.2% in 1997-98. Net NPAs to total assets declined from 4% in 1994-95 to 3.3% in 1997-98. (Table 6.3) The NPA figures incidentally do not include advances covered by government guarantees which have turned sticky). The reduction in the level of NPAs partly reflects banks efforts at recovery and the write offs of losses and provisioning for non-performing loans which banks were enabled to do so a result of infusion of government funds as part of a recapitalisation programme.

TABLE 6.3

Gross and Net NPAs of Public Sector Banks—1992-93 to 1997-98

(Amount in Rs. crore)

End-March	*Gross NPAs*	*% to Gross Adv.*	*% to Total Assets*	*Net NPA's*	*% to Net Adv.*	*% to Total Assets*
1993	39,253	23.2	11.8			
1994	41,041	24.8	10.8			
1995	38,385	19.5	8.7	17,567	10.7	4.0
1996	41,661	18.0	8.2	18.297	8.9	3.6
1997	843,577	17.8	7.8	20,285	9.2	3.6
1998 (Provisional)	45,653	16.0	7.0	21.232	8.2	3.3

Source: RBI Report on Trend and Progress of Banking in India 1997-98.

So long as NPA's remain on the books, it is difficult for banks to raise their profitability to desired level. banks have accordingly been designing strategies for restructuring bad debts, improving recovery and reducing NPAs. The Government and the Reserve Bank are committed to perservere with efforts in several directions which would bring down the level of NPA's.

(J) IMPROVED DISCLOSURE REQUIREMENTS

RBI has taken a number of measures to improve transparency and disclosure in the published accounts of banks. Banks are required to disclose under 'Provisions and Contingencies' in the Profit and Loss account, details of provision for bad and doubtful debts, provision for dimunition in the value of investments, provisions for tax separately instead of showing it as a conglomerate item. Banks are also required to disclose the Capital adequacy ratio as well as percentage of net NPA to net advances. This information will also have to be audited.

Additionally, banks are required to disclose business and accounting ratios relating to capital, income, operating profit, per employee etc. Banks have been advised to furnish information about seven additional financial ratios viz. (i) CAR separately for Tier I and Tier II capital; (ii) interest income as a percentage of average working funds; (iii) non-interest income as a percentage of average of average working funds; (iv) operating profits as a percentage of average working funds (v) return on assets; (vi) business per employee; and (vii) profit per employee, in the 'notes on account' effective the balance sheet date of March 31, 1998.

CONCLUSION

Thus the banking sector has been significantly restructured in 1990's. Capital base of the banks has been strengthened by recapitalisation. Prudential norms have been introduced and progressively tightened for income recognition, classification of assets, provisioning of bad debts and pre-emption of bank resources by the government has been reduced sharply. New private sector banks have been licensed. Interest rates have been deregulated. Disclosure requirements have improved. The government has moved to market determined interest rates on its borrowing.

The second phase of restructuring has been launched. In this phase action is being taken to strengthen the foundation of the banking system, to streamline procedures, upgrade technology and human resource development and to affect structural changes in the system.

REFERENCES

1. Allahabad bank (Rs. 90 crore), Andhra bank (150 crore), Bank of Baroda (400 crore), Bank of India (625 crore), Bank of Maharashtra (150 crore), Canara Bank (365 crore), Central Bank of India (490 crore), Corporation Bank (55 crore), Dena Bank (130 crore),

Indian Bank (220 crore), Indian Overseas bank (705 crores), Oriental Bank of Commerce (50 crore), Punjab and Sind bank (160 crore), UCO bank (535 crore), Union Bank of India (200 crore), United Bank of India (215 crore), Vijaya Bank (65 crore).

2. Allahabad Bank (160 crore), Syndicate Bank (172 crore), Bank of Maharashtra (80 crore), Punjab and Sind Bank (72 crore), UCO Bank (110 crore) and United Bank of India (256 crore).
3. Andhra Bank (165 crore), Central Bank of India (500 crore), Punjab and Sind Bank (150 crore), UCO Bank (302 crore), United Bank of India (338 crore) and Vijaya Bank (302 crore). The Government contributed a sum of Rs. 2,700 crore during 1997-98 towards recapitalisation of three banks viz., Canara Bank (600 crore), Indian Bank (1, 750 crore) and UCO Bank (350 crore).
4. Indian Bank (100 crore), UCO Bank (200 crore) and United Bank of India (100 crore).
5. To enable the nationalised banks to raise capital funds from the market by way of public issue of shares, the Banking Companies (Acquisition and Transfer of Undertakings) Acts 1970/1980 were amended effectively July 15, 1994, permitting the nationalised banks to raise capital upto 49% from the public.
6. The earlier eight health codes were (i) Satisfactory (ii) Irregular (iii) Sick; viable/under nursing (iv) Sick: non-viable/sticky (v) Advances recalled (iv) Suit-filed accounts (vii) Decreed debts and (viii) Debts classified by the banks as bad/doubtful, were reduced into four groups, of these four categories were deemed as non-performing assets.
7. Total assets consists predominantly of loans and advances and SLR investments in addition to other assets.
8. Net NPA is derived from gross NPA by excluding (i) balance in interest suspense account i.e. interest due but not received, (ii) DICGC ECGC claim received and kept in suspense account pending adjustment (for final settlement); (iii) part payment received and kept in suspense account, and (iv) total provisions held.

Restructuring in Indian Capital Markets in 1990's

The capital market in India is undergoing a process of structural transformation. The chief aim of the exercise to restructure capital markets is to improve market efficiency, make stock market transactions more transparent, curb unfair trade practices and to bring capital markets upto international standards. With this objective in mind, several institutional changes have been made, e.g., The National Stock Exchange has been set up with a screen based limit order book market, the National Securities Clearing Corporation Ltd. (NSCCL) has been set up to guarantee settlements, NSDL has been established to improve settlement process etc. These institutional developments have resulted in a drastic reduction in transaction costs and have made the markets fair and safe for investors.

This chapter seeks to highlight the chrohological sequence of capital market reforms in 1990's and to identify some of the notable developments in Indian equity market and debt market in 1990's.

CHRONOLOGICAL SEQUENCE OF ATTEMPTS TO RESTRUCTURE CAPITAL MARKETS IN 1990'S

The process to restructure capital markets began in 1992

with the establishment of SEBI. Persistent efforts have been made since then. An array of capital market reforms encompassing primary and secondary markets, equity and debt have been announced. These reforms have significantly restructured capital markets.

That the Capital market has been restructured can be gauged from the following chronological sequences of major developments during the period 1990 to 1998-1999:

1. IFCI and a number of financial institutions set up ICRA (Investment Information and Credit Rating Agency of India Ltd.) in 1991 to undertake rating of debt instruments.
2. SEBI was established in February 1992 with the twin objective of investor protection and capital market development. Statutory recognition was given on January 30, 1992. It has been vested with powers such as regulating the stock exchanges, various intermediaries (such as custodians, depositories, venture capital funds, credit rating agencies, FIIs), mutual funds as also promoting investors' education and training of intermediaries. The powers also require SEBI to take steps to prohibit fraudulent and unfair trade practices as also insider trading in the securities market. SEBI's autonomy was reinforced by allowing it to issue regulations and file suits without prior approval of central government. The Department of Company Affairs delegated to SEBI powers to file complaints against violations of Companies Act.
3. Capital Issues (Control) Act, 1947 was repealed in May 1992 and the Office of Controller of Capital Issues was abolished. Share-pricing was decontrolled and companies were permitted to

approach the capital market after clearance from SEBI.

4. During 1992-93, foreign institutional investors were allowed to make direct investment both in the primary and secondary markets on registration with SEBI. Further, investment norms for NRI's were liberalised so that NRI's and overseas corporate bodies could buy shares and debentures with prior permission of RBI. Moreover, Indian companies were permitted to access international capital markets through euro-equity issues.
5. Over the Counter Exchange of India (OTCEI), a nationwide, screen based trading exchange was set up in 1992 to provide the small and medium sized companies an access to capital markets. Trading in debt-instruments began on OCTEI. The debt-instruments traded were non-convertible debentures of Grasim Industries, Hindalco and Gujarat Ambuja. The UTI was the 'initiator' for all the debentures and Infrastructure Leasing and Finance Services Ltd. (ILFS) was the market maker.
6. The Bombay Stock Exchange introduced the Circuit-break system to regulate trading in shares in 1993. It is a system in which exchange temporarily suspends the trading in a security when its prices are volatile and tend to breach the price band. SEBI has tried to control price volatility by instituting circuit breakers.
7. The RBI announced the setting up of Securities Trading Corporation of India in 1993 to develop a secondary market in government dated securities and public sector bonds.
8. IDBI jointly with Canara Bank, UTI, private sector

banks and financial services companies promoted CARE (Credit Analysis and Research Ltd.) to offer credit rating information and equity research services to Indian industry and institutions. CARE, incorporated on April 21, 1993, commenced its operations in October 1993. CARE undertakes rating of all types of debt instruments.

9. The badla system was discontinued by SEBI in December 1993. The SEBI directed stock exchanges on December 13, 1993 to enforce that all transactions in securities are concluded by delivery and payment and not to allow any carry forward of transactions. This was done in order to ensure the safety of the market in the context of building up of excessive speculative positions.
10. The National Stock Exchange of India (NSE) with nationwide stock trading, electronic display, clearing and settlement facilities was incorporated in 1992. It was granted recognition as a stock exchange in April 1993; it started operations in wholesale debt market in June 1994 and equity trading in November 1994. On the NSE, all types of instruments are being traded viz. equity, debt and hybrids.
11. To enable the nationalised banks to raise capital funds from the market by way of public issue of shares, the Banking Companies (Acquisition and Transfer of Undertakings Acts 1970/1980) were amended effective July 15, 1994 permitting nationalised banks to raise capital upto 49% from the public.
12. An ordinance was promulgated on January 25, 1995 for amending Securities Contract (Regulation)(SCR) Act, 1956. Section 20 of the

Act which refers to 'prohibition of option' was deleted. Trading options is permitted now. This has enhanced liquidity in the market.

13. Stock exchanges introduced fully computerised screen based trading. The efforts of progressing from floor-based trading to scripless floorers trading began in 1995, with the Bombay Stock Exchange deciding to computerise its operations. Computerisation has removed common investor's biggest complaint viz. unfair dealing practices and delays in settlement.
14. Carry forward deals (or badla) were resumed on the Bombay Stock Exchange from 15 January 1996 in conformance with the recommendations of the G.S. Patel Committee. Badla was resumed after almost two years since it was banned in December 1993.
15. The Government of India promulgated the Depositories ordinance in September 1995, paving the way for setting up depositories in the country. The Depositories Act was passed by the Parliament in August 1996. The Act provides that a . depository, which is required to be a company under the Companies Act, 1956 and depository participants need to be registered with SEBI. The depository shall carry out dematerialisation of securities and transfer of beneficial ownership through electronic book entry. This will overcome the problem of bad deliveries, fake shares, lost shares etc. Besides this, dematerialisation (a) does not attract stamp duty on transfer of shares, (b) reduces costs of handling large volumes of paper, storage, transportation and other back office costs, (c)

eliminates share transfer delays due to signature mismatches.

16. On October 29, 1996, the restriction that debt instrument of a corporate could be listed only after its equity had been listed on any exchange was removed thus easing the listing of debt instruments for infrastructure projects.
17. Noteworthy developments in government securities market have been the introduction of subsidiary general ledger (SGL) transactions in government securities and setting up of primary dealers system. Moreover, guidelines were issued for setting up of satellite dealers system.
18. Consequent upon enactment of Depositories Act. the National Securities Depository Limited (NSDL) the first depository In India commenced operations from November 8, 1996. NSDL was set up to provide an efficient solution to the Us associated with paper, reduce settlement risk and facilitate movement towards rolling settlement.
19. Effective January 15, 1997, FII's were allowed to invest upto 100% of the funds in debt instruments of Indian companies through 100% dedicated debt funds. Such investment may be in listed or to be listed corporate debt securities or in dated government securities, and will be treated as part of the overall limit on external commercial borrowings.
20. The SEBI introduced Securities Lending Scheme on February 7, 1997. Securities lending has been thought of as a measure of improving availability of the scrips for an active secondary market.

21. On February 28, 1997, the Union Budget 1997-98, announced the abolition of tax on dividends in the hands of shareholders, thus, offering a strong incentive for investing in shares.
22. Effective April 1, 1997, adhoc and on tap treasury bills were discontinued. According to the supplemental agreement signed by the Reserve Bank with the Central Government on March 26, 1997, temporary mismatches between receipts and expenditures of the Central Government are to be met through a system of Ways and Means Advance (WMA) on certain terms and conditions to be agreed between the two parties from time to time.
23. Effective April 1, 1997, with the discontinuance of tap treasury bills, the Central Government introduced the scheme of 14-day intermediate treasury bills to provide state governments, foreign central banks and specified bodies with an alternative arrangement to invest their surplus funds.
24. In order to help form a complete yield curve for aiding in the pricing of debt instruments, the Reserve Bank introduced 14-day auction treasury bills on a weekly basis, effective June 6, 1997.
25. On June 17, 1997, SEBI advised stock exchanges to set up either Trade Guarantee Fund or Settlement Guarantee Fund to eliminate counterparty risk.
26. On October 21, 1997, the RBI permitted money market mutual funds (MMMFs) to invest in corporate bonds and debentures with a residual maturity of one year. The total investment on CPs and debentures/bonds of a company should,

however, not exceed 3% of the total resources of MMMFs.

27. In October 1997, the Modified Carry Forward system recommended by J.R. Verma Committee was approved by SEBI and all exchanges desirous of implementing modified carry forward system were advised to apply to SEBI for prior approval.
28. On November 13, 1997, SEBI allowed institutional investors, stock brokers, stock exchanges etc. to make use of 'warehousing' of trades subject to certain conditions. This facility is helpful where large orders, are to be executed but due to liquidity constraint it is either costly or not possible to execute the orders immediately.
29. The Government of India, on November 18, 1997 directed that entities which issue instruments like agro-bonds, plantation bonds etc. would come under the regulatory purview of SEBI and such entities would be treated as 'collective investment schemes'.
30. In 1997-98, in an effort to provide necessary liquidity to the comparatively less traded though fundamentally good scrips, the SEBI constituted a committee under the chairmanship of G.P. Gupta to study the concept of market making and to revive the institution of market makers.
31. During 1997-98, SEBI granted recognition to two new stock exchanges viz. Capital Stock Exchange Kerala Limited (CSEKL) and Inter Connected Stock Exchange of India (ICSI). ICSI is the 23rd stock exchange of India.
32. SEBI (Depository and Participants) Regulations, 1996 were amended to allow dematerialisation of government securities during 1997-98.

33. On January 5, 1998, RBI decided in principle to permit FII's to invest in treasury bins. FII's were permitted to purchase/sell treasury bills within the overall approved debt ceiling of 30%.
34. SEBI introduced compulsory trading of shares in dematerialised form in specified scripts by institutional investors (FII's, MF's, banks and Fi's) with effect from January 15, 1998.
35. SEBI introduced TF rolling settlement cycles from January 15, 1998 in the dematerialised segment of all companies.
36. SEBI accepted recommendations of LC. Gupta Committee on Derivatives on May 11, 1998 and announced a phased introduction of derivatives trading beginning with stock index futures. The Union Budget for 1998-99 announced necessary amendments to the Securities Contracts (Regulation) Act to enable derivative instruments to be treated as securities.
37. Indian companies were permitted to buy-back their own shares with effect from October 31, 1998. On November 10, 1998 SEBI formulated regulations governing buy back of shares by Indian companies. The SEBI regulations on buy-back cover only listed securities and unlisted securities issued through private placement or otherwise fall outside the purview of SEBI regulations.
38. The Central Depository Service (India) Ltd. (CDL), the second depository in the country was granted certificate of registration during 1998-99.
39. On February 28, 1999. the Union Budget 1999-2000, announced that there would be no discrimination between the rate of long-term

capital gains tax on transfer of shares between residents and non-residents. The LT capital gains tax for resident Indians on transfers of shares and securities shall be 10% instead of 20% earlier.

Thus, we find that capital markets have seen considerable reforms. The above mentioned intiatives by both government and SEBI have focussed on regulatory reform as well as market modernisation do as to promote investors as well as market modernisation so as to promote investor interest and ensure investor protection. What have been the notable developments in the equity and debt market in 1990's is discussed next.

NOTABLE DEVELOPMENTS IN INDIAN EQUITY MARKET IN 1990'S

1. Reduction in Spreads and Costs

NSE introduced for the first time in India a transparent screen based trading system, which did not require intervention of any broker or jobber. Thus the investor is assured of a price which is not vulnerable to manipulation. The national reach of the NSE has enabled it to have a deeper and more liquid market and hence lower costs. The NSE also introduced the concept of 'novation' through clearing house to guarantee trades executed on NEAT (trading system of NSE). All these factors have contributed to reducing the costs of trading. Table 7.1 gives a broad estimate of transaction costs on India's equity markets. It is important to bear in mind that NSE has become the driving force behind this drastic reduction in transaction costs.

TABLE 7.1

Transaction Costs on India's Equity Market

	INDIA			*NEW YORK*
COST COMPONENT	*1993 (Before NSE)*	*1997 (NSE)*	*FUTURE*	*TODAY*
TRADING	3.75%	0.70%	0.40%	1.23%
Brokerage	3.00%	0.50%	0.25%	1.00%
Market Impact Cost	0.75%	0.15%	0.15%	0.23%
CLEARING				
Counter Party Risk	Present	In part	0.00%	0.00%
SETTLEMENT	1.25%	1.50%	0.10%	0.05%
Back office	0.75%	0.75%	0.10%	0.05%
Bad Paper Risk	0.50%	0.75%	0.00%	0.00%
TOTAL	5.00%	2.20%	0.50%	1 .28%

Source: Securities Market by Ajah Shah and Susan Thomas, in K. Parikh (ed.), India Development Report, 1997.

Table 7.1 also shows that there has been an almost 50% reduction in transaction costs after NSE was established and commenced operations. The numbers are only indicative in nature, but nevertheless point to an all-pervasive reduction in costs on a broad front.

Inter-exchange competition and transparency of screen-based trading have resulted in slashing transaction costs to less than half.

2. Fully Computerised Stock Exchange Trading

This was pioneered by NSE in India in 1994. The competitive pressure made the Bombay Stock Exchange to computerise in 1995. Other exchanges viz. Delhi Stock Exchange, Pune, Vadodara, Bangalore, Coimbatore, Ahmedabad followed suit in 1996. Cochin and Calcutta stock exchange were among those who commenced screen-based trading in 1997. As on March 31, 1998, 20 stock exchanges accounting for almost 99.8% of the total all-

India turnover, had shifted to on-line screen based trading. This has removed the common investors biggest complaints viz. unfair dealing practices and delays in settlement. It has improved transparency and trading efficiency.

3. Setting up of Depositories and Shift to Paperless Trading

The Depositories Act was passed by the Parliament in August 1996. The Depositories Act provides for multiple depository system. Consequent upon enactment of Depositories Act to enable scripless trading, the National Securities Depository Limited - the first depository in India - was set up by IDBI, UTI and NSE. It started operating from November 8, 1996. NSDL carries out its operations through participants and the clearing corporation of the stock exchange, with participants acting as market intermediaries through which NSDL interacts. NSDL performs a wide range of securities related functions through the depository participants viz.

- maintenance of individual investors beneficial holdings in an electronic form.
- dematerialisation and rematerialisation of securities.
- account transfer for settlement of trades in electronic shares.
- allotments in the electronic form in case of initial public offerings.
- distribution of non-cash corporate actions.
- facility for pledge and hypothecation of securities.

As on June 6, 1998, 208 companies had entered into agreements with NSDL. Amongst these, dematerialisation facilities were available for shares of 186 companies and trading facilities were available for 183 securities.

Many organisations are in the process of setting up depositories. The BSE has decided to set up its own depository (with capital of Rs. 100 crore). The Central Depository Services (India) Ltd. (CDL), the second depository in India has been granted certificate of registration in 1998-99.

The setting up of depository has helped to overcome the major problem of handling physical share certificates such as problem of theft, fake and/or forged shares, share transfer delays, particularly due to signature mismatch. Transaction holding costs (costs of handling, storage, transportation and other back office costs) in the depository environment are cheaper when compared to same in the physical and Demat segments.

TABLE 7.2

Cost comparison for Trading in Physical and Demat Segments

A comparison of cost for a long term investor who buys and trades shares worth Rs. 10,000

(Figs. in basis points)

	Without Transacting			*With transacting 10 times/year*		
	Physical Shares	*Demat Shares*	*Savings*	*Physical Shares*	*Demat Shares*	*Savings*
Brokerage	75-100	50-75	25-50	750-1000	500-750	250-500
Stamp duty	50	—	50	—	—	—
Postal charges	10-30	—	10-30	—	—	—
Company objection (notarisation etc.)	10-30	—	10-30			
Settlement Charges	—	5-10	-(5-10)	—	50-100	-(50-100)
Custody (5 years)	—	—	-(25-50)	—	5-10	-(5-10)
Total	—	—	**35-100**	—	—	**140-445**

Source: An Investor's Guide to Depositories, NSDL.

In the depository, an electronic record of share ownership is maintained. The maintenance of records of ownership in electronic form resolves almost all the problems of handling physical share certificates and improves the efficiency of the market.

4. Setting up of Trade/Settlement Guarantee Fund by Stock Exchanges

During 1997-98, SEBI advised stock exchanges to set up either Trade Guarantee Fund or Settlement Guarantee Fund to eliminate counterparty risk.

One of the shortcomings of the clearing and settlement process of Indian stock markets was the absence of a system to reduce counter-party risks. Managing this risk is an essential need of a safe and efficient market, which can be achieved through setting up of a Trade or Settlement Guarantee Fund. The principal objective of this fund is to provide the necessary funds and ensure timely completion of settlements in cases of failure of member brokers to fulfill their settlement obligations. Thus establishment of such funds would give greater confidence to investors in the settlement and clearing procedures of the stock exchanges.

The corpus of the Settlement Guarantee Fund of NSE as on 31 August 1998 was Rs. 493.44 crore. During 1997-98, settlement guarantee funds of Mumbai, Ludhiana, Calcutta and Bangalore stock exchanges were granted approval by SEBI. In addition, the stock exchanges at Delhi, Hyderabad and Cochin were also granted in principle approvals to set up settlement guarantee funds.

This move has strengthened the safety and integrity of the secondary securities market.

5. Buy Back of Sares by Companies

The buy back of shares was prohibited in India until October 31, 1998 when the Union Government amended the Companies Act to allow this.

Under the new provisions, a company may buy-back its own shares or other specified securities from (i) its free reserves, (ii) securities premium account, or (iii) the proceeds of an earlier issue other than fresh issue of shares made specifically for buy-back purposes. Buy-back is permitted only when the company satisfies the following conditions: (a) it is authorised by its articles, (b) a special resolution has been passed in general meeting of the company authorising the buy-back, (c) the buy-back does not exceed 25% of the paid-up capital and free reserves of the company concerned, (d) the debt-equity (including free reserves) ratio is not more than 2:1 after such buy-back, (e) al! shares and other specifiedsecurities are fully paid-up and (0 the buy-back is in accordance with the SEBI regulations framed for the purpose.

Following amendment to the Companies Act, SEBI on November 10, 1998 formulated the regulations governing buy-back of shares by Indian companies. The SEBI regulations apply only to listed securities and as such unlisted securities issued through private placement or otherwise fall outside the purview of the regulations.

The Union Budget 1999-2000 announced that on buy-back of shares, the shareholders will not be subject to dividend tax, and would only be liable to capital gains tax.

6. Insider Trading and Takeovers Regulated by SEBI

Till 1991, there was no law in India which specifically dealt with the menance of insider trading. The Central Government granted its approval to the SEBI (Insider Trading) Regulations in 1992 and insider trading has now been made an offence w.e.f. 19 November 1992. SEBI has been made the administrative authority of the regulations against insider trading. During 1997-98, MLL was held to have violated the provisions of the SEBI (Prohibition of Insider Trading) Regulations, 1992 and SEBI passed an order directed MLL to compensate UTI to the extent of Rs. 3.04 crore. It also ordered that prosecution proceedings should be initiated against HLL and its five directors who were party to the decision of the purchase of shares.

SEBI (Substantial Acquisition of Shares and Takeovers) Regulations were notified in November 1994 bringing all parties in a substantial acquisition under SEBI's regulatory umbrella. The regulations set out a procedure for substantial acquisition of shares. This will protect the rights of minority shareholders providing an exit route at a price which is fair and transparent. They also aim at making the takeover process transparent. SEBI approved the modified takeover code based on the recommendations of the Bhagwati Committee and SEBI (Substantial Acquisition of Shares and Takeovers) Regulations, 1997 were notified in February 1997. The 1997 regulations aimed at (a) investor protection in the takeover process, (b) greater transparency, (c) fairness and equity of treatment to all investors, (d) timeliness and accuracy of disclosure of information to investors, (e) prevention of frivolous offers and (f) enforcement against violations.

7. Regulated Market Intermediaries

SEBI regulations cover primary market intermediaries viz. merchant bankers, underwriters, portfolio managers, bankers to an issue, registrars to issue, share transfer agents and secondary market intermediaries viz. stock brokers, sub-brokers.

Amendments to SEBI (Merchant Bankers) Regulations, 1992 were made during 1997-98.

The SEBI (Registrars to an Issue and Share Transfer Agents) Regulations 1993 were amended during 1997-98 to provide for an arms length relationship between the issuer and the Registrar to the issue.

The SEBI regulations relating to stock brokers, registrars to an issue, portfolio manager, underwriters, bankers to an issue were amended on January 5, 1998 to provide that applicant should be a fit and proper person.

8. Book Building

The book-building method of pricing of securities is slowly becoming popular in India. During 1997-98, various issuers like IPCL, HUDCO, HAL, IOC and Hindalco Industries used the book-building route to fix the coupon rate on their bond issues.

Book building is a mechanism through which an offer price for IPOs is determined. The normal method of offering shares at a price fixed by the issuers is not efficient in the sense that it does not take into account the investors demands. The book-building method, on the other hand, explicitly uses investor demand for shares at various prices as an important input to arrive at the offer price. The book building is done in following steps:

(a) The company wishing to issue shares approaches its merchant banker and informs him of the number of shares it wishes to issue and other material information on the company. The company would like to get as high a price as possible.

(b) The merchant banker and underwriter a promised a fee which aligns the interests of the issuer and the merchant banker.

(c) The merchant banker now invites his own investors to bid for company's shares. The investors are generally institutional investors. These investors are asked to indicate the number of shares they would like to buy at different prices. Thus the merchant banker gets the demand function of each investor. Once the offer price is finalised, allocation is done on the basis of highest bid price.

(d) Based on the demand function known to him, the merchant banker arrives at a final offer price. At this point the company still has the option to cancel the issue if it feels the price is too low. If the company agrees with the offer price, the issue goes through and shares are allocated based on the bids. Thus the investor who bids the highest gets the maximum pro-rata allocation of shares. The trading typically commences from the next day.

SEBI guidelines for new. issuers through book building became operational with effect from September 1997.

NOTABLE DEVELOPMENTS IN THE DEBT MARKET IN 1990'S

The debt market in India is conventionally classified into three segments, viz., (i) Government Securities Market, (ii) Public Sector Units (PSU) Bonds Market, and (iii) Corporate Debt market. In India, the Government securities segment has remained predominant due to large Government deficits. Central to the development of debt market in India is the development of the Government Securities market. Several policy initiatives have been undertaken by the RBI and the Government of India for the development of the Government securities market. The reforms in Government Securities market since 1991-92 are directed towards:(a) instrument development; (b) institutional development; and, (c) strengthening market transparency and efficiency with particular reference to secondary market development.

(A) Instrument Development

1. Since 1992, Central Government borrowings have been undertaken at market related rates, primarily through auctions of government securities of different maturities. The new instrument of 364-day treasury bills was introduced in April 1992 replacing 182-day treasury bills. The auction system for sale of GOI dated securities was introduced in June 1992 for 91-day treasury bills in January 1993.
2. Consequent upon the primary market acquiring depth with market related rates, some innovative instruments were introduced viz. conversion of auction treasury bills into term security, zero coupon bonds (January 18, 1994), Tap stocks (29 July 1994), Partly paid government stock (November 15, 1994), Floating Rate Bonds (September 29, 1995).
3. Effective April 1, 1997, with the discontinuance of adhoc and 91-day tap treasury bills, a scheme of 14-day intermediate treasury bills was introduced to enable State Governments, foreign central banks and other specified bonds with whom the Reserve Bank has an arrangement to invest their temporary surplus funds.
4. Since June 6, 1997 a new instrument called 14-day auction Treasury bill has been introduced.
5. It was decided in August 1997 to issue treasury bills of varying maturities to facilitate better cash management for the Government as also the investor. 28-day treasury bills and re-introduction of 182-day treasury bills are also proposed to be introduced.
6. During 1997-98, the Government introduced capital indexed bond as a hedge against inflation.

7. Recently, uniform price auction (dutch auction) system was introduced for 91-day treasury bills on an experimental basis on November 6, 1998. Uniform price auction method is expected to eliminate the problem of winners curse and encourage more aggressive bidding in the primary market.

(B) Institutional Development

1. With a view to developing an efficient institutional infrastructure for an active secondary market in Government securities and public sector unit bonds, the Securities Trading Corporation of India (STCI) was set up in May 1994 which commenced its operations in June 1994.
2. In order to strengthen the securities market infrastructure, improve secondary market trading, liquidity and turnover and encourage voluntary holding of Government securities amongst a wider investor base, a system of primary dealers (PDs) has been operating since March 1996 with six PDs offering two way quotes with bidding commitments in the auction of dated securities and 91/364 days treasury bills.
3. A scheme for payment of underwriting fees to primary dealers was introduced on June 2, 1997 replacing the earlier system of payment of commission on primary purchases of PDs. All auctions conducted since June 2, 1997 fall under the new scheme.
4. With a view to broadening the market with a second tier of dealers system and imparting greater momentum in terms of increased liquidity and turnover, guidelines for Satellite Dealers (SDs) were issued in December 1996.

5. The scheme for approval for both primary and satellite dealers has been made as an ongoing process. The RBI has recently enlarged the number of PDs from 6 to 13 by announcing in principle agreement to register 7 PDs.
6. The guidelines for the scheme of liquidity support to mutual funds dedicated exclusively to investments in Government securities, either by way of outright purchases or reverse repos in Central Government securities outstanding as at end of previous calender month were issued on April 20, 1996.
7. Effective January 15, 1997, FIIs have been allowed to invest in the category of 100% debt funds to invest in debt instruments of Indian companies, dated Government securities.
8. Permission has also been given to NSDL, SHCI and NSCCI to open subsidiary General Ledger (SGL) Accounts with the RBI, which would enable dematerialisation of Government securities.

(C) Strengthening Market Transparency and Efficiency

Several policy measure have been undertaken to strengthen the market transparency and efficiency. They are:

(i) Large percentage of marked to market valuation of investment portfolio of banks.

(ii) Delivery vs payment system.

(iii) Publication of SGL data.

(iv) Changes in strategics of open market operations and repo auctions.

(v) Liberalisation of policy on banks investment.

(vi) Rationalisation of under writing commission fees for primary dealers.

(vii) Abolition of TDS on interest income from government securities.

- Mark to market requirements for banks in respect of their investment portfolio have been increased to 70% for 1998-99.
- In order to ensure settlement by synchromising the transfer of securities with the cash payment, delivery Vs payment system has been introduced in Mumbai w.e.f. July 1995 in dated securities and February 1996 in Treasury bills and the system has been extended to all public debt offices by May 1996.
- Greater transparency has been introduced since September 1994 with publication of transactions in government recorded by RBI under SGL accounts. Soon, the RBI proposes to publish data on banks investments in corporate and PSD debt in the weekly statistical supplement to the RBI Bulletin.
- In the recent past, policy on banks investments in PSU bonds/private corporate debt has been considerably liberalised, taking into account the increased market preference for these instruments vis-a-vis bank credit. Banks had been allowed to invest in debentures/bonds/shares of private corporate bodies and PSU shares upto 5% of their incremental deposit in the previous year. As part of the Monetary and Credit Policy for the first half of 1997-98, bank's investment in debt instruments was exempted from investment ceiling of 5% of incremental deposit. The limit is now appriable for investments only in respect

of ordinary shares of corporates including PSU's.

- As a part of the budget announcements for 1997-98 government has exempt interest income on government securities from the provision of tax deduction at source (TDS) under section 193 of Income Tax Act, 1961 w.e.f. June 1997. Abolition of TDS has facilitated quotations at clean prices and genuine trading in secondary market.

Reforms in Non-Government Debt Market in 1990's

Several new instruments were added to the debt segment in the recent past such as deep discount bond, securitised debt, PSU infrastructure bond, government index bond, corporate floating rate bond and institutitonal tax free bonds.

National and local stock exchanges have been established where trading in corporate and government debt is done on the exchange through screen based systems. The National Stock Exchange of India with nationwide facilities started operations in wholesale debt market in June 1994.

Securities and Exchange Board of India (SEBI) was established in February 1992 which regulate the primary issuances in debt markets other than government securities and ensures sound trading practices in the secondary market through stock exchanges.

Depositories have been set up for equity and debt to facilitate dematerialisation and easier and safer transfer and settlement. The settlement of debentures is not yet possible through electronic book entry with NSDI as transfer of debentures have not been exempted from payment of stamp duty.

Also there is complete transparency in debt transacted through the National Stock Exchange. Information on trades settled through the central depository with RBI is disseminated to market participants to enable them to have access to data on volumes and prices in the secondary markets.

CONCLUSION

During 1990's, significant efforts have been made to restructure Indian Capital market. Many of the weaknesses and inefficiencies of the Indian Capital Market have been removed. Today, a sound regulatory framework is in place for floatation of primary issues, operation of stock exchanges and working of market intermediaries like brokers, merchant bankers, registrars and custidians. Screen-based trading has been introduced in 19 out of 23 stock exchanges in the country. Trades on leading exchanges are now guaranteed. Depository has become a reality and transactions through depository will bring down the cost and risks of trading associated with paper-based trading. Cost of transaction has come down from an average of 5% prevailing in 1991 to an average of 1.5% now, and it is expected to go down to 0.5% over the next few years. Stock exchanges have strengthened their internal operating practices, surveillance system and infrastructure. Stock brokers and merchant bankers are now better capitalized, more professionally organized and more accountable. Margining system is now better implemented and defaulting members are not allowed to continue trading.

When we reflect upon the improvement in the capital

market, we can draw satisfaction from how much the financial infrastructure has improved over the past few years. However, the restructuring excercise, is by no means complete. The future course of reform will have to be based on the need to integrate the Indian financial markets more completely with the global financial sector, and to iron out the systemic deficiencies still present in the system.

Attracting and Sustaining International Financial Flows: Restructuring Needed

Having gained insight into restructuring process that is already underway in banking sector (chapter 5) and capital markets (chapter 6) and why it is underway, the present chapter and the next seek to answer the question what restructuring is needed in Indian financial system in response to financial flows.

India needs to accord attention to attracting and sustaining international financial flows. But why? It is necessary for India to attract financial flows viz. private, non-debt flows because such flows are just 3-4% of total private, non-debt flows to developing countries; these flows are not likely to dry up in future but are projected to rise and because these flows offer potential benefits for recipient countries. Another factor that makes it necessary for India to attract such flows is the savings investment gap in India.

It is necessary for India to accord attention to sustaining international financial flows because portfolio investment —an important component of financial flows is inherently volatile. Several countries have experienced sudden reversals of inflows e.g. Mexico, South East Asia. Their reversal can affect the domestic economy through a decrease in asset prices, a jump in interest rate, liquidity problems in the banking sector or a devaluation of the currency. A financial flow reversal can cause a crash of financial system.

Does the Indian Financial System need any restructuring to attract and sustain these flows is the key issue to which an answer is sought in the present chapter.

ATTRACTING FOREIGN INVESTORS

Financial flows make it necessary to reform market infrastructure and to establish an appropriate regulatory structure [World Bank (1996)]. Strengthening and expanding the underlying infrastructure facilitates the development of effective capital markets, which will make them more attractive to foreign investors, increase their ability to absorb financial flows. The process of building market infrastructure, establishing the necessary regulatory institutions is a long one that requires constant support from the authorities.

Attracting foreign investors entails the following:

(i) Permitting Greater Competition in the Financial Sector

Permitting foreign banks and non-bank financial institutions is an important condition for attracting foreign direct investment and portfolio investment [World Bank (1996)]. This is because foreign investors usually feel more comfortable dealing with familiar financial institutions with which they can also do business elsewhere. International money centre banks often provide a wide range of services for interfacing with world markets that are not available from domestic banks. These services are critically important to international investors.

(ii) Improving Accounting and Auditing Rules

One impediment to participation by foreign investors is that recipient country's accounting rules do not conform to international standards. If accounting and auditing rules are incomplete or inconsistent across countries, investors cannot ascertain the true meaning of the reports provided or can do so only at great cost, which makes evaluation of investments much more difficult. These failings exacerbate information asymmetry, reduce investor confidence and sap the attractiveness of domestic issues to international investors.

Since major cross-country differences in accounting and auditing standards are an impediment to portfolio equity flows to the extent that financial statements are not transparent for international investors, it is necessary to work towards harmonising accounting standards and to improve auditing standards and practices to ensure reliability of disclosed information [World Bank (1996)].

(iii) Prudential Regulation

Prudential regulation and supervision are crucial to maintaining the soundness of finance system. Well-designed and well-implemented prudential regulations and supervision increase investor confidence and reduce risks. The primary regulations should cover the following elements for all financial institutions:

a) requirements for minimum capital, reserves and bad loan reserves
b) licensing provisions on ownership and branching
c) public disclosure of information
d) operating guidelines on mergers and consolidation
e) early warning system, supervision and examination

f) enforcement of sanctions on both firms and individuals when rules have been violated.

Additional prudential regulations would be appropriate for enterprises that issue securities and for non-banking institutions that deal in securities, including securities dealers and brokerage firms, investment banks, finance companies, mutual funds and other institutional investors.[1] The most important of these additional regulations should include:

a) registration and capital requirements for securities issuers
b) registration requirements for corporation to be listed on exchanges
c) restrictions on insider-trading-based information
d) rules for soliciting business by securities dealers, brokers and mutual funds.
e) regulations on, for example, margin requirements and trading of futures and options.

(iv) Stability

Stability is of prime importance for international financial flows since an unstable finance system has an adverse impact on financial flows. Financial stability can be enhanced by increasing capital and reserve requirements, strengthening financial supervision and enforcing sanctions when rules have been violated. Adequate supervision and examination in the field and an effective early-warning system are more important than simply setting up requirements on paper.

(v) Effective Law Enforcement

It is necessary to ensure effective enforcement of regulations. Poor law enforcement has serious consequences - international investors' confidence falls when they do not believe their interests will be protected, and their willingness to invest in that particular market diminishes. International investors are most wary of fraud-prone markets. Attracting a wider range of investors will be easier with tighter rules that promote fairness. Some basic rules, such as disclosure of information by listing corporations and prevention of outright fraud, would have to be strictly enforced. Brokers and other dealers should be subject to similar rules to maintain confidence.

Effective enforcement requires clarifying the mandate and powers of different regulatory institutions. With regard to official regulator, the consensus is that one independent agency should be responsible for the oversight of capital markets [World Bank (1997)].

(vi) Operating Infrastructure

Without a basic infrastructure to complete transactions reliably, capital flows very slowly. This is particularly true of portfolio investment, but onerous registration and approval procedures also discourage FDI.

International investors are concerned about delays in settlement and failed trades. Slow settlement and delivery add to uncertainty and dissuade foreign investors. It becomes necessary to introduce well-synchronised comparison, clearance, settlement and central depository systems so as to attract financial flows.

(vii) Establish Credit Rating Agencies

Credit rating agencies are important for attracting foreign investment since foreign investors are often unfamiliar with the accounting rules and corporate laws of the issuing countries. The existence of rating agencies lessens the need for investors to do independent credit analysis and hence reduces their transaction costs.

(viii) Increase Market Capitalisation

When an asset market is 'thin', liquidity is low and transaction costs are high, both of which reduce the market's attractiveness to foreign investors. Liquidity is an important desirable feature for foreign investors, since it reduces the risks and costs associated with their eventual withdrawal from a market. In an illiquid market, foreign investors fear that they will not be able to liquidate their interests quickly without incurring a substantial loss.

Transaction costs in a thin market are high - bid-ask spreads are large - because dealers have to bear higher risks than in deeper market.

It is necessary to increase market capitalisation so as to improve liquidity and reduce transaction costs. Market capitalisation can be increased by privatising state owned enterprises, encouraging healthy corporations to seek listing on the stock market, allowing broader foreign ownership and generally easing regulations and taxes on transactions, subject to prudential concerns.

(ix) Eradicate Insider Trading

To attract foreign portfolio investment it is necessary to eradicate insider trading. Insider legislation develops confidence among foreign investors. Based on U.S. experience, Strahota[21] (1996) suggests that emerging markets should not try to eliminate insider trading by relying solely on criminal prosecution. It is more effective according to him, to have the full range of sanctions (civil, administrative and criminal). [3] To further facilitate enforcement World Bank (1997) suggests that insider rules should include incentives for market participants to monitor compliance, such as making managers and firms responsible for breaches of insider rules committed by their subordinates or employees, requiring security houses to institute internal control procedures, and holding responsible both the giver and receiver of information.

(x) Improve Corporate Governance

Laws and regulations that improve corporate governance make a capital market significantly more attractive for foreign investors [World Bank (1997)]. Effective corporate governance involves essentially the promotion of shareholders rights and responsibilities, including those of minority shareholders. Two basic principles are fair treatment for all shareholders and shareholder approval of key corporate decisions. More broadly, corporate governance also refers to shareholders and their representatives at the board being more independent and active in corporate affairs, monitoring and demanding more transparency from management.

Has the Indian financial system been restructured (seen any progress) on these grounds - is a natural question that needs to be answered in this context so that further restructuring that is needed in Indian financial system to attract financial flows can be suggested.

Over a period, India has been created a more **competitive environment** in the financial sector. There is a more liberal policy of permitting branches of foreign banks in India. By end of 1998-99, total number of foreign banks and their branches in India stood at 44 and 180 respectively. Further, Indian banks are also opening branches abroad - the total number of such branches being 95 till 1998-99.

In respect of **accounting rules,** we find that accounting standards in India do not reflect international practices, e.g., in India preparation of consolidated accounts of a group company is optional. This is in contrast to the international accounting standards and it makes the assessment of real financial health of the group difficult. Accounting rules are not consistent across companies e.g. AS-2 on inventory valuation is not mandatory and consequently wide disparities in inventory valuation are taking place. Further, absence of disclosure of earnings per share provides only insufficient information to investors.

With respect to **prudential regulations,** it is important to note that India introduced prudential norms and regulations in 1992 as an element of financial sector reforms. Prudential norms introduced in India relate to income recognition, asset classification, provisioning for bad and doubtful debts and capital adequacy. Over a period of time, these measures have been tightened. The prudential rules apply to banks and non-banks (viz. NBFC's and DFI's), various market participants and intermediaries in the capital market (viz. brokers, registrars to an issue, banker, merchant banker, underwriter, portfolio managers, custodians and credit rating agencies, FII's, venture capital funds, asset management companies etc.). The abolition of Controller of Capital Issues (CCI) in May 1992 and setting up of SEBI (February 1992) have been two important steps in the move from control to fundamental regulation in the case of capital markets.

With respect to **supervision,** the position in India is that out of 25 core principles of banking supervision released by Basle Committee on Banking supervision and endorsed by Bank for International Settlements (BIS), 13 legal provisions have been enshrined in the Banking Regulation Act, RBI Act and/or in executive instructions issued by RBI.

With regard to **disclosure of information,** SEBI has issued guidelines on disclosure of information by all players in the capital market. Efforts are already in place in India to improve disclosure of information by corporates, banks, financial institutions etc. Effective October 1998, banks are required to disclose in a phased manner the maturity pattern of loans and advances, investments in securities, foreign currency assets and liabilities, movements in non-performing assets, lendings to sensitive sectors etc., in order to bring the disclosure of Indian banks on par with international accounting standards. A scheme of disclosure of information about defaulters of banks and financial institutions has also been operating in India since April 1994. Further, actions have been initiated in India against errant NBFC's and unincorporated bodies for various defaults and violations of the Reserve Bank of India Act. The actions include prohibition from accepting further deposits, filing of winding up petitions and launching of criminal proceedings against the errant companies and their management.

With regard to **operating infrastructure,** we find that India has made institutional and infrastructural improvements in stock market practice. Bourses have been modernised by introducing screen-based trading, scriples trading system (depository). The former has helped to overcome the problems of unfair dealing practices, delays in settlement and improved transparency and trading efficiency. The latter has dealt with the problem of delays in share transfer etc. apart from minimising costs (holding, back office cots). Substantial progress has been made in demat trading coupled with introduction of rolling settlement in the demat segment. The vigilance and surveillance system has also seen improvement and capital adequacy norms for market intermediaries have been tightened. The initiatives taken to introduce derivatives trading on stock indices and the approval for buy-back of shares should attract investors.

With respect to establishment of **credit rating agencies,** it is heartening to note that India has established its own credit rating agencies. The major credit rating agencies in India being - CRISIL (Credit Rating and Information Services of India Limited), ICRA (Information and Credit Rating Agency of India Ltd.), CARE (Credit Analysis and Research Limited) and Deff and Phelps Credit Rating India (P) Limited. To make sure that these credit rating agencies do not work against the interest of investors who rely upon their rating results, the power to regulate credit rating agencies have been vested with SEBI in India and they are regulated by SEBI via SEBI (Credit Rating Agencies) Regulations, July 1999.

The **market capitalisation** in India has seen an increase. The market capitalisation of BSE increased from Rs. 3,23,363 crore in 1991-92 to Rs. 5,60,325 crore in 1997-98 (source CMIE) and the BSE turnover for all companies increased from Rs. 71.777 crore in 1991-92 to Rs. 78,989 crore at the end of December 1997. The market liquidity, too, has marginally increased as indicated by growth in market capitalisation alongwith an increase in turnover ratio (turnover as percentage of market capitalisation) from 22.19% in 1991-92 to 22.70% at end of December 1997.[4]

With respect to **insider trading,** it is worth noting that in India insider trading is an offence w.e.f. November 19, 1992. SEBI is the administrative authority of the regulations against insider-trading. SEBI (Insider Trading Regulations), 1992 relate to insider trading in India. Thus, SEBI takes action against anyone found guilty of insider trading in India e.g. during 1997-98 it asked HLL (found guilty of insider trading) to compensate UTI to the tune of Rs. 3.04 crore and initiated criminal proceedings against HLL and its five directors.

Corporate governance has become an important issue in India since 1991. The Companies Act, 1956; the SEBI Act, 1992; public financial institutions and institutional investors - all are playing a role in evolving good corporate governance practices in India. The Companies Bill, 1997 and the Ordinance of Companies (Amendment) Bill, 1997 have amended several provisions of the existing Act and introduced new provisions incorporating some internationally accepted corporate governance practices aimed at strengthening corporate democracy, protecting the interests of minority investors and providing increasing flexibility to the corporates in responding to market conditions. The capital market developments in recent years have considerably improved corporate governance mechanisms for large and small investors, i.e. with detailed disclosure requirements, greater investor protection, screen-based trading and move towards integrated markets, investors are becoming increasingly well informed about true company performance and are also being able to respond quickly to any market information, good or bad. The Confederation of Indian Industry (CII) has also come out with a code for corporate governance in 1998. Further, the Finance Ministry has asked FI's in India to take 'full responsibility' for corporate governance in companies where they have substantial stakes - the object being to boost investor confidence and pep up the capital market. UTI has spearheaded many governance reform campaigns in companies where it has substantial stakes. The UTI is asking leading corporates where it has sizable stakes to make presentations outlining their plans and expected performance after declaration of half-yearly results. The objective of the exercise is to give more hands-on governance to give confidence to unit holders. FII's have implemented new norms for appointment of nominee directors, are in the process of revising guidelines for nominee directors and are insisting on setting up of audit subcommittees to strengthen internal control structures and safeguard shareholder interests. The participation by FII's has led to improved corporate governance at ICICI.

RESTRUCTURING NEEDED TO ATTRACT FINANCIAL FLOWS

Thus, we find that attempts that are necessary in a financial system so as to attract these flows has already been initiated in India. Gradual efforts are in progress on the various fronts mentioned above. These need to continue in a non-disruptive manner. More specifically, the process to restructure the financial system to attract financial flows in future should entail the following:

- Capital adequacy of all securities market intermediaries should gradually be raised to the norms prescribed by International Organisation of Securities Commission (IOSCO) of which SEBI is a member.
- Accountability and the enforcement of contracts requires that we have a legal system that dispenses justice quickly, inexpensively and sensibly. Reform of our legal system to make it so is vital. We should strive for the adoption of International Accounting Standards by Indian companies and the strengthening of auditing procedures through the formation of audit sub-committees. This would help ensure the disclosure of comparable, consistent and complete information. The task here is particularly challenging given that international best practice mechanisms are continuously evolving even in rather mature capitalistic economies like USA and UK.
- There is need to further strengthen the prudential regulations to cover exposures in short-term foreign currency loans and other cross border operations in case of Indian banks, keeping in view international best practices and specific

requirements. In respect of prudential regulation it is important to note that the central objective of prudential regulation should be to set an upper bound to the insolvency probability of financial intermediaries. Capital adequacy ratio (CAR) are an imprecise tool for achieving this outcome. An approach based on 'Value at Risk' (VAR) which is phrased in terms of insolvency probabilities rather than capital ratios is better.

- Specific action is needed in respect of supervisory co-operation with regulators inside and outside the country, consolidated supervision of institutions and their subsidiaries as conglomerates, cross-border supervision, inter-agency cooperation.
- India's financial system needs a well-functioning derivatives exchange, which trades futures and options on currencies, interest rates, equities and commodities. The regulatory structure of derivatives in India is fragmented between SEBI (which has jurisdiction over exchanges), the RBI (which has jurisdiction over fixed income and currency markets and banks), and the Forward Markets Commission (which regulates commodity futures markets) and needs to be unified.

ENHANCING SUSTAINABILITY OF FINANCIAL FLOWS

To continue to attract/sustain financial flows, particularly portfolio flows, requires developing countries to provide for:

(i) A Stable Macroeconomic Environment

Large budget deficits, excessive monetary expansion,

erratic exchange rate policies, repressed financial system are symptoms of chronic instability. To provide a stable macroeconomic environment, developing countries should pursue sound financial policies, correct structural problems such as excessive government intervention, labour market distortions and inefficient tax and trade policies.

(ii) Provide for the Proper Use of Funds

If the financial flow proceeds are being used for consumption they are less sustainable. On the other hand, if such flows are used for domestic investment they are more sustainable.

(iii) Rapid Export Growth

Rapid export growth tends to enhance sustainability of flows, particularly portfolio flows, as it improves future repayment capacity.

or (iv) Maintain a Stable, Investor Friendly Economic and Political Environment in the Long Run

A sudden large and relatively long-lasting reduction in financial flows may arise when the perception is created that a devaluation, non-payment of public sector debt or the imposition of restrictions of capital outflows is about to occur. Such expectations are likely to arise when the real exchange rate is perceived to be out of line, the governments debt obligations are large, fiscal adjustment is perceived as politically or administratively infeasible, or the country's growth prospects are bleak. From the prospective of creditors, therefore, a high share of investment in absorption and a strong record of growth, a low stock of government obligations coupled with demonstrated fiscal flexibility (in the form of small deficits and low inflation) and a real exchange rate broadly perceived to be in line with fundamentals all augur well for future debt service. From a policy perspective, countries need to have an active exchange rate policy that avoids substantial appreciation of the real exchange rate and responsible fiscal policies.

To sustain portfolio flows, it is necessary to have stable real exchange rates, a relatively large share of investment in GDP and faster economic growth. By having well established policy and performance track records, strong macroeconomic, banking sector and institutional underpinnings vulnerability to reversals of flows can be reduced.

How is India posed in these respects? - is a question that is sought to be answered in this context so that it can suggest further restructuring that is needed in Indian financial system to sustain financial flows (particularly portfolio flows).

India has been characterised by persistence of high and unsustainable level of fiscal deficits in the recent past. Unsustainable fiscal deficits pose a threat to macroeconomic stability and growth through pre-emption of scarce financial resources on repayment and interest obligations. Along with the increase in gross fiscal deficit, revenue deficit has soared. Over the years, revenue deficit as a percentage of gross fiscal deficit has risen from an average of about 32% in 1985-86 to 1989-90 to 53% in 1998-99. (Economic Survey, 1998-99)

On the export front, India has been experiencing a decelerating trend since 1996-97. After three years of robust growth at an annual average of 19.7% (in U.S. dollars) during 1993-94 to 1995-96, export momentum slowed in 1996-97, with exports registering a modest growth of 5.3% and decelerating further to 1.5% in 1997-98. The performance in 1998-99 was worrisome with exports having registered a decline of 2.9% over April-December 1998 over the corresponding period of last year. Both global and domestic factors have contributed to the slow down in export growth since 1996-97.

Further, India has seen four governments in the last three years - (the second United Front Government fell in early 1998, coalition government led by BJP came to power in March 1998, then on April 17, 1999 Vajpayee Government fell). The political parties seem to be unable and unwilling to confront the deeper problems plaguing the economy. The environment of political instability, coupled with nuclear tests and sectarian violence, has not provided atmosphere conducive to domestic and foreign investment.

The exchange rate system in India is intermediate between fully managed and fully floating exchange rate regime. The managed float system of exchange rate that India has adopted since March 1993 has helped to protect India from erratic exchange rate movement. Maintaining stable external value of rupee is one of the prime objectives of RBI. RBI's intervention in the foreign exchange market coupled with monetary policy measures has helped to contain volatility and speculative activities in the foreign exchange market. Indeed, despite the negative US sanctions, downgrading by rating agencies, withdrawal of FII investments and decline in exports, the RBI has protected the rupee through a combination of market operations and interest rate changes.

RESTRUCTURING NEEDED TO SUSTAIN FINANCIAL FLOWS

India is not favourably poised to sustain financial flows - particularly portfolio flows. Further, it is noted that India has experienced outflows of portfolio flows particularly FII investment since November 1997. A number of factors have had an adverse impact on capital flows including exchange rate uncertainties associated with the Asian currency crisis, investors concerns about nuclear test of May 1998, subsequent G7 sanctions on aid and multilateral lending and loss of confidence in the regions stock process.

To enhance the sustainability of portfolio flows, then, the Indian financial system needs to be restructured. Herein, the process to restructure should include the following:

- Controlling the high fiscal deficit - It is essential to put the fiscal deficit on an irreversible and unambiguously declining trend. This requires removal of nonmerit[5] subsidies, disinvestment of public sector units, widening the tax net and more effective collection of taxes. Subsidies on non-merit goods currently account for an astonishing 11% of GDP. One way to phase out subsidies is to raise user charges at a rate which holds the quantum of subsidies constant in absolute terms. The next step could be a regime where user charges rise at inflation rates. Quite clearly, fiscal consolidation is absolutely necessary for containing inflation, reducing interest rates, promoting investment and growth and fostering reasonable stability in the financial system and the foreign exchange market. Thus, there is a need to improve the overall quality of fiscal adjustment, change the composition of expenditure towards investment and restrain the growth in revenue expenditure.
- Vigorous efforts are required to reverse the current deceleration in exports and achieve a rapid growth of exports, especially in the context of difficult international trading environment brought about by economic and financial crisis in East Asia. To achieve export targets in the light of the difficult external environment, we should endeavour to

address the more long-standing and intractable structural disadvantages faced by our exporters (relative to exporters in China, Malaysia and Thailand). A sea change in approach is required in respect of routine interaction between exporters and the organs of the state such as customs, exchange control, tax authorities and licensing authorities (DGFT) - to bring in on par with successful exporters of East Asia. The policies applicable to export production need to be transformed to remove the controls and constraints facing exporters. This requires a comprehensive examination of labour laws and SSI reservation as applicable to exporters, with a view to bring them on par with successful exporting countries like China. Warehousing and cargo handling of exports at airports and ports remains a monopoly of the state, with the consequent deleterious effect on service. The supply of infrastructure services like electricity, telephone and rail transport to exporters, remain of as poor quality as for general economy. Better export promotion policies also require a clear recognition that high import tariffs discourage exports, while lower tariffs enhance the relative profitability of exports.

The sharp depreciation of the competing East Asian currencies adversely affected India's exports to other economies. In 1998, this was partly alleviated because of a depreciation of the rupee in combination with recovery of currencies in East Asia. We need a further depreciation of the rupee to boost exports. Depreciation would also lead to a rise in the price of imports and a decline in the relative profitability of import dependent sectors. Hence the right strategy to promote exports would be to permit an export neutral devaluation, where the devaluation would be accompanied by tariff reductions, so as to leave import prices unchanged.

- Government should accord top most priority to eliminate red tapism which continues to be cited as main complaint of potential foreign investors.
- We must ensure that the regulations governing the inflow of foreign investment are transparent and attractive in comparison with other Asian countries.
- Exchange rate management should continue its focus on smoothing excessive volatility in the exchange rate and maintaining orderly market conditions to ensure that exchange rate remains constant with economic fundamentals.

CONCLUSION

It is necessary to restructure the Indian financial system to attract and sustain these flows. Right efforts have been initiated in India to attract these flows. These need to continue in a non-disruptive manner. India however, is not favourably poised to sustain these flows particularly portfolio flows. To enhance the sustainability of these flows Indian financial system need further restructuring.

NOTES

1. An important consideration in this area is the extent to which countries ought to allow universal banking, under which commercial banking and securities and investment banking activities are merged or require a separation of these functions. There are strong views on both sides.
2. Strahota, Robert D. (1996), "Securities Regulation in Emerging

Markets: Some Issues and suggested Answers" (paper prepared for SEC International Institute for Securities Market Development, Washington, D.C., April), processed.

3. Civil and administrative penalties for insider offences include loss of profits, warnings, fines and temporary suspension or cancellation of registration.
4. The capital market in India is relatively illiquid by developed country standards.
5. Primary health care, sanitation and environmental protection, fall in the list of 'merit goods' while electricity, fertilizer and higher education are treated as 'non merit goods'.

9

Minimising Risks Posed by Financial Flows: Restructuring Needed

Financial flows pose several problems for recipient countries - overheating of macroeconomy, lending boom that may exacerbate macroeconomic and financial vulnerability and volatility of asset prices and returns. The steps to combat these problems are:

(I) Steps to Avert Overheating

To control overheating, developing countries can attempt to (a) reduce net inflows of foreign flows on domestic monetary aggregates and (b) offset the impact of monetary expansion on aggregate demand.

(a) To reduce net inflows of foreign exchange following may be attempted:

i) The magnitude of gross financial flows can be reduced by imposing a variety of direct or indirect **controls on inflows.**

ii) Even if gross inflows are freely allowed, the **liberalisation of capital outflows**[1] or the **accelerated repayment of public debt** can be undertaken to attempt to reduce net flows.

iii) The implications of a net capital account surplus on the foreign exchange market can be counteracted by accelerating **trade liberalisations** to increase the current account deficit.

iv) The most extreme option could be to eliminate all foreign exchange intervention by **floating the exchange rate.**[2] A move toward a floating exchange rate regime, e.g., by establishing or widening the band within which a fixed exchange rate is allowed to fluctuate – increases the exchange risk that market participants face, with correspondingly less incentive for short-term financial flows.

(b) To offset the impact of financial flows on domestic monetary aggregates, following policies may be adopted:

(i) Sterilisation - i.e. contracting domestic credit to offset the expansion of net foreign assets of the central bank, through mechanism such as open market operation or transferring public sector deposits from commercial banks to the central bank, and

(ii) Increasing reserve requirements - This reduces the impact of the expansion of monetary base on the growth of broader monetary aggregate.

The impact of monetary expansion on aggregate demand can be neutralised through fiscal contraction. A tighter fiscal stance during the inflow episode does help reduce aggregate demand pressures.

(II) Measures to Contain Lending Boom While Strengthening Banking Sector

Lending booms can be curbed through a combination of macroeconomic and banking sector policies.

(a) Macroeconomic policies: Fiscal, monetary and exchange rate policies can all help to mitigate the lending boom. Tight fiscal policy helps to reduce overheating caused by the lending boom and helps keep interest rate low. A semi-floating exchange rate system (band), by increasing banks and other domestic borrowers exposure to foreign exchange risk, induces a more cautious approach towards external borrowing, resulting in smaller financial flows and less bank lending and overheating. A tight monetary policy may also help to reduce overheating and contain the lending boom. However, it also exacerbates capital inflows by keeping domestic interest rates high.

(b) Banking sector policies: Banking sector policies directed at containing the lending boom include:

(i) increasing banks capitalisation requirements, i.e. **increasing banks risk-adjusted-capital-asset ratios** - this makes banks more resilient to shocks, induces sound banking practices and may reduce the growth in lending,

(ii) **increasing provisioning for non-performing loans** - this makes banks more resilient to shocks, it may induce a portfolio shift toward safer assets. By reducing banks net profits and capital, this may constrain the growth in bank lending with a direct negative effect on credit growth.

(iii) **raising banks reserve requirements** - this restricts credit growth and minimises the risk of overlending.

(iv) **improving ceilings on commercial bank lending and external borrowing** - this limits the lending boom and the overheating. It is most effective if directed toward specific uses of credit such as consumption loans, credit cards and mortgages.

(v) **imposing indirect (economy-wide) capital controls** - Capital controls appear to change the composition of flows toward longer maturities. This may have the positive effect of biasing expenditures (and bank lending) toward investment rather than consumption.

Restructuring of finance system by adopting above mentioned macroeconomic and banking sector policies can help to contain lending boom and minimise the impact of financial flows on macroeconomic and financial sector vulnerabilities.

(III)Measures to Reduce Volatility of Asset Prices and Returns

This requires undertaking policy reforms aimed at:

i) improving domestic fundamentals and stabilising economic policies,
ii) diversification of economy,
iii) improving the attributes of the capital markets.

Improvements in capital markets are a significant factor in reducing volatility of asset prices and returns. To improve the capital market requires:

i) Well-synchronised comparison, clearance and settlement and central depository systems be established, sound links with banking and payment systems be laid down.
ii) Two basic principles of shareholder governance be followed: fair treatment for all shareholders and shareholder approval of key corporate decisions.
iii) International best practice on disclosure (including accounting) be adopted.

iv) Government regulatory functions (starting with oversight of trading activities) be devolved to Self Regulatory Organisations.

v) Improve enforcement of rules.

In general, improvements that increase the attractiveness of markets for foreign investors also serve to reduce volatility.

Finally, an attempt should be made to **create a domestic investor base -** to develop domestic institutional investors. They can serve as a counterweight to foreign investors and thereby assuage fears of excessive foreign presence. Domestic institutional investors can ensure that a large pool of dedicated money will be available for bottom fishing - value picking which will reduce the vulnerability of domestic capital markets to a rapid liquidation of assets by foreign investors. In addition, domestic institutional investors will increase the depth and liquidity of domestic capital markets.

In the light of the above framework, an attempt has been made to ascertain **what restructuring is needed in the Indian financial system so as to tackle the risks posed by financial flows? The first question that needs to be answered in this context is—Financial flows to India have posed what risks to India?**

Our analysis in chapter 4 for India reveals that:

1) Indian economy has not got overheated as a result of financial flows so far. Financial flows to India have not posed the risk of inflation, real exchange rate appreciation and widening of current account deficit till now. Infact, in India inflation has marginally dropped, current account deficit (as a % of GDP) has narrowed down and real exchange rate has depreciated.

2) The volatality in domestic stock markets has not increased during the period of study with the onset of financial flows. Share price volatility has infact declined and share return volatility shows no significant difference with the onset of financial flows.
3) The Indian economy has not experienced a lending boom during the financial flow period. Bank lending (as a % of GDP) has infact declined with the onset of financial flows.
4) Financial flows have not exacerbated macroeconomic vulnerability in India. Financial flows to India have not been accompanied by over-consumption and under-investment.
5) Financial flows have not exacerbated financial sector vulnerability. All scheduled commercial banks have improved their capitalisation ratio, profitability ratios and reduced their NPA's (as % of total assets) thereby increasing their capacity to absorb negative shocks.
6) Inflows of portfolio capital have fluctuated but they did not turn negative even in 1997-98 during the East Asian Crisis. India has not experienced sudden and massive reversal of financial flow as was evident in East Asian countries in 1997-98.[3] There have been modest outflows on account of FII's since November 1997. These outflows have not exposed the Indian financial system to those risks that its East-Asian counterparts were exposed to viz currency crisis, banking crisis.

Thus, India has averted most of the risks that these flows may pose. That India has escaped relatively unhurt from the surge in financial flows and sudden outflows of financial flows - is not a matter of chance - but due to sound management of financial flows. A co-ordinated policy framework and careful calibration of policy instruments resulted in an effective management of financial flows in India without intolerable shocks to the performance of the economy. How has India coped with problems resulting from surges in financial flows? - is discussed in the next section.

MANAGEMENT OF SURGE IN FINANCIAL FLOWS: INDIAN EXPERIENCE

India has been able to ensure finance system stability during the period of surge in financial flows and sudden outflows. This is because government has drawn up economic policies to handle this surge in financial flows. These policies have been drawn in the light of following principles. First, India has adopted a progressive approach to capital account liberalisation taking into account the overall macroeconomic conditions and the progress in the development of the financial & foreign exchange markets. Secondly, stability - oriented macroeconomic policies have been put in place to alleviate the impact of surging financial flows on the economy. Third, prudential supervision has been strengthend to improve the soundness of the financial institutions.

(A) Capital Account Liberalisation

Most economists agree that countries should liberalise their domestic financial system before opening up to foreign capital. By & large the countries of East Asia failed to do this. Interest rate ceilings, government-directed lending and insider relationships between banks & borrowers had all served to channel credit without regard for rates of return. Foreign money was pushed in the same directions, leading to excessive investment.

India, however, has adopted policy of cautious movement towards capital account liberalisation. It seeks to move over to capital account convertibility over time in a phased manner. Tarapore Committee's recommendation of achieving certain pre-conditions before liberalising the capital account are noteworthy for hasty capital account liberalisation without strong economic fundamentals, a well-functioning market mechanism and healthy financial institutions may cause immense damage to the national economy. India seeks to meet the following preconditions : to reduce fiscal deficit GDP ratio to 3.5% by 1999-2000, achieve an inflation rate of 3-5% mandated by Parliament with empowerment for the Central Bank, maintain REER in a 5% band around a target level to be announced publicly, reduce average effective CRR to 3% by 1999-2000 and reduce gross NPA of banking system to 5% - before liberalising its capital account. Thus, one reason why India has avoided the risks posed by financial flows is because it has been careful in avoiding capital account liberalisation without prior action for strengthening its finance system and because it has paid careful attention to co-ordinating the sequence, speed and timing of capital account liberalisation.

(B) Management of External Debt

India's management of external debt has hovered around building adequate reserves to tide over sudden outflows, monitoring maturity profile of external debt portfolio at a macro level and restricting short-term flows. As regards, *adequacy of reserves,* India has been steadily building up reserves by encouraging non-debt creating flows and de-emphasising debt-creating flows. India's foreign exchange reserves have been steadily increasing over the years. For instance, the last three years saw increase in reserves in the range of $4.7 billion in 1996-97 ; $2.9 billion in 1997-98 and $3.1 billion in 1998-99 i.e. acumulative

$10 billion.[4] However, between end-March 1996 and December 1998, India's total external debt increased by a mere $2 billion.[5] Thus, India's policy of building and maintaining adequate level of reserves while at the same time constraining debt, especially short-term debt has helped India to ensure finance system stability.[6]

Further in India, with deregulation and liberalisation, adequate attention has been paid to the *maturity profile of external debt portfolio.* Appropriate maturity structure is not a micro decision in India that is left to the final borrower whose main consideration is cost. Rather it is recognised as a macro aspect and a stability issue. Accordingly, in India, from 1992, emphasis has been laid not only on the cost and size of debt, but also on the maturity. The desired maturity profile is taken into account in policy articulation and clearance of individual cases. The average maturity of our ECB is five years. Basically, consideration, of the size, cost and maturity are embedded in the clearance mechanism for ECB.

A major source of vulnerability in the Asian crisis was the large stock of *short-term liabilities* of banks and corporates and their linkage to foreign exchange reserves. For example, short-term debt as a % of foreign exchange reserves rose from 89% (End-1993) to 153% (Mid-1997) for Thailand; in case of Indonesia it increased from 171% to 182%; Malaysia saw an increase in this ratio from 28% to 62% while for South Korea the ratio increased to 214% from 148% during the same period. In India, as opposed to East-Asian countries, we carefully monitor short-term debt. We maintain a difference in treatment between trade and non-trade related debt. The authorities sanction short-term debt over six months on a case-by-case approval of purpose, amount and terms, within a sub-ceiling of total external commercial borrowings ceiling. NRI deposits are controlled through specification of interest rate or interest rate ceilings for different maturities in respect of deposits in select schemes India's external debt scenario is healthy as short-term external debt is just 5%-6% of total external debt[7] and less than 20% of country's foreign exchange reserves. India's approach to management of external debt has also helped India to avert the risks of financial flows and ensure financial stability.

(C) Our Approach to Tackle Macroeconomic Risks of Financial Flows

India has tackled the macro-economic risks of financial flows by pursuing following policies: sterilisation through open market operations, sterilisation through other means, restrictions on financial inflows, liberalisation of the current account and selective capital outflow liberalisation.

The surge in financial flows to India since 1993 led to a spurt in foreign exchange reserves. This brought in its wake the problem of large increase in primary liquidity which resulted in unacceptable growth in M3 in 1993-94 (18.4%) with the attendant problem of acceleration of inflation. The problem of excess liquidity has been tackled by India through a combination of policy measures including a drastic reduction in the monetisation of the budget deficit, an increase in cash reserve ratio, resort to open-market operations and restructuring of non-resident deposit schemes to reduce the element of high cost borrowing. In 1993-94, as part of sterilisation policy, large open market operations were conducted by RBI equivalent to a cash reserve ratio increase of 2.8 percentage points. During 1993-94, RBI undertook aggressive open market operations and sold government securities worth $ 3 billion to mop up liquidity. Unlike in 1993-94 when CRR's of banks were lowered and the burden of sterilisation was entirely on open market operations, in 1994-95, a multi pronged strategy was followed. First, there was a phased increase in CRR of banks. Secondly, moderate OMO were conducted. Thirdly, the growth of foreign exchange reserves was moderated by discouraging short-term inflows and regulation of inflows under euro-issues. Further, Indian authorities have imposed direct or indirect controls on financial flows. India imposed guidelines to limit access of Indian companies to eurobond market. In May, 1994, India's Central Bank stipulated that any group of companies will not be allowed more than two euro-issues during a financial year and there must be a minimum gap of twelve months between two issues floated by a single firm. In addition, the guidelines stipulated that 85% of the receipts from these issues should be used within one year for import of goods and services. Indian government is also trying to sterilise the burgeoning foreign exchange reserves by liberalising current and capital account transactions to increase imports. Capital outflows, too, have been liberalised to some extent e.g. Foreign investors are allowed to repatriate dividends and capital freely but Indian residents are not free to take capital out of the country, a restriction which makes it easier to avoid panic overreaction in foreign exchange markets. Further, in managing our external account, we ensure a sustainable current-account deficit[8] policymakers in India have been extremely conscious (after the crisis of 1991-92) of the need to ensure that the CAD remain at an appropriate level. Price stability is also an important objective underlying monetary policy in India.

(D) Strengthening of Financial Sector

The East Asian experience shows that a loose domestic financial system and large financial flows are the worst combination. Weaknesses in the financial sector - was one of the several causes for the East Asian crisis. Banks wee not subject to prudential regulation and supervision or asset liability management. This coupled with poor governance and lack of internal controls resulted in excessive leverage and excessive credit expansion directed to unproductive investments. Financial reporting and disclosure norms in these countries were far from satisfactory. This kind of regime encouraged large domestic credit expansion. The pegged exchange rate system also resulted in investments being financed by short-term external debt Globalisation of the financial market was not accompanied by an appropriate information system. Lack of transparency delayed public realisation of the magnitude of the problem. Heavy lending against real estate put several banks into difficulties when land prices began to fall.

However, India has strengthened its financial system since the onset of financial flows. RBI has been making continuous efforts towards strengthening financial soundness by prescribing capital adequacy norms for banks and financial institutions, advising improvements in asset classification and accounting systems and establishing best practice norms for income recognition and provisioning against exposures faced by them. A Board for Financial Supervision has been set up for exercising integrated supervision both, on-site and off-site over banks, financial institutions and finance companies. Besides several steps have been taken to improve the audit system in general. There is midely recognised transparency in operations of banks. We have taken various measures to ensure that the banking system does not get into a maturity mismatch bind. Liquidity position of banks is being closely monitored. We discourage banks investments in real estate and stock market, corporate exposure to debt especially external debt is within reasonable limits.

Prudential regulations in India pertain to capital adequacy, income recognition, asset classification, marking investments to market, portfolio concentration and large exposures, connected lending, country and transfer risk, market risk, risk management system in banks & internal controls.

Prudential supervision in India consists of both on-site and off-site supervision. On-site inspections are based on CAMELS (Capital adequacy, asset quality, management, earnings, liquidity and systems and controls). The domestic banks are rated on CAMELS model while foreign banks are rated on CACS model (capital adequacy, assets quality, compliance and systems). The OSMOS - off-site monitoring and surveillance system that is prevalent in India with respect to supervision consists of 12 returns (called DSB returns) focussing on supervisory concerns such as capital adequacy, asset quality, large credits and concentrations, connected lending, earnings and risk exposures (viz. currency, liquidity and interest rate risks). The supervisory intervention power rests with RBI and the process is triggered by the deterioration in the level of capital adequacy, NPAs, credit concentration, lower earnings and larger incidence of frauds which reflect the quality of control.

Further, RBI has made continuous efforts to impart greater *transparency* to the balance sheets of banks. Commercial banks in India are required to disclose capital adequacy ratios (both Tier/and Tier II Separately), percentage of NPA's to net advances, provision made towards NPA's, gross and net value of investments. From April 2000, banks are also required to disclose maturity profile of loans and advances, investments and lending to sensitive sectors.

The RBI has also accorded attention to strengthening *internal control systems* in banks. Banks have been advised to introduce the system of concurrent audit in major and specialised branches and are required to set up audit committees to follow up on the reports of the statutory auditors and inspection by RBI.

Thus, we find that India has taken steps to strengthen supervision and regulation of financial system while liberalising its financial markets.[9] Since attempts to liberalise[10] financial markets in India have been accompanied by attempts to tighten the system for effective supervision and regulation, India has been successful in ensuring financial system stability during period of surge in financial flows and sudden outflows.

(E) Position of Indian Banks in Respect of Certain Factors that Increase Financial Sector Vulnerability

If an increase in bank lending is associated with declining liquidity ratio's, increased exposure to real estate or stocks, increased exposure to foreign exchange risk, portfolio concentration, connected lending it reflects increased vulnerability of financial sector to banking crisis. How is India poised in respect of these factors?

India is favourably poised in these respects since to *avoid portfolio concentration,* India sets limits on lending to individual borrowers and group borrowers. Exposure to a single borrower can not exceed 25% of the banks capital funds (i.e. paid up capital and free reserves). The Mid-term review of Monetary and Credit Policy for 1999-2000 has introduced reduction in this from existing level of 25% to 20% effective from April 1, 2000. Existing level of exposures in excess of 20% as on October 31, 1999 are sought to be brought down to 20% over a period of two years (i.e., by end October, 2001). Group exposure can not exceed 50% of the capital funds of the bank. Additional 10% is allowed in respect of exposure to infrastructure projects (power, telecom, roads and ports).

Exposure of banks to real estate operations is limited in India to less than 1%.[11] Of the gross bank credit amounting to Rs. 2,58,991 crore; Rs. 3,00, 283 crore and Rs. 3,42,012 crore at end March 1997, 1998 and 1999 respectively — Rs. 1,546 crore, Rs. 1899 crore and Rs. 1625 crore had been in the form of real estate loans. Thus, real estate loans by banks in India have been 0.60%, 0.63% and 0.48% of gross bank credit respectively at end — March 1997, 1998 and 1999.[12]

Further, India seeks to ensure adequate *liquidity* within the financial system by closely monitoring liquidity position of banks and requiring banks to maintain CRR and SLR as per section 42(1) of the RBI Act, 1934 and Section 24(2A) of the Banking Regulation Act, 1949 respectively. The method of computing these ratios has been defined in the respective sections of the Acts. The RBI has powers to modify CRR between 3% to 20% and SLR between 25% to 40%.[13] The RBI has advised banks to monitor liquidity through maturity or cash flow mismatches. RBI by enforcing liquidity risk management system on banks in India seeks to prevent financial institutions from facing a liquidity crisis in the light of financial flows.[14] As part of the liquidity risk management system, banks are required to bracket future cash flows in different time buckets. The banks are required to fix tolerance levels for various maturity mismatches depending upon the bank's asset-liability profile, extent of stable deposit base, nature of cash flows etc. Further, prudential limit on mismatches (negative gap) in cash flows during 1-14 days and 15-28 days should not exceed 20% of each of the cash outflows during these time buckets as per RBI guidelines. The RBI monitors the liquidity position of banks through a periodic return on structural liquidity. The objective of RBI is to move to fortnightly reporting by April 1, 2000.

As regards *banks investments in stocks* that exposes the banks to market risks, RBI has placed quantitative restrictions on the extent of exposure that banks can have in equity.[15] The overall ceiling of investment by banks in ordinary shares, convertible debentures of corporates and units of mutual funds etc. is limited to 5% of banks incremental deposits. This limit has been enhanced to the extent of banks investment in venture capital in accordance with the Monetary and Credit Policy Statement for 1999-2000. The banks in general are not allowed to trade in commodities. Recently, however, select banks have been permitted to deal in gold/silver/platinum. These banks must maintain 9% capital adequacy on all risk weighted assets including on the open position in gold/silver/platinum that carries 100% risk weight w.e.f. 31March, 1999. To control banks exposure to 'market risk', investment portfolio of banks is classified into 'permanent' & 'current' categories w.e.f. 1992. At present, banks are required to mark to market at least 70% of all approved securities and 100% of non-approved securities. The ratio of marking to market has been fixed at 75% of approved securities w.e.f. March 31, 2000. In addition, effective from March 31, 2000. Government and other approved securities are to be assigned 2.5% risk weight instead of 'nil' risk weight as earlier and requisite capital has to be maintained thereon.

To avoid increased *exposure* of Indian banks *to foreign exchange risk,* banks are required to assign 100% risk weight to their open position in foreign exchange w.e.f. March 31, 1999. Besides, they are required to fix aggregate and individual gap limits for each currency with the approval of RBI. They are required to adopt Value at Risk Approach to measure the risk associated with forward exposures. The RBI monitors currency risk through a monthly return on maturity and positions for both on and off balance sheet items in foreign exchange.

Connected lending is India is governed by the regulations of Section 20 of Banking Regulation Act. In order to strengthen the provisions relating to connected lending and making their application more stringent, the Reserve Bank is seeking legislative amendment to empower it to take appropriate steps to safeguard against siphoning of bank's funds through connected lending and to initiate criminal prosecution in such cases.

That India has instituted adequate safeguards in respect of these factors implies that financial sector vulnerability has not increased in India. Increased financial sector vulnerability in the presence of large financial flows is likely to lead to fiscal sector distress and crisis (instability in the financial system) once any untoward event occurs. Since in India financial sector has been strengthened during the period of surge in financial flows, financial flows have not led to financial distress and banking crisis.

(F) Management of Exchange Rate

India has avoided another of the serious mistakes of several East Asian countries, most notably Korea, the Philippines and Thailand. These countries pegged their currencies to the US dollar in the early 1990's; then experienced inadvertent and sharp currency appreciation vis-a-vis Europe and Japan when the dollar strengthened after 1995; and then ran down foreign exchange reserves vainly trying to defend the overvalued exchange rate when market sentiment turned against the currencies in late 1996 and in the first half of 1997. By spending reserves in a failed attempt to defend the currency, the central banks also left their economies exposed to subsequent financial panic when short-term debts came to exceed the dwindling level of foreign exchange reserves. In the end, the currencies collapsed in any case, but only after a deep financial crisis had already gotten under way. Fortunately, the Reserve

Bank of India has been more circumspect in exchange rate policy, letting the rupee weaken in the face of Asian crisis.

Free capital movement and pegged exchange rates are a dangerous mix. India has avoided this. India has a unified, market determined exchange rate regime since March 1993. However, the central bank intervenes to regulate the market. It is more a system of managed float. The primary objective of the Reserve Bank in regard to the management of the exchange rate has been to ensure that the external value of the rupee is realistic and credible as evidenced by a sustainable current account deficit and manageable foreign exchange situation. Subject to this predominant objective, the exchange rate policy is guided by the need to reduce excess volatility, prevent the emergence of destabilising speculative activities, help maintain adequate level of reserves and develop an orderly foreign exchange market. The Indian market is not yet very deep and broad and is characterised by uneven flow of demand and supply over different periods. The market is also characterised by a few major players, and lumpy public sector demands, particularly on account of payment for oil imports and servicing of public debt. In this situation, the Reserve Bank has been making sales and purchases of foreign currency in order to even out lumpy demand and supply in the relatively thin forex market and to smoothen jerky movements. However, such intervention is not governed by a predetermined target a band around the exchange rate.

India has been able to keep the spill over effects of the Asian crisis to a minimum through constant monitoring and timely action, including recourse to strong monetary measures, when necessary to prevent the emergence of self-fulfilling speculative activities.

(G) Capital Market Reforms

The development of effective and efficient transaction infrastructure in capital markets is as essential as appropriate macroeconomic policy and prudential regulations and supervision for managing financial flows. In this respect, we find major changes have taken place in the capital market during the period of financial flows. In 1991, India's capital market did not have a statutory regulatory framework. The Securities and Exchange Board of India (SEBI) was given statutory powers in 1992 and has since laid down a structure of regulations governing various participants in the capital markets; including rules for insider trading, takeovers and management of mutual funds. The stock exchanges, which were earlier dominated by brokers and lacked effective supervision, are now much better governed. The focus of the new regulations is to ensure investor protection through transparency and full disclosure. The technology of trading has been modernised. There is now automatic matching of buy and sell orders with price time priority. The fully computerised stock exchange trading system ensures transparency for investors and assurance of the best price. The settlement system has also seen major improvement. Earlier, completion of a trade involved physical transfer of share certificates from seller to buyer followed by submission of the certificates to company registrars to effect changes in the register of stockholders. The process was vitiated by long delays, frequent loss of certificates, return of certificates because signatures of the seller on the certificates did not match with signature on record with registrars, and also the danger of forged certificates. In 1996, a National Depository commenced operations offering investors the facility of holding securities in dematerialised form and settling trades through book entries in the depository, eliminating delays and uncertainties in transfer of ownership. These changes are putting in place a set of capital market institutions which can generate confidence among investors. The presence of FII's has been an importance force in pushing the capital market to come closer to international standards.

The process of capital market reforms aimed at improving market efficiency, making stock market transactions more transparent, curbing unfair trade practices and bringing the Indian capital market upto international standards has helped to promote investor interest and ensure investor protection and has contributed to arresting the rise in volatility in domestic stock market. Another factor that has gone in India's favour is the fact that Indian stock market is not fully integrated with the world markets. Therefore, volatility spillover effects have been guarded against. Further imposition of ban on short sales by SEBI (as on June 15, 1998 — July 6, 1998) has helped India to counter volatility in share prices. In order to tighten the measures aimed at curbing volatility in share prices, SEBI prescribed additional volatility margins (AVM) (w.e.f. July 6, 1998).

Thus, India has avoided the risks posed by financial flows so far on account of its strong fundamentals and introduction of prudential regulation and supervision alongwith financial liberalisation. India, we find, has been pursuing sound policies in areas where serious concern has been expressed in the light of South East Asian crisis. Hence, India has been successful in ensuring financial system stability in the light of surge in financial flows and sudden outflows.

RESTRUCTURING NEEDED TO AVERT RISKS POSED BY FLOWS

India has avoided the risks posed by financial flows since many of the policy prescriptions to avert the risks are already in place in India. These policies have served us well so far. It seems that the efforts are in the right direction. However, India cannot afford to pause and relax. Rather, efforts need to continue relentlessly/vigorously and progress so far achieved needs to be accelerated. Specifically, concerted action on following lines is needed.

(A) Capital Account Liberalisation

India's policy of cautions movement towards capital account liberalisation that has been adopted by us needs to continue since premature opening of the capital account could lead to massive capital outflows from the country. Liberalisation of capital account needs to be viewed as a process to be implemented in phases and not as a single event that can be attained overnight. India needs to embark upon it cautiously as part of overall economic reforms as well as assessment of emerging scenario relating to international, economic and financial architecture. There should be full convertibility on capital account only after India has achieved a consistent macroeconomic framework, stable exchange rate policies and strong institutional framework in its financial markets. Otherwise, large capital outflows may develop and government could then end up bailing out the weakened domestic financial system at a significant cost to the taxpayer.

India should strive to achieve the following preconditions before opening its capital account:

a) *Fiscal deficit GDP ratio* needs to be brought down from a budgeted 4.5% in 1997-98 to 3.5% in 1999-2000. This is essential because a large fiscal deficit financed through central bank credits to the government typically leads to high inflation and/or large exchange rate depreciation and because a large fiscal deficit as a proportion of

GDP is taken as a proxy for the risks of macroeconomic instability. The key to achieving this target would be the maintenance of the growth momentum and reduction of subsidies.

b) *Inflation* rate should remain at an average 3-5%. The inflation rate should be mandated by Parliament with empowerment for RBI. This would make the RBI an independent authority.

c) *Gross NPA's* of the public sector banking system need to be brought down to 5% by 2000. Reducing NPA's would in effect mean writing them off, since a large proportion is irrecoverable.

d) *Average CRR* needs to be brought down to 3%. Reducing CRR will increase bank profitability, but if growth picks up, a CRR reduction could fuel inflationary pressures. This well amount to an injection of funds close to the tune of Rs. 35,000 crore in the system. This holds the potential to fund development projects -especially in the infrastructure sector on a much larger scale and to remove the various bottle necks that constrain the growth of GDP beyond 6.5-7%.

e) RBI should have a monitoring *exchange rate band* of plus-minus 5% around a neutral REER, RBI should be transparent about the changes in REER. This will enable the market to predict the value of the rupee reasonably accurately.

f) a consolidated sinking fund be set up to meet the governments debt repayment needs, to be financed by the RBI's profit transfer to the government and disinvestment proceeds. This implies rolling over of public debt will be avoided. We also need to review our disinvestment policies.

g) Transparent and globally comparable procedures for fiscal accounting should be in place.

h) External sector policies should be designed to increase current receipts to GDP ratio. This requires a dynamic export growth to be sustained at over 20% of the GDP. It is important to remember that our exports are price sensitive and the appreciation of the rupee in the event of capital account convertibility (CAC) might impede our export growth.

i) Dept servicing ratio needs to be brought down to 20%.

j) The conventional measure of measuring an optimal level of forex reserves expressed in terms of adequacy of financing a number of months of imports should be replaced by other indicators to evaluate adequacy of foreign exchange reserves. Adequate foreign exchange reserves are necessary to provide a buffer against any seasonal and cyclical shortfalls in balance of payments and to be able to hold on to the required market exchange rate.

Progress on these prerequisites will help improve India's creditworthiness and attractiveness to foreign investors. These pre-conditions will encourage financial flows (such as foreign direct investment) based on long-term fundamentals rather than short-term returns. The attainment of these preconditions will ensure that financial flows are well used ultimately. Finally, the more robust, India is with regard to these preconditions, the greater will be its latitude in responding to surges and volatile flows. Poor macroeconomic policies and CAC are likely to generate large outflow of funds and price volatility.

(B) External Debt Management

Government needs to prudently manage the size, maturity profile and currency structure of its own debt because one of the many causes of the East Asian crisis was high percentage of external debt, systematic mismatching of maturities[16] and matching of denominations.[17]

We need to continue with the objective of restricting short-term flows though the means of doing[18] it could be refined from time to time in consonance with domestic and to some extent global developments. There is need to restrain short-term flows until markets, institutions and regulatory framework have been sufficiently strengthened.

Our policy of building and maintaining adequate level of reserves while at the same time constraining debt, especially short-term debt should continue. This, is necessary because one of the causes of East-Asian crisis was a very high ratio of short-term debt to reserves — this ratio was well over 100% in case of East Asian countries. The international debate on adequacy of reserves should continuously be monitored[19] in this respect.

ECB policy should ensure built in measures towards optimal maturity. There can be several views on what an optimal maturity itself is. There is one influential view that the average maturity of country's external liabilities should exceed a certain threshold, say three years.

(C) Efficient functioning of financial system

Our efforts to provide India with:

a) well designed infrastructure-legal and judicial framework, good corporate governance, accounting standards, system of independent audits, efficient payments and settlement systems;
b) effective market discipline — good credit culture, well developed and functioning equity and debt

markets and wide variety of instruments for risk diversification; and

c) strong regulatory and supervisory framework — need to be continued endlessly. The presence of these conditions will ensure efficient functioning of financial sector and serve to attract investors. These pre-requisites are also necessary to reduce vulnerability of banking system; to channel flows into productive uses. Proper & effective regulation and supervision also serves to provide early warning signals of impeding crisis apart from increasing resilience of banks to shocks. The development of well-functioning capital markets will reduce risks of potential instability as well as attract the growing pool of portfolio investment.

(D) Shock Absorbers

India needs to build better shock absorbers and develop mechanisms to respond to instability that may arise in future. Three types of shock-absorbers need to be built.

First, the level of international reserves needs to be established in relation to the variation in the capital account, rather than in terms of months of imports; since the levels of gross flows is likely to be higher in future due to opening of the capital account. International reserves can also be buttressed with contingent lines of credit (as Argentina has done recently) when investor confidence is less firm.

Second, increased financial flows in future heighten the need for fiscal flexibility, which in turn will depend on the level of public debt, among other things.

Third, cushions should be built in the banking system. Authorities should use periods of credit boon to increase capitalisation and provisioning requirements as a way to promote sound banking practices and increase the resilience of banks.

To ensure that India has resilience to handle outflows net foreign assets to currency ratio (NFA/Currency Ratio) should be monitored. This ratio provides a rough and ready rule of thumb to judge whether or not the country has followed prudent monetary management. The ratio indicates whether currency expansion has been lower/higher than the financial inflow during the period of upswing in foreign exchange reserves and as such when a capital outflow emerges whether the foreign exchange reserves would be large enough to meet the outflow. This ratio should be fixed by law at not less than 40%.

(E) Strengthening Banking System

India must continuously strive to strengthen its banking system by adopting best practices and best international standards of performance and prudence. Actions in following areas are needed in this respect:

i) **Further tightening of prudential norms** e.g. the present norm of 18 months for categorising a sub-standard asset as doubtful needs to be brought down to make it at par with the international practice of 12 months. As regards income recognition, it is important to pursue implementation of international norm of 90 days in a phased manner by 2002, as against current practice of 180 days. We should strive to come closer to the international norm of 15% for exposure to a single borrower from current practice of 20%.

ii) **Problem of weak banks:** In view of the adverse implications that weak banks have on the stability of banking system, there is need to restructure weak public sector banks - banks which are grappling with profitability and ensuring compliance with prescribed norms.

To identify weak banks following parameters may be used:

- **Solvency parameters** viz. capital adequacy ratio and coverage ratio i.e. ratio of equity capital and loan loss provision less non-performing loans to total assets.
- **Earnings capacity parameters** viz. return on assets and net interest margins; and
- **Profitability parameters** viz. ratio of operating profit to average working funds, cost to income and staff cost to net interest income plus all other income.

There parameters can be supplemented with criteria for detecting bank weakness, as provided by Narasimham Committee to detect bank weakness.[20]

Banks where none of the criteria are met should receive primary attention. Attempts should be made to restructure these weak banks. The exercise to restructure such banks should be done in stages. In stage one the focus should be on restoring competitive efficiency through operational, organisational, financial and systemic restructuring. And the options of privatisation and/or merger should assume importance in stage two of the restructuring process. In stage, one, operational restructuring should comprise (i) basic changes in mode of operations, (ii) adoption of modern technology, (ii) resolution of problem of high non-performing assets through the setting up of a government owned Asset Reconstruction Fund (ARF) and (iv) drastic reduction in the cost of operations, through, among others, staff rationalisation measures. Organisational restructuring should encompass improved governance practices of the banks and enhancement in management involvement and efficiency. Financial restructuring may be achieved via the recapitalisation route, which may be done for specific purposes, and with conditions which the banks management, including its Board of Directors, and the employee agree to fulfill before the restructuring process is initiated. Finally, systemic restructuring should involve, interalia, changes in the legal system and formulation of appropriate measures aimed at institution building so as to support the restructuring exercise.

For speeding up the recovery process of weak banks and ARF, an arrangement could be worked out so that Debt Recovery Tribunals (DRT's) attend to their cases on a priority basis.

The above exercise to restructure weak banks (where none of above criteria are met) is likely to be substantial (around Rs. 5,500 crore) and hence restructuring of the other category of weak banks (where some criteria are met) should await till the more chronic cases are restructured.

iii) **Reducing NPA's:** Reducing NPA's is crucial to maintaining the viability of the banking system. NPA's of large magnitude are a major hindrance to the profitability of banks. Gross NPA's of public sector banks have moved up from Rs. 39,253 crore in 1993 to Rs. 51,710 crore in 1999. As a percentage of gross advances, NPA's of public sector bank stood at 15.9% as at end March, 1999 and these were significantly higher than that of the developed economies like U.S. (1.1%), Finland (2.7%), Norway (3.2%) and even the Asian economies like Malaysia (3.9%) and Japan (3.4%).

It is necessary to reduce the average level of net NPA's for all banks to 3% by 2002 and to zero for banks with international presence (Narasimham Committee Report, 1998) Gross NPA's should be reduced to 5% by 2000 and 3% by 2002.

Both internal and external factors are responsible for NPA in case of Indian banks. Internal factors that have led to NPA include weak credit appraisal, non-compliance and willful default while external factors include factors such as pre-ponderance of certain traditional industries in the credit portfolio of certain banks, majority of which are suffering from serious inherent operational problems, natural calamities, policy and technological changes which increase the incidence of sickness, labour problems and non-availability of raw materials and other such factors which are not within the control of banks. While banks cannot be blamed for advances becoming non-performing due to external factors, there is an urgent need that the banks address the problems arising out of internal factors and this requires organisational restructuring of banks, a change in the approach of banks towards legal action and a clear thrust on improving the skills of officials for proper assessment of credit proposal, risk factor and repayment possibilities. Though there are problems in effecting recoveries and write offs and in compromise settlements, it is of utmost importance that necessary changes are brought about in the related legislations for making recovery process more smooth and less time consuming and also to create other alternative channels/agencies for recovery of debt/reduction of non-performing advances. As the Lok Adalat have proved a very good agency for quick justice and recovery of smaller loans, their efforts should supplement efforts of recovery by debt recovery tribunals. The setting up of Asset Reconstruction Company (ARC) can also be used to reduce NPA's and provide necessary liquidity to banks through securitisation of banks loan assets. Further attempts should be undertaken to make

DRT's more effective in operation as ARC's could engender moral hazard problems. Moreover, government and other authorities should devise policies having a bearing on the industrial sector, agriculture and trade with a long term perspective to avoid sickness in the industry and adverse impact on borrowers because of sudden shift in the policy. Reduction of NPA's in the banking sector should be treated as a priority item to make the Indian banking system more strong and resilient to shocks. It is also necessary to work out the levels of NPA's at which the confidence in banking can be maintained at high levels.

iv) **Full implementation of Basle Core Principles for Effective Banking Supervision: RBI** should strive towards full implementation of Basle Core principles for Effective Banking Supervision. Many of the prudential norms are already enshrined in our existing legislation or current regulations. However, there are gaps in areas of risk management in banks, consolidated supervision, inter-agency co-operation with other domestic/international regulators and consolidated supervision. Concerted action in these areas is called for. For example, the regulatory and supervisory functions are presently performed by a number of agencies - the RBI, SEBI, NABARD, Registrars of Co-operative Societies. Within these organisations, these functions are performed in different departments/sections/units. While each organisation attempts to co-ordinate its supervisory concerns and works out the required regulations, a co-ordination of oversight functions among the organisations through a firmly established institutional arrangement is vital for avoiding any systemic problems that may develop on account of the existence of interfaces among financial entities.

(F) Development of Forex Market

Development of forex market is required to channel

the increased flow of funds that will take place once capital account convertibility is achieved. All the funds that flow in will have to go through the dollar - rupee market then and an illiquid dollar - rupee market will display spurious volatility under the pressure. Hence, institutional development of India's forex market is necessary if India has to have an open capital account and financial flows. The two key approaches for this are:-

a) transition of the spot market away from the inter-bank market to modern screen-based trading that is widely accessible all over the country; and

b) transition away from the inter-bank dollar rupee forward market to a modern dollar - rupee futures market without entry barriers. Further, there is a need to develop strong linkages among the markets - stock, forex, debt and money markets. These markets need to be integrated before we move on to Capital Account convertibility.

(G) Strengthening Risk Management Systems

Risk management system needs to be strengthened as capital controls are lifted by India in the presence of financial flows. Exposure to interest rate volatility and exchange risk (due to increased dollar-rupee volatility) are part of the transition to capital account convertibility. This raises the urgency of developing futures and options on interest rates and on the dollar-rupee which would give people a method of managing these risks. Thus, future development of forex derivative market is necessary to significantly reduce exchange rate risk.

Risk management systems needs to be devised by banks to address the various risks they are likely to be exposed to viz. credit risk, foreign exchange risk, liquidity risk, market risk etc. when they increase their lending activity (especially in a deregulated environment) in response to financial flows. Banks need to develop and implement integrated risk management system. In this respect, banks need to take concerted actions simultaneously in nine areas. **One,** banks must lay down clear and meaningful policies on identificaiton, measurement, monitoring and control of various risks (such as credit risk, liquidity risk, interest rate risk, currency risk) and to review the policy from time to time to incorporate changes in business environment and perception of top management about the risks. **Two,** banks need to improve the skills of its staff members. This is necessary because a bank may formulate robust policies and strategies for risk management, but unless its staff members are adequately trained and skilled manpower is available, there would be difficulty in implementation of risk-management process. **Three,** banks need to devise suitable systems to measure risks. Simple gap statements can be used to measure liquidity risk and currency risk. Interest rte risk can be measured via. gap analysis, duration analysis, Value at risk (VAR), simulation.[21] **Four,** banks should have a committee that constantly monitors banks exposure to various risks e.g. Credit Policy Committee may monitor credit risk, likewise there may be other committees to monitor other risks. The efforts of all these committees however need to be integrated by Assets-liability Committee (ALCO). The ALCO should be headed by the Chief Executive Officer/Chairman and Managing Director or the Executive Director of the Bank. **Fifth,** banks need to maintain adequate capital base in conformity to risks faced by them. In this respect, it is essential to bolster capital adequacy ratio from 8% specified by Basle Accord because this ratio is based only on recognition of credit risk faced by banks. Since banks are exposed to other risks apart from credit risks, the Basle Committee on Banking

Supervision has come out with a consultative paper on capital adequacy framework (in the light of other risks faced by banks) in June, 1999. These recommendations should form the basis of our standard for capital adequacy ratio for banks. **Sixth,** it is necessary that effective implementation of risk management policies takes place. Implementation could be assigned to a committee or a committee of top executives that reports to the Board. **Seventh,** banks should develop good management information system. Strengthening of information technology is an important pre-requisite for affective implementation of risk management system in banks. The data base of banks has to be exhaustive to cover all operations of braches for a detailed analysis of assets and liabilities and for forecasting a comprehensive projection of liquidity conditions under various scenario. The software packages used must be well tested and have extensive computing power to analyse the massive amount of asset/liability data under alternative scenarios. **Eight,** the risk management systems of banks should be examined during on-site inspections to assess how comprehensive bank's system of risk management is. **Lastly,** risk management has to be a culture that has to develop from within the internal management system of banks since it is not possible to have a uniform risk management system for all banks due to diversity and varying size of balance sheet items. The risk management systems should be suited to banks own requirement dictated by size, complexity of business, risk philosophy, market perception, existing level of capital. Thus, banks need to evolve their own system compatible with type and size of operations as well as risk perception.

It would be necessary to adopt stricter prudential norms and disclosure standards for banks once capital account convertibility is achieved. This is because CAC may increase risk (foreign currency exposure) for the banking system with increased interface with international markets and increased exchange rate volatility.

(H) Further Development of Capital Market

There are no simple solutions to preparing capital markets for financial flows. There is need to improve the market infrastructure and regulatory framework. International standards for market infrastructure provide excellent medium-term benchmarks for India, though they need to be tailored to fit our circumstances. In this respect, it is important that the speed of settlement and custody functions should not be improved at the expense of reliability; membership standards in key capital market institutions should be set high to bolster market safety and improve investor confidence.

An important development that is needed in Indian capital market is development of a market for derivative products. It is imperative that investors are provided with instruments such as future and options which allow them to hedge their risks in investment in securities. With the introduction of derivative trading, liquidity of the markets is also likely to improve as also the price-discovery process. Quick action is required on developing a regulatory system for derivatives trading in India.

Another area that needs attention is introduction of market-marking mechanism for illiquid scrips. This will help to improve the liquidity in the stockmarkets. Liquidity can also be improved by other measures like enhancing the minimum public offer for qualifying for listing from 25% to 40% of issued capital of the company, directing companies numbering about 5,000 to raise the minimum issued capital to atleast 3 crore for continuing as listed companies etc.

Thus, since FII's may lead to market volatility in future (as their presence in Indian market increases) due to their operations of buying and selling the equities in bulk at regular intervals, it is of utmost importance that India develops financial derivatives and risk management products in its capital market and provides adequate training to market participants in derivative trading. In this respect, SEBI may send team to markets and exchanges overseas for a better understanding of derivative trading.

CONCLUSION

India has averted most of the risks that these flows may pose. That India has escaped relatively unhurt from the surge in financial flows and sudden out flows—is not a matter of chance—but due to sound management of financial flows. India has avoided the risks posed by financial flows since many of the policy prescriptions to avert the risks are already in place. These policies have served us well so far. However, India cannot afford to pause and relax. Rather, efforts need to continue relentlessly/vigorously and progress so far achieved needs to be accelerated.

NOTES

1. Liberalising capital outflows may induce domestic investors, such as pension finds, to take their capital aboard. This may partially compensate for the effects of financial flows, although this result is uncertain : some models predict a larger financial flow from liberalisation of capital outflows.
2. The resulting appreciation of the domestic currency would both reduce net inflows through the capital account and create a current account offset.
3. There was a net reversal of flows of $105 billion from Indonesia, Korea, Malaysia, Philippines & Thailand - this represented approximately 11% of the pre-crisis GDP of the five countries.
4. In the East-Asian countries, however, foreign exchange reserves dipped. For example, for Thailand the foreign exchange reserves stood at $25.7 billion in December 1997 as comared to $37.2

billion on December 1996. In Indonesia, foreign exchange reserves fell from $18.6 billion (Dec. 1996) to $16.1 billion (Dec. 1997). For Malaysia, the decline was to $20 billion (Dec. 1997) as compared to $26.2 billion (as on Dec. 1996) and in Korea's case foreign exchange reserves fell from $33.2 billion (as on Dec. 1996) to $19.7 billion (as on December 1997).

5. Adequacy of reserves is linked not only to imports now but also to short-term liabilities, particularly short-term debt.
6. Central banks in both Thailand & Korea went out of their way to take gambles in forward markets until their reserves were gone. Lack of adequate reserves magnified problems as the East crises unfolded.
7. In Thailand short-term debt constituted around 30% of external debt. A high level of short-term debt makes the country vulnerable because of continuous need of rollovers which can be extremely difficult at times of crisis.
8. When the CAD exceeds 5% of GDP, it is generally regarded as high and in most cases, where it persists over a relatively long period of time, it would turn out to be unsustainable. The sustainability of a large CAD depends mainly on how the capital inflows financing the deficit are used and whether the external liabilities associated with the capital inflows are consistent with the country's debt servicing capacity.
9. Financial liberalisation when accompanied by strict bank regulation & supervision prevents reversal in financial flows or a sharp rise in interest rates from breaking the banks.
10. It is important to note that liberalisation introduces greater competition leading to a squeeze on profit margins in traditional business and therefore requires restructuring and competence building in the banking sector.
11. If funds are invested in unproductive sectors, they may give rise to rash of non-performing assets resulting in a fragile banking system and weakened macro-economic fundamentals.
12. In Malaysia in mid-90's the real estate loans accounted for about 25% of outstanding bank loans & about 20% in Thailand & Indonasia.
13. The SLR ratio for banks has been reduced progressively from 37.5% to 25% on an incremental basis and the CRR, including incremental CRR from 25% to 10%. The CRR to be maintained by scheduled commercial banks is to be reduced by one percentage point from 10% to 9% in two instalments, effective from the fortnight beginning November 6, 1999 and the fortnight beginning November 20, 1999 respectively.

14. A sudden reversal of financial flow may cause financial institutions to face a several liquidity crisis. Similarly, if there is mismatching of maturities - the banks may be exposed to liquidity risk - the sudden inability to roll over debts.
15. One reason for East Asian crisis was banks exposure to market risk-borrowing to carry assets that are exposed to large fluctuations in their capital value : stocks, commodities, foreign exchange or high risk instruments such as Brady bonds. Korean Fl's, e.g, had taken a large position in Russian bonds and Brazilian Brady bonds. When their prices fell sharply, the balance sheets of the Koreans had instantly a huge hole.
16. Banks and firms in South East Asia borrowed short either becuase it was cheaper or becuase nobody was willing to lend them at long maturities. On the assets side, they were funding with these loans long-term investment such as real estate development, corporate capital formation or even infrastructure. The resulting vulnerability took the form of liquidity risk - the sudden inability to roll over debts.
17. Asia borrowed in dollars or yen to fund investment with payoffs in local currency. As a result, balance sheets were exposed to the risk of currency movements. A major currency depreciation carried the risk of bankrupting a large part of the finance system or their loan customers. In such a scenario, absence of a currency hedge came in disastrously expensive.
18. The means by which short-term inflows can be controlled are - effective monitoring, tax on spot transactions, varied reserve requirements, increased capital requirements on interbank transactions, changes in capital adequacy requirements of lending banks to non-OECD countries and discouraging local firms from undertaking external borrowing by imposing taxes. Quantitative controls have also been recognised as effective. The oft-quoted measure relates to reserve requirements imposed on short term flows. Chile and Columbia imposed unremunerated reserve requirements of 30% on short-term flows, subsequently reduced to 10%. This represented a tax on short-term holdings. The empirical evidence on its effectiveness is inconclusive.

    A favourite for economists has been the never tried Tobin-tax- it envisages a levy of uniform tax on all spot transactions in foreign exchange. The objective is to discourage a one-night stand by speculators in the foreign exchange market as the tax burden will be inversely proportional to the maturity of flows.

    Alan Greenspan has proposed imposing increased capital requirements on borrowing banks to bring greater discipline on cross-border interbank market.

Most of the above proposals have the effect of increasing cost of short-term debt.

19. Traditionally, adequacy of reserves was linked to import requirements. Now, the emphasis has shifted from measuring the adequacy of reserves only in relation to imports, to short-term liabilities, in particular short-term debt. Two notable suggestions in this regard have emanated. One is that countries should manage their external assets and liabilities in such a way that they are always able to live without new foreign borrowing for upto one year. In other words, usable foreign exchange reserves should exceed scheduled amortisation of foreign currency debts (assuming no rollovers) during the following year. In terms of debt management, this implies limit on the size of debt, in particular short-term debt and debt that is falling due for repayment. The other suggestion - by BIS - is to run trade surpluses and to borrow reserves and arrange contingent lending facilities with the private sector. According to Alan Greenspan, countries could adopt a" liquidity - at-risk" standard to manage their exposure to financial risks. This standard would give the ex-ante probability that a country would avoid new borrowing for one year, based on the level of reserves.

20. According to Narasimham Committee a weak bank is one whose accumulated losses and net NPA's exceed its net worth (definition 1), alternately, a weak bank is one whose operating profits less its income in recapitalisation bonds is negative for three consecutive years (definition 2).

21. Gap analysis measures the difference between a banks assets and liabilities and off-balance sheet positions which will be repriced or will mature within a predetermined period (Gap is the difference between the rate sensitive assets minus rate sensitive liabilities). The duration analysis estimates the average amount of time required before the discounted value or the present value of all cash flows (e.g. principal and interest) can be recovered by an asset holder including that of bank's depositor. The concept can be used for all assets, liabilities and off-balance sheet items Value at Risk (VAR) model estimates the maximum potential loss in a position over a given holding period for a given confidence level. Simulation model attempts to determine whether the model adequately captures the bank's current and projected cash flows, taking into account the different interest rate and market price scenarios. Simulation model is simply an interactive process and not an optimisation model.

10

Summary Conclusions and Tasks Ahead

INTERNATIONAL FINANCIAL FLOWS

The study has concerned itself with drawing implications for restructuring Indian financial system in response to international financial flows. The international financial flows are not a new phenomenon and have existed since a long time viz. 1870. Though international financial flows are not new, such flows have shown some marked departure in the 1990s from the earlier flows, viz. there has been a surge in international financial flows in 1990s, the surge is concentrated in a few developing countries - so called emerging markets in 1990s, financial flows in 1990s have not been pulled by deficit running government budgets and public enterprises but essentially by private investors and private firms, the private flows dwarf official flows in 1990s, the share of aid in financial flows has declined in 1990s, the commercial bank loans, an important flow in 1970s, has disappeared since debt crisis of 1980s, the share of debt in private financial flows has declined and the share of non-debt (FDI and FPI) has increased in 1990s. There is a spurt in the inflow of portfolio investment in the 1990s. The international financial flows of the 1990s warrant detailed analysis and a fresh look because of their changed nature and composition as compared to international financial flows of earlier decades and, therefore, the present study focuses on international financial flows of the 1990s.

The book first examines international financial flows to developing countries/emerging markets in 1990s and next studies the financial flows to India in the 1990s. In respect of international financial flows to developing countries during 1990-97, the study found that (i) 74.7% of financial flow is private flow while 25.3% is official flow, (ii) 32% of private flows are debt flows while 68% of private flows have been non-debt flows, (iii) in non-debt flows though a major amount has flowed to developing countries in form of FDI, yet portfolio flows have exhibited a rise (10 fold increase) much rapid than rise in FDI flows (five fold increase).

An analysis of international financial flows to emerging market economies revealed the following:

i) Private flow have been almost seven times the flow on official account during 1991-98 and it is projected that proportion of such flows shall rapidly pick up in 1999 and 2000 to reach almost 19 times of official flows.
ii) Portfolio flows have dominated private flows to emerging markets during 1991-94. However, since 1995 there has been a turnaround in these flows with net direct investment overtaking portfolio flows to emerging markets.
iii) During 1991-98, Western Hemisphere countries have received the largest proportion (about 34%) of financial flows (official plus private) and Asian countries have secured the next largest chunk (31%). Further, it is projected that in 1999 and

2000 Asia is expected to experience outflows amounting to 8.29% of total capital flow to emerging market economies in 1999 and 2000.

iv) There has been a drop in net financial flows to emerging market economies in 1994, 1997 and 1998. The most affected region being Western Hemisphere in 1994 and East Asia in 1997 and 1998.

Having gained some broad insight into nature of international financial flows, the book looks into the flow of funds into India in the 1990s to ascertain whether these generalizations about behaviour of international financial flows have held good for India in 1990s, specifically, whether India has experienced a surge in financial flows in the 1990s, have private flows increased proportionately in 1990s, has there been an increase in private non-debt flows to India in 1990s, has there been a spurt in portfolio flows to India in the 1990s?

On examining financial flows to India in the 1990s, it is found:

i) There has been a surge in financial flows to India in the 1990s as foreign investment has increased quite dramatically from US$ 103 million in 1990-91 to US$ 4,993 million in 1997-98 - an increase of 48 times.

ii) Official flows have declined in 1990s - This is borne out by the fact that total external assistance has declined from US$ 2210 million in 1990-91 to US$ 899 million in 1997-98 - a decline of 59.3%.

iii) Private flows viz. foreign investment and commercial borrowing have increased, commercial borrowing has increased from US$

2248 million in 1990-91 to US$ 3999 million in 1997-98 (an increase of 1.8 times) and foreign investment has increased almost 48 times during this period.

iv) Private non-debt flows to India have recorded a 20 times increase during 1990-1999.

v) During 1990-1999 much of private, non-debt flows to India (54%) is accounted for by portfolio investment.

vi) There has been a spurt in portfolio investment to India in the 1990s. Portfolio flows have increased at a faster rate as compared to direct investment in India. Between 1990-91 and 1997-98, portfolio investment to India has recorded three hundred times increase (from US$ 6 million to US$ 1828 million) whereas direct investment exhibited an increase of thirty-six times (from US$ 97 million to US$ 3557 million).

Since financial flows to India also portray picture similar to behaviour of international financial flows then it implies that macroeconomic concerns as well as other concerns (regarding banking sector and capital market) raised by international financial flows of the 90s for recipient countries are also relevant for India. A literature review on the subject revealed the concerns raised by international financial flows of the 1990s - the risks they pose to financial system of recipient country.

ISSUES/CONCERNS RAISED BY INTERNATIONAL FINANCIAL FLOWS OF 1990S

A survey of literature revealed that while such flows can bring benefit of economic growth for recipient country by relaxing balance of payments constraint and facilitating investment, such flows also pose risks to recipient countries.

Typical macroeconomic repercussions of such flows being increase in inflation, appreciation of real exchange rate, widening of current account deficit. Further it was observed that recipient countries may experience a lending boom consequent to the surge in financial flows and the lending boom may exacerbate macroeconomic vulnerability and financial sector vulnerability. A large and sudden outflow can inter alia, produce a liquidity problem brought on by the need to refinance a large volume of short-term external debt and difficulties in the banking system caused by the increase in domestic interest rates. Another risk that such flows may pose to the recipient country is that it may increase volatility of domestic asset prices and returns. The experience of Mexico in 1994-95 and South-East Asia in 1997-98 vividly illustrates the impact of a sharp increase in financial flows followed later by an abrupt and sudden outflow. Given the above framework regarding the concerns raised/risks posed by international financial flows of the 1990s, the study sought to ascertain the impact of international financial flows of the 1990s on Indian financial system.

IMPACT OF FINANCIAL FLOW OF 1990S ON INDIAN FINANCIAL SYSTEM

The impact on Indian financial system was studied under three headings viz. impact on macro economy, impact on capital market, impact on banking sector. In respect of impact on macro economy, the study sought to ascertain whether foreign exchange reserves have increased as a consequence of financial flows, whether Central Bank has intervened in foreign exchange market in response to financial flows, whether money supply has increased consequent to financial flow in India, whether increase in money supply, if any, has led to inflation in India, whether real exchange rate has appreciated with the onset of financial flow and whether appreciation of real exchange rate has led to widening of current account deficit and finally, whether Indian economy has got overheated as a consequence of surge in financial flows. In respect of capital market, the study sought to ascertain whether FIIs are influencing equity price movement in India or not, whether volatility of asset price and returns has increased with the surge in financial flows to India and whether stock price volatility is related to volatility of portfolio flows.

In respect of impact on banking sector, the study sought to ascertain whether the surge in financial flow has led to lending boom in India, whether increase in bank lending has exacerbated macroeconomic vulnerability (by biasing expenditure towards consumption rather than investment), whether increase in bank lending has been associated with increased vulnerability of banking sector.

EMPIRICAL FINDINGS

The study found that financial flows to India in the 1990s have had the following impact on Indian financial system:

(A) Impact on Macroeconomy

- The study found that **foreign exchange reserves** in India have increased with the onset of surge in financial flows in 1990s - specifically, the study found that since 1992-93 till 1997-98, international financial flows to India have increased foreign exchange reserves by Rs. 69,750.3 crore. During this period, 44.5% of the inflows have been channeled to reserves, while the remainder has been used to finance wider current account deficits in India.
- The **Central Bank** has **intervened** in foreign exchange market to prevent nominal appreciation of rupee. Specifically, the study found that as

the exchange rate regime in India is managed float, RBI has been actively intervening in foreign exchange market to mop up the condition of excess supply in the foreign exchange market created by financial flows. The surge in financial flows in the absence of any widening of current account deficit have necessitated intervention purchases by RBI in foreign exchange market. The study found that RBI has consistently purchased foreign exchange from 1993-94 till 1997-98 except during April 1995-December 1995 and October 1997-December 1997 when it sold foreign exchange.

- **Money supply** has increased consequent to financial flow to India: The study found that the arrival of financial flow together with central bank intervention has resulted in substantial upward pressure on money supply in India - the Broad money (M3) increasing from Rs. 3,17,049 crore in 1991-92 to Rs. 8,25,389 crore in 1997-98 - an increase of 160%. On the basis of hypothesis testing, the study found that money supply in India has significantly increased during financial flow period (January 1993 - December 1997) as compared to pre-financial flow period (January 1985 - December 1992) - the monthly mean of money supply during 1985-92 was found to Rs. 2,09,661.44 crore as compared to Rs. 5,59,267.48 for 1993-97.
- **FII Investment and Money Supply:** The study found that percentage variation in money supply (M3) seems to be correlated with some factor other than FII investment since correlation between FII investment and percentage variation in M3 was found to be very weak (r = 0.110053).

- An increase in **money supply** has not been associated with **inflation** in India. Percentage variation in money supply is negatively correlated to inflation (r = - 0.16664. Inflation in India has declined from 13.7% in 1991-92 to 4.8% in 1997-98 despite an increase in money supply from Rs.3,17,049 crore in 1991-92 to Rs.8,25,389 crore in 1997-98.
- **Financial flow** to India in the 1990s have not increased **inflation** in India: Hypothesis testing revealed that there is no significant difference in inflation in the two periods studied viz. during financial flow period (January 1993 to January 1999) and pre-financial flow period (May 1988 - December 1992). Further, the study found that average monthly inflation has marginally dropped during the period of surge in financial flow (it was 0.0078 in the pre-financial flow period and 0.0059 in financial flow period).
- **FII flow and inflation**: The study found that FII investment and inflation are negatively correlated. An increase in FII flow has led to a decline in inflation. There is in fact very weak relationship between FII investment and inflation since r = - 0.159. Inflation, in India, the study found is more strongly correlated to factors other than FII flow.
- **Real effective exchange rate** in India has not appreciated with the onset of financial flows: Hypothesis testing revealed that there is no significant difference in both trade-based and export-based REER during the two periods studied viz. during financial flow period (January 1993 to March 1999) and pre-financial flow period (January 1985 - December 1992). Further, the

study found that real effective exchange rate (both trade based and export based) has depreciated in India during the financial flow period since average trade-based REER has fallen from 80.78 (in pre-financial flow period) to 62.67 (during financial flow period) and export-based REER has fallen from 79.51 in pre financial flow period to 60.77 in financial flow period.

- The **current account deficit** has not widened in India with the onset of financial flows: Hypothesis testing revealed that there isn't significant difference in current account deficit during the two periods studied viz. during financial flows period (1993 Q_1 - 1999 Q_4) and pre-financial flow period (1985 Q_1 - 1992 Q_4). Further, the study found that the current account deficit has shown greater fluctuation/ variability since 1993 onwards.
- **Current account deficit (as a % of GDP)** has not widened in India due to financial flows to India: Hypothesis testing revealed that there is not significant difference in current account deficit as a percentage of GDP in the two periods - during financial flow period (1992-93 to 1996-97) and pre-financial flow period (1985-86 to 1991-92). The Current Account Deficit as a percentage of GDP has in fact not widened during financial flow period since average annual CAD (as percentage of GDP) was 2.4333% for pre-financial flow period and 1.4130% for during-financial flow period.
- **Real exchange rate** has not appreciated in India as a consequence of financial flows: The average annual real exchange rate was 97.82 for pre-financial flow period (1985-92) and was 136.789 for during financial flow period (1993-97) - the

rise in the index denoting depreciation of rupee. The study held that the theoretical prediction that if real exchange rate appreciates, current account deficit widens has not held good for India as CAD (as percentage of GDP) has narrowed down and Real-exchange rate has depreciated during financial flow period.

- India has avoided the overt symptoms of **overheating** except for acceleration of economic growth. Average annual GDP has recorded an 110.23% increase in inflow period (1993-93 to 1996-97) as compared to immediately preceding period of equal length (1987-88 to 1991-92). Average annual inflation has declined by 9.02% during inflow period as compared to pre-inflow period; average annual current account deficit (as percentage of GDP) has narrowed down to the tune of 42.2% in the inflow period as compared to pre-inflow period; average annual real exchange rate has depreciated by 27.33% during inflow period as compared to pre-inflow period and average annual real effective exchange rate has depreciated by 20.94% (trade based) and 23.56% (export based) during inflow period as compared to pre inflow period of equal length.

(B) Impact on Capital Market

- **FII investment** is one of the factor influencing **equity price movement** in India since FII investment and share price movement exhibited positive correlation = 0.5993187 for the period 1991-92 to 1997-98; with lag FII investment was found to be correlated to share price index to the tune of 0.780449.
- **Financial flows** to India in the 1990s have not

increased **share price volatility** - Hypothesis testing revealed that there is a significant difference in share price volatility in the two periods viz. during financial flow period (January 1993 - September 1998) and pre financial flow period (January 1985 - December 1992). However, the study did not find an increase in share price volatility during the financial flow period since during financial flow period average annual coefficient of variation was found to be 9.2991% which was less as compared to 12.8745% for pre-financial flow period.

- **Share price volatility** is not related to **volatility of FII flows** in India i.e. volatility of FII flows does not help to explain much of the change in stock price volatility in India or volatility in share prices is not due to volatility of FII flows: The study found weak and negative correlation between volatility of FII flows and volatility of share prices (r = - 0.358). The study further found that only 12% of volatility in share prices can be explained by volatility of FII flows.
- **Financial flows** to India in the 1990s have not increased **share return volatility** - the analysis revealed that there is no significant difference in share return volatility in the two periods (during financial flow period and pre-financial flow period). Further, the study found that there exits almost no relationship between volatility of FII flows and volatility of share prices since r = 0.2294. Only 5% of the volatility in share return can be explained by volatility of FII flows.

(C) Impact on Banking Sector

- **Financial flow and lending boom**: India has

not experienced a lending boom with the surge in financial flows to India. Hypothesis-testing revealed that there is a significant difference in bank lending (as a percentage of GDP) in the two periods viz. during financial flows period (1992-93 to 1997-98) and pre financial flow period (1985-86 to 1991-92). Though there is a significant difference in bank lending (as a percentage of GDP) in the two periods the study found that such lending has not increased during financial flow period: Rather it found that average annual bank lending (as percentage of GDP) declined to 33.6121% during financial flow period as compared to 35.9491% in pre-financial flow period.

- An increase in bank lending during financial flow period has not exacerbated **macro economic vulnerability** in India: Hypothesis testing revealed a significant difference in monthly bank lending in the two periods viz. during financial flow period (January 1993 - March 1998) and pre-financial flow period (April 1990 - December 1992) - the average monthly bank lending during the two periods being Rs.3,02,291.9365 crore and Rs.1,76,218 crore respectively. Further, the study found that this increase in bank lending has not been associated with over consumption and under investment. Though the study found that annual consumption (as a percentage of GDP) during financial flow period was significantly different as compared to pre-financial flow period (on the basis of hypothesis testing) it also found that the financial flow period has not been a period of over-consumption in India as compared to pre-financial flow period since average annual consumption (as percentage of GDP) declined during financial flow period to 78.23% as compared to 86.34% in pre-financial flow period. As regards investment, the study found (on the basis of hypothesis testing) that there is no significant difference in investment (as a percentage of GDP) in the two periods - during financial flow period (1992-93 to 1996-97) and pre-financial flow period (1985-86 to 1991-92) and further that financial flow period has not been a period of under-investment since average annual investment (as percentage of GDP) increased during financial flow period to 27.31% as compared to 26.65% in pre-financial flow period.

- An increase in bank lending during financial flow period has not exacerbated **financial sector vulnerability** in India: since all scheduled commercial banks in India have shored up their capitalisation ratio by 122.4% between 1992 and 1999. Further, non-performing assets of public sector banks in India have declined - gross NPA as percentage to total assets have declined from 11.8% in 1993 to 6.7% in 1999 and net NPAs as percentage to total assets have declined from 4% in 1995 to 3.1% in 1999. Profitability ratios, too, have shown an improvement for all scheduled commercial banks in India - gross profit/loss (as percentage to total assets) has recorded an increase of 42.7% since 1992-93 to 1998-99; net profit/loss (as percentage to total assets) has increased by 145.4% in case of all scheduled commercial banks during the period of increase in bank lending (1992-93 to 1998-99) and finally net interest income (spread) has recorded an increase of 10.8% for all scheduled commercial banks since 1992-93 to 1998-99. Only in respect of provisions and contingencies all scheduled commercial banks in India have weakened themselves. Provisions and contingencies (as percentage to total assets) have declined by 53.6% during 1992-93 - 1998-99.

OBSERVATIONS ON EMPIRICAL FINDINGS

(A) Macroeconomy

- The study found that there has been a sharp build up in foreign exchange reserves in India during financial flow period. The study felt that this is highly desirable for India since the recent crises in South-East Asia has brought into sharp focus the need to maintain high level of reserves to counter the increased volatility in short-term capital inflows.
- Timely intervention by the RBI has helped to prevent undue exchange rate appreciation and helped to maintain India's external competitiveness.
- Though money supply has increased in India during financial flow period, the increase in money supply is not on account of spurt in FII flows. The study felt that money supply in India is correlated with some factor other than FII investment and that percentage variation in money supply may be more closely related to NRI flows.
- The puzzle of low rate of inflation and relatively high growth in money supply can be explained for India through the concept of core inflation (Reddy, 1999). The decline in inflation can also

be explained in terms of slack in export demand and sluggish industrial growth.

- India has not experienced the overt symptoms of overheating - acceleration of inflation, real exchange rate appreciation and widening of current account deficit - because many of the policies to avert these risks have been pursued by India. Specifically, India has sought to tackle the problem of excess liquidity in the system by drastic reduction in monetization of budget deficit, by increase in cash reserve ratio, sterilizing inflows by open market operations. Further, India has imposed direct/indirect controls on financial inflows: it has regulated inflows under euro-issues, discouraged high-cost short term inflows. Moreover, India has liberalized current and capital account transactions to increase imports. Thus, India has not experienced overheating due to economic measures adopted by it viz. sterilization through open market operations, sterilization through other means, restrictions on financial inflows, liberalization of the current account and selective liberalisation of capital outflows.

(B) Capital Market

- FIIs have exerted some influence on share price movement of Bombay Stock Exchange since FIIs have practically invested in all SENSEX companies. FII investments have generally been confined to the set of high turnover companies at the Bombay Stock Exchange.[1]
- The study felt that volatility in domestic stock markets has declined with the onset of financial flows due to economic reform and stabilisation measures introduced by the Government since

1991-92. The process of capital market reforms that has aimed at improving market efficiency, making stock market transactions more transparent, curbing unfair trade practices and bringing the Indian capital market upto international standards has helped to promote investor interest and ensure investor protection and has contributed to arresting the rise in volatility in domestic stock market.[2] Other factors that may have prevented stock price volatility from increasing in India could be that Indian capital market is not fully integrated with world capital markets (its exposure to foreign stock markets is low) thereby minimizing the spillover effects from other stock markets; foreign investors have not been able to liquidate their position quickly in India due to infrastructural constraints (lack of speedy settlement); measures have been taken consistently by SEBI to counter volatility in share prices e.g. on June 15, 1998, SEBI banned short sale and further to tighten the measures aimed at curbing volatility in share prices, it prescribed additional volatility margins (AVM) w.e.f. July 6, 1998. Further Indian stock market have a low, even negative correlation with the stock markets in industrial nations. So when the latter goes down, FIIs invest more in the former as a means to reduce overall portfolio risk.

- Though FIIs have influenced share price movement, volatility in FII flows has not had much impact on stock price volatility (there being weak negative correlation between the two) because of the presence of large domestic investor viz. UTI. The presence of UTI has served as a counterweight to FIIs and has helped to prevent

FIIs from influencing capital market in India in a significant manner.

(C) Banking Sector

- One possible explanation for the absence of lending boom in India during inflow period is that banks in India, under heavy pressure to avoid taking on loans that might turn out non-performing, tended to use the increased liquidity with them primarily to purchase government securities rather than to increase credit availability. Domestic interest rates declined under the pressure of the growing liquidity, which further encouraged the banks to purchase government securities for capital gains. Towards the end of 1994, however, when the capital inflows eased off and interest rates began to rise, commercial banks in India began expanding their loan books and reducing their holding of government securities.
- Increase in monthly bank lending during financial flow period has not exacerbated macroeconomic vulnerability in India because banks have not used excess liquidity with them to lend excessively for consumption purposes, for speculative purposes and activities (e.g. real estate).
- Though India has experienced a significant increase in lending activity in the financial flow period, this increase in lending has not exposed the Indian banking system to potential instability.[3] This is mainly because we have been pursuing sound policies in areas where serious concern has been expressed in the context of Asian crises. In fact, India has installed effective regulatory

and supervisory controls in banking sector to stall banking crises that have often resulted from a surge in financial flows and sudden outflows to countries whose banking systems are not well managed and supervised. India has been successful in minimizing the impact of surge in lending on financial sector vulnerabilities because we have meshed banking sector reforms with the opening up of the Indian market to overseas investors. Banking sector vulnerabilities have not increased in the presence of financial flows because India has been making continuous effort to strengthen its financial soundness since the onset of financial flows by introducing and subsequently tightening prudential norms and prudential supervision.

RESTRUCTURING INDIAN FINANCIAL SYSTEM

The study noted that attempts to restructure the Indian financial system have been underway in 1990's. Some of the measure that have been implemented in 1990's to restructure the Indian financial system include:

a) Liberalisation of financial policies in pace with Government of India's programme of fiscal and balance of payments adjustment;
b) Restoration of health to banking institutions (through introduction of international standards of prudential regulations for asset classification, income recognition, provisioning requirements and adoption of Basle Accord capital adequacy norms for commercial banks and term lending institutions, establishing an improved legal mechanism for the recovery of non-performing loans and recapitalisation of public sector banks);

c) Reinvigoration of competition in financial service industries through the entry of private sector in banking and mutual fund industries, opening India's capital markets to foreign investment, allowing large and reputable Indian corporations to tap Euro-issues market and lowering/ removing various administrative barriers to competition in the term lending market;

d) Broadening the ownership of public sector banks (by permitting to issue equity in the capital market, enhancing managerial autonomy in line with increased private shareholder representation on board of banks and transforming these banks into competitive and commercially oriented business enterprises;

e) Development of an active government securities market (involving regular auctioning of treasury bills and long-dated securities and secondary trading in the National Stock Exchange as a basis for better management of monetary policy and development of a deep and liquid debt market;

f) Modernisation of clearing and settlement system, introduction of screen-based trading, setting up securities depository and strengthening of investor protection; and finally,

The study felt that the process to restructure Indian financial system is not complete and policies are needed to attract, absorb and sustain these flows and to deal with the risks posed by these flows.

CONCLUSION

Based on analysis of nature of international financial flows, financial flows to India and empirical findings on impact of financial flows on Indian financial system the study has drawn following conclusions:

- Financial flows necessitate restructuring of financial system. It is necessary to restructure financial system so as to be able to attract foreign investors and to enhance the sustainability of financial flow. Restructuring of financial system is also required to tackle problems/risks posed by financial flows.
- It is necessary to attract financial flows to India viz. private, non-debt flows because such flows are just 3-4% of total private, non-debt flows to developing countries; that these flows are not likely to dry up in future[4] but are projected to rise and that these flows offer potential benefits for recipient countries. Another factor that makes it necessary to attract such flows is the savings investment gap.[5]
- Indian financial system needs to be restructured to sustain the flows because portfolio investment - an important component of financial flows is inherently volatile. Several countries have experienced sudden reversals of inflows e.g. Mexico, South East Asia - there being abrupt and sudden outflows of capital on account of the inflows being of a short-term nature (as in the case of FII flows) and being invested long-term. When financial flows (particularly portfolio flows) find their way into the banking system and push up domestic expenditure and increase the current account deficit, their reversal can affect the domestic economy through a decrease in asset prices, a jump in interest rate, liquidity problems in the banking sector or a devaluation

of the currency. A financial flow reversal can cause a crash of financial system.[6]

- The process to restructure Indian financial system so as to attract such flows should entail the following: permitting greater competition in the financial sector, improving accounting and auditing rules, introducing prudential regulation, enhancing stability, ensuring effective law enforcement, having basic operating infrastructure, establishing credit rating agencies, increasing market capitalization, eradicating insider trading and improving corporate governance.
- To enhance sustainability of flows India should have a stable macro-economic environment,[7] provide for proper use of funds,[8] rapidly expand export growth and maintain a stable, investor-friendly economic and political environment in the long run.
- Appropriate macroeconomic policies such as direct or indirect controls on inflows, liberalization of capital outflows or accelerated repayment of public debt, trade liberalization, floating the exchange rate, sterilization, increasing reserve requirements, fiscal contraction can help to avert the risk of overheating. Further, increasing banks risk-adjusted capital asset ratios, increasing provisioning for non-performing loans, raising banks reserve requirements, imposing ceilings on commercial bank lending and external borrowing, imposing indirect economy-wide capital controls can help to avert the risk of lending booms. Finally, improvement of domestic fundamentals and stablilization of economic policies, diversification of economy and

improving attributes of the capital markets may help in reducing volatility of asset prices and returns.

- Restructuring that is necessary to attract these flows to India has already been initiated. A more competitive environment has been created in the financial sector, India has introduced prudential norms in 1992 as an element of financial sector reforms, 13 of the 25 core principles of banking supervision and endorsed by BIS have been enshrined in the Banking Regulation Act, RBI Act, and/or in executive instructions issued by RBI; guidelines on disclosure of information by all players in the capital market have been issued, efforts are in place to improve disclosure of information by corporates, banks, financial institutions etc.; actions have been initiated in India against errant NBFCs and unincorporated bodies for various defaults and violations of Reserve Bank of India Act; improvements have been done in institutional and infrastructural practices in stock market; India has established its own credit rating agencies; market capitalization in India has seen an increase; insider trading is an offence in India w.e.f. November 19, 1992; corporate governance has become an important issue in India and Companies Act; SEBI Act; public financial institutions and institutional investors - all are playing a role in evolving good governance practices in India. These efforts need to continue in a non-disruptive manner.
- The study concluded that India is not favourably poised to sustain these flows - particularly portfolio flows since it is characterized by

persistence of high and unsustainable level of fiscal deficits - the level increasing from an average of about 32% in 1985-86 to 1989-90 to 53% in 1998-99; on the expert front India is experiencing a decelerating trend since 1996-97; India has seen four governments in the last three years, the environment of political instability, coupled with nuclear tests and sectarian violence has not provided atmosphere conducive to domestic and foreign investment.

- India has avoided the risks posed by financial flows because it has drawn policies based on three principles. First, India has adopted a progressive approach to capital account liberalization taking into account the overall macroeconomic conditions and the progress in the development of the financial and foreign exchange markets. Secondly, stability-oriented macroeconomic policies have been put in place to alleviate the impact of surging financial flows on the economy. Third, prudential supervision has been strengthened to improve the soundness of financial institutions.
- Though India has avoided the risks posed by financial flows, India cannot afford to pause and relax. Rather efforts need to continue relentlessly/vigorously and progress so far achieved needs to be accelerated. India's policy stance that has helped India to avert risks should continue. Specifically, India needs to pursue a policy of cautions movement towards capital account liberalization, prudently manage the size, maturity profile and currency structure of its own debt. Short-term debt needs to be controlled, provide well designed infrastructure, effective

market discipline, strong regulatory and supervisory framework, build better shock absorbers, strengthen banking system.

- To avert/minimize the risk posed by flows, India needs fiscal tightening to handle expansionary effect of flows and needs to further strengthen its banking system which is weak in respect of NPAs of private banks and foreign banks and provisions and contingencies of banks.

TASHS AHEAD

- To continue to attract such flows, further restructuring is needed on following lines: capital adequacy of all securities market intermediaries should gradually be raised to the norms prescribed by International Organization of Securities Commission (IOSCO) of which SEBI is a member; accountability and enforcement of contracts should be ensured through a legal system that dispenses justice, quickly, inexpensively and sensibly; prudential regulations need to be strengthened further to cover exposures in short-term foreign currency loans and other cross border operations in case of Indian banks keeping in view international best practices and specific requirements, specific action is needed in respect of supervisory co-operation with regulators inside and outside the country, consolidated supervision of institutions and their subsidiaries as conglomerates, cross-border supervisioin, inter agency cooperation; India's financial system needs a well-functioning derivatives exchange, which trades futures and options on currencies interest rates, equities and commodities. Thus to attract these flows our efforts to provide India with well designed infrastructure - (legal and judicial frame work, good corporate governance, accounting standards, system of independent audits, efficient payment and settlement systems), effective market discipline - (good credit culture, well developed and functioning equity and debt markets and wide variety of instruments for risk diversification); and strong regulatory and supervisory framework need to continue endlessly.

- To sustain such flows Indian Finaicial System needs further restructuring. The process to restructure should include: controlling the high fiscal deficit, reversing the current deceleration in exports; according top most priority to eliminate red tapism which is main complaint of potential foreign invetors ensuring that regulations governing the inflow of foreign investment are transparent and attractive in comparison to other Asian countries, exchange rate management should continue its focus on smoothing excessive volatility in the exchange rate and maintaining orderly market conditions to ensure that exchange rate remains consitent with economic fundamentals.
- To minimize risks posed by these flows Indian Banking system needs to be further strengthened. The process to strengthen banking system should include further tightening of prudential norms to bring them at par with international standards, restructuring weak public sector banks (viz. operational, organisational, financial and systemic restructuring should be attempted for weak banks), capital adequacy ratio needs to be

bolstered from its level of 8% specified by Basle accord, NPA's should be reduced especially for priviate banks & foreign banks, provisions and contingency position of banks needs to be improved further.

- Volatility in capital market can be controlled partly by a strict check on 'badla' or forward trading and partly by a curb on portfolio capital inflows and outflows. Domestic capital market reforms that reduce information asymetries and thereby promote liquidity can help reduce excess volatility/vulnerability to reversals. Some measures adopted by countries to reduce volatility in asset markets and to limit downside risks are - restrictions on margin purchases of securities and short selling, prohibition of certain derivative products, limitations on foreign ownership, transaction taxes and direct government intervention in equity and real estate market. Such temporary prudential regulations, if applied selectively and sparingly, can be helpful in maintaining market stability.
- To deal with volatility of portfolio flows India needs to take action on following lines. First, it should try to reduce those components of volatility that are under its control. Secondly, India should try to hold a larger cushion of financial resources against volatility induced losses. Thirdly, India should reduce exposure to volatility through aggressive diversification (e.g. opening the current account) and lastly, India can buy insurance against volatility. The risk of a reversal in flows of portfolio investment is better dealt with through mechanisms that absorb negative shocks and minimize their effects on

the economy rather than restricting capital outflows. India had sought to deal with the volatility accompanying FPI through short-term capital gains tax. FIIs were allowed lower rates for capital gains. However, volatility in portfolio flows can be better handled by making the economy more resilient to economic shocks, so that foreign investors will be less inclined to flee if a shock occurs. This calls for maintaining long-term fiscal and monetary targets, sustaining a balanced budget and building a large stock of international reserves because of its buffer effect. The short-term capital gains tax should be harmonized across countries and to prevent outflow macro-economic, financial conditions should be strengthened.

- To avert risks these flows may pose in future when capital controls are lifted by India in the presence of financial flows risk management system needs to be strengthened. It is utmost necessary to develop futures and options to enable people to manage interest rate and other risks. Banks need to develop and implement integrated risk management system to handle the various risks they are likely to be exposed to viz. credit risk, foreign exchange risk, liquidity risk, market risk etc. Further, to avert/minimize downside risks in future, India needs to build shock-absorbers or the emphasis should be on generating long-term inflows like FDI.
- To prevent volatility in portfolio flows leading to increased volatility in stock markets, it is necessary to develop large domestic investors as counter-weight to FII's (who have large pool of funds) - like UTI in India- till other measures

to deal with volatility are in place. Further, hedging tools should be available to FII's to minimize their downside risks.

- To reduce influence of FII's on stock price movement, more broad based trading by FII's should be encouraged - FII's have invested in practically all the SENSEX companies implying that their operations could potentially influence the index. FII investments have, historically, been confined to the set of high turnover companies on BSE. This suggests that FII operations have progressively been confined to liquid shares. The thinness in market trading can lead to volatility. Hence, there is need for broader trading by FII's as growing concentration of trading reduces stability base of stock market.
- Asset-liability management has to be given crucial attention - this is extremely essential for the flow of funds into infrastucture sector.
- Action in needed on part of SEBI, Government and RBI. SEBI should concentrate on strengthening capital markets and regulating activities of FII's; Government should regulate euro-issues by Indian companies and devise appropriate fiscal, monetary and exchange rate policies to sustain such flows and lastly, RBI should strive to strengthen banking system through prudential regulation and prudential supervision.

LIMITATIONS OF STUDY

The focus of the present study is on foreign portfolio investment flows since FDI has different characteristics and implications as compared to FPI. However, inadequate institutional monitoring of portfolio investment flows has hampered analytical research on foreign portfolio investment in India. There is a need to improve data monitoring capacity on private capital flows, particularly portfolio investment flows. Comprehensive analysis of FPI could not be attempted because of lack of consistent and comprehensive data series. To carry out the present study, some proxy variables were introduced. These proxies have their own weaknesses. The findings of the study are subject to this limitation. However, the findings are reliable to the extent data is reliable. There are differences in data reported by different institutions - Economic Survey (Government), Report on Currency and Finance (RBI), CMIE, SEBI etc. However necessary adjustment have been made to make the data uniform.

NOTES

1. Out of around 6000 companies listed at the BSE, the largest 500 companies in terms of market turnover account for over 99% of the total turnover. FII investments have generally been confined to this set of high turnover companies.
2. Improvements that help to improve the attractiveness of market to foreign investors also serve to reduce volatility.
3. Banking system is exposed to potential instability when the increase in liquidity in the banking system is associated with deterioration in quality of loans or there is mismatch between maturity of assets and liabilities.
4. These flows will not dry up in future because of growing institutionalization of saving in the mature economies (assets of pension funds, insurance companies and mutual funds) and the quest for international diversification.
5. According to Economic Survey 1999-2000 the Saving Investment Gap was -1% of GDP at current market prices (Gross Domestic Savings being 22.3% of GDP at current market prices and GDI being 23.4% of GDP at current market price.
6. If the Central Bank does not react quickly enough and the stock of international reserves is low, the reversal may cause a balance of payment crisis. When FIIs react by selling their domestic stock holdings and buying foreign currency with the proceeds -

this causes a fall in the general stock price index and depending on the exchange rate system, either a loss of international reserve and an increase in domestic interest rates or a depreciation of the nominal exchange rate or both. All these price movements can create considerable uncertainty, discouraging investment, whether foreign or domestic. At the same time, they can be very damaging for the economy as a whole if interest rates, asset prices or exchange rates fluctuate too widely - because of bankruptcies and hysterisis effects when interest rates increase and in the case of exporting and import-competing sectors, when the exchange rate appreciates. Thus, short-term flows including portfolio flows of FIIs to developing countries in particular are inherently instable and increases volatility of the emerging equity markets.

7. An unstable macroeconomic environment results from large budget deficits, excessive monetary expansion, erratic exchange rate policies and repressed financial system.

8. If the financial flow proceeds are being used for consumption they are less sustainable and if such flows are being issued for domestic investment they are more sustainable.

Select Bibliography

Agenor, Pierre-Richard (1998), "Capital Inflows, External Shocks and the Real Exchange Rate", *Journal of International Money and Finance*, 17:5, October, pp. 713-740.

Aggarwal, R. N. (1997), "Foreign Portfolio Investment in Some Developing countries: A Study of Determinants and Macroeconomic Impact", *Indian Economic Review*, Vol. XXXII, No. 2, pp. 217-229.

Agosin. M. R. and French-Davis. R. (1999), "Managing Capital Inflows in Chile", in *Global Financial Turmoil and Reforms-UNU Policy Perspectives*, edited by Barry Herman, United Nations, pp. 161-187.

Ajit, D. (1997), "Para Banking in India: Some Issues," *Economic and Political Weekly*, October 18.

Arias, E. F. and Montiel, P. J. (1996), "The Surge in Capital Inflows to Developing Countries: An Analytical Overview", *The World Bank Economic Review*, Vol. 10, No. 1, Jawary, pp. 51-77.

Asian Development Bank (1995), *Asian Development Outlook* 1995 and 1996 Manila.

Bank for International Settlements (1996), 66th Annual Report, Basle, 10 June, pp. 115-137.

Beckerman and Das (1998), "Risk-Capital Inflows, Inflation and Maacroeconomic Policy in India", *Quarterly Review of Economics and Finance*, Vol. 38, Fall, pp. 359-383.

Bekaert, G. and Harvey, C. R. (1995), "Emerging Equity Market Volatility", *NBER Working Paper* 5307, Massachusetts, Cambridge, October.

Bhalla. V. K. (1999), "Global Financial Flows: Derivative Markets and Developments in Emerging Stock Markets", *Chartered Secretary*, November, pp 1292-1303.

Calvo, G. A. Leiderman, L. and Reinhart, C. M. (1996), "Inflows of Capital to Developing Countries in the 1990's", *Journal of Economic Perspectives*, Vol. 10, No. 2, Spring, pp. 123-139.

Calvo, G.A., Leiderman, L. and Reinhart, C. M. (1994), "The Capital Inflows Problem-Concepts and Issues", *International Center for Economic Growth, Occasional Papers, No. 56*, (San Francisco, California).

Calvo. G. (1996), "Capital Flows and Macroeconomic Management: Tequila Lessons", *International Journal of Finance And Economics* 1 (July): pp 207-22360.

Calvo. G. A and Reinhart. C. M. (1999), "Capital Flow Reversals, the Exchange Rate Debate, and Dollarization", *Finance and Development*, September, pp 13-15.

Capoor Jagdish (1998), *"Emerging Trands in Regulation and Supervision,"* RBI Bulletin, October.

Chen Edward K. Y. (1992), " Changing Pattern of Financial Flows in the Asia-Pacific Region and Policy Responses", *Asian Development Review*, Vol. 10, No. 2, pp. 46-85.

Chen, Z. and Khan, M. S. (1997), "Patterns of Capital Flows to Emerging Markets: A Theoretical Perspective", *IMF Working Paper WP/97/13*.

Cherunilam. F. and Thomas B (1996), "Changing Composition of Financial Flows to Developing Countries", *The Indian Journal of Commerce*, Vol XLIX, No 189, Part IV, December.

Chuhan P., Claessons. S and Mamingi. N. (1993), "Equity and Bond Flows to Latin America & Asia. The Role of Global & Country Factors." *Policy Research Working Paper 1160*. World Bank, International Economics Department, Washington D. C.

Chuhan Punam et al. (1998), "Equity and Bond Flows to Latin America and Asia: The Role of Global and Country

Factors", *Journal of Development Economics*, 55:2, April, pp. 439-463.

Claessen, S., Dooley, M.P. and Warner (1995), "Portfolio Capital Flows: Hot or Cold?", *The World Bank Economic Review*, Vol. 9, No. 1, pp. 153-174.

Claessens. S. and Gooptu. S. (1993), *Portfolio Investment in Developing Countries* (eds.), World Bank Discussion Paper 228, Washington, D. C.

Collyns Charles (1995), "Recent Experience with a Surge in Capital Inflows", *IMF Occasional Paper 134*, December, Washington D.C., pp. 41-53.

Corbo, V. and Hermandez, L. (1994), "Macroeconomic Adjustment to Capital Inflows Latin American Style Vs East Indian Style", *World Bank Policy Research Working Paper 1377*, November.

Cordoso, Eliano and Ilan Goldfain (1998), "Capital Flows to Brazil: The Endogeneity of Capital Controls," *IMF Staff Papers 45: 1*, March, pp. 161-202.

Fernandey – Arias, Eduardo (1994), "The New Wave of Private Capital Inflows: Push or Pull?", *Policy Research Working Paper 1312*. World Bank, International Economics Department, Washington, D. C.

Fernandix-Arias, Eduard (1996), "The New Wave of Capital Inflows: Push or Pull?", *Journal of Development Studies, 48: 2*", march, pp. 389-418.

Folkerts-Landau, David and Others (1995), "Effects of Capital Flows on Domestic Financial Sector in APEC Developing Countries", in Capital Flows in APEC Region, (ed.) by Mohsin, S. Khan and Carmem: M. Reinhart, *IMF Occasional Paper 122* (Washington: IMF), March, pp. 31-57.

Gangadhar, V. and Yadagiri, M. (1997), "Emerging Dimensions of International Financial Flows in India," *Management Accountant*, pp. 180-184.

Garber, Peter (1996), "Managing Risks to Financial Markets from Volatile Capital Flows: The Role of Prudential

Regulation", *International Journal of Finance And Economics* 1 (July): pp 183-195.

GOI (Government of India) *Economic Survey* (New Delhi: Ministry of Finance) (various issues)

Gooptu S. (1993), "Portfolio Investment Flows to Emerging Markets" *Policy Research Working Paper WPS 1117*, World Bank, International Economics Department, March

Gooptu Sudarshan and Ahmed Masood (1993), "Portfolio Investment Flows to Developing Countries", *Finance and Development*, March 1993.

Gooptu, S. (1996), "The Analysis of Emerging Policy Issues in Development Finance—A Survey of the Literature", *World Bank Policy Research Working Paper 1589*, World Bank, April.

Gopinath, T. (1997), "Foreign Investment in India: Policy Issues, Trends and Prospects", *RBI Occassional Papers*, Vol. 18, No. 2&3, June and September, pp. 453-470.

Gruben, William, C. and Darry, C. Mcleod (1998), "Capital Flows, Savings and Growth in the 1990's", *The Quarterly Review of Economics and Finance*, 38: 3, Fall, pp. 287-301.

Herman. B. and Sharma. K. (1998), "Financial Flows, Financial Crises, Financial Policy Needs", in *International Finance and Developing Countries in a Year of Crises*, edited by B. Herman and K. Sharma, (Tokyo: United Nations University Press.

Hernandez, L. and Rudolph, H. (1995), "Sustainability of Capital Flows to Developing Countries—Is a Generalized Reversal Likely?", *World Bank Policy Research Working Paper 1518*.

IFR *International Financing Review*, "Global Financing Directory", 1988, 1989 and January-June 1991.

IIF (1999), "Capital Flows to Emerging Market Economies", *Institute of International Finance*, April 25.

IMF (International Monetary Fund)

International Capital Markets: Development, Prospects, and Key

Policy Issues. World Economic and Financial Surveys. Washington, D.C. (various issues)

International Financial Statistics, (various issues). Washington, D.C.

IMF (1995), *International Capital Markets: Developments, Prospects and Policy Issues,* World Economic and Financial Surveys (Washington: International Monetary Fund, August), pp. 109-119.

IMF (1995). Capital Flows in the APEC Region, Edited by Mohsin, S. Khan and Carmen, M. Reinhart, *IMF Occasional Paper 122,* (Washignton D.C.), March.

IMF (1997). *International Capital Markets: Developments, Prospects and Policy Issues.* World economic and Financial Surveys (Washington: International Monetary Fund) November, pp. 234-251.

ISID (1999), "Foreign Institutional Investments and the Indian Stock Market," April 5-6 *Institute for Studies in Industrial Development,* Narendra, Niketan, IP Estate, New Delhi-110002.

Jain. N. (1998), "India Is In Asia But It Is Not Asia", *Chartered Secretary,* Volume XXVIII, No. 10, April, pp. 1016—1020.

Jain. N. (1998), "Policy Options In Managing Capital Flows", *Business Analyst,* Vol. 19, No. 2, July-Dec, pp. 41-54.

Jain. N. (1998), "Sterilizing Capital Inflows", *Chartered Secretary,* Volume XXVIII, No. 4, April, pp. 309—314.

Jain. N. (1999), "Restructuring Banking Sector," in *Contemporary Issues In Finance,* edited by V.K. Bhalla, Anmol Publications Pvt. Ltd., New Delhi-2, pp. 81-114.

Jain. N. (1999), "South East Asian Crisis: Lessons For India", in *Contemporary Issues In Finance,* edited by V. K. Bhalla, Anmol Publications Pvt. Ltd., New Delhi-2, pp. 377-398.

Jain. N. (1999), "Restructuring Capital Markets", *Chartered Secretary,* Volume XXIX, No. 9, September, pp. 982-990.

Jalan, Bimal (1998), "Trends in International Banking," *RBI Bulletin*, October.

Joshi. V. and Little, I.M.D. (1997), "India- Reform on Hold", *Asian Development Review*, Vol. 15, No. 2, pp. 1-42.

Jutnani. S. (1997), "Emerging Dimensions of International Financial Flows: Global Scenario", *The Indian Journal of Commerce*, Vol. L, No. 190, Part I, March, pp. 63-76.

Khan. M. S and Mathieson. D. M. (1996), "The Implications of International Capital Flows for Macroeconomic and Financial Policies", *International Journal of Finance And Economics* 1 (July): pp 155-160.

Kim, E. H. and Singal, V. (1993), "Opening up of Stock Markets by Emerging Economies: Effect on Portfolio Flows and Volatility of Stock Prices", in *Portfolio Investment in Developing Countries*, World Bank Discussion Papers 228, pp. 383-403.

Koenig, L.M (1996), "Capital Inflows and Policy Responses in the ASEAN Region", *IMF Working paper WP/96/25*, International Monetary Fund, South East Asia and Pacific Department, April.

Lane. T. (1999), "The Asian Financial Crisis What Have We Learned?", *Finance and Development*, September, pp 44-47.

Loon, F. D and Dijk, M. P. (1995), "Financial Flows to and Emerging Capital Markets in Asia", in *Regional Co-operation and Integration in Asia* Edited by Kuchiro Kukasaku, OECD.

Lopez-Mejia. A. (1999), "Large Capital Flows Causes, Consequences and Policy Responses", *Finance and Development*, September, pp 28-31.

Mani, S. and Nandakumar, P. (1993), "Aggregate Net Financial Flows to India: Private Loans vis-a-vis Foreign Direct Investment", *International Journal of Development Banking*, Vol. 11, No. 1, January, pp. 63-83.

Martin. W. (1998), "Ins and Outs of Capital Flows", *Financial Times* (16 June).

Mussa. M, Swoboda . A, Zettelmeyer. J. and Jeanee O. (1999), "Moderating Fluctuations in Capital Flows to Emerging Market Economies", *Finance and Development*, September, pp 9-12.

OECD (Organization of Economic Cooperation and Development), *Financial Market Trends*, Various Issues

— 1992, *Financial Market Trends*, Paris, February.

— 1992, *Financial Statistics Monthly*, Paris, March.

— 1992, *Economic Outlook*, Vol. 51, June.

Pal, P. (1998), "Foreign Portfolio Investment in Indian Equity Markets—Has the Economy Benefited?", *Economic and Political Weekly*, March 14, pp. 589-598.

Pfeffermann, G. (1992), "Facilitating Foreign Investment—Some dos and don'ts", *Finance and Development*, March.

Pohit Sanjib (1993), "Capital Flows, Domestic Savings, Investment and Fiscal Balances in India: Some Tests for Causality", *Asian Economic Review*, Vol. 35, pp. 1-11.

Rangarajan, C., (1997), "Financial Sector Reforms: The Indian Experience," *RBI Bulletin*, July.

Rajan Goyal (1995), "Volatility in Stock Market Returns", *RBI Occasional Papers* Vol. 16, No. 3, September, pp. 175-195.

Razin, Assaf et al. (1998), "A Pecking Order of Capital Inflows and International Tax Principles", *Journal of International Economics*, 44:1, February, pp. 45-68.

RBI, "Harmonising the Role and Operations of Development Financial Institutions and Banks—A Discussion Paper," Mumbai, January, 1999.

RBI (Reserve Bank of India)

— RBI Bulletin (various issues)

— Report on Currency And Finance (various issues)

— Report on Trend And Progress of Banking in India (various issues), Bombay

— Statistical Tables Relating to Banks in India (various issues)

— Handbook of Statistics on Indian Economy, December, 1998.

Report of the Committee on Banking Sector Reforms, April 1998.

Report of the Khan Working Group on Harmonising, the Role and Operations of DFI's and Banks, May 1998.

Reddy. Y. V. (2000), *Monetary and Financial Sector Reforms in India-A Central Banker's Perspective,* UBS Publishers Distributors Ltd., 5 Ansari Road, New Delhi-2.

Reisen, H. (1996), "Managing Volatile Capital Inflows: The Experience of the 1990s", *Asian Development Review,* Vol. 14, pp. 72-96.

Reuven Glick (ed.) (1998), *"Managing Capital Flows and Exchange Rates: Perspectives from the Pacific basin"*, Cambridge University Press, Cambridge.

Salomon Brothers (1992), "Private Capital Flows to Latin America", *Emerging Markets (Weekly)* February 12, 1992.

Samal, K. C. (1997), "Emerging Equity Market in India: Role of Foreign Institutional Investors", *Economic and Political Weekly,* October 18, pp. 2729-2732.

Schadler, S., Carkovic, M., Bennett, A. and Kahn, R. (1993), "Recent Experiences with Surges in Capital Inflows", *IMF Occasional Paper 108,* IMF (Washington D. C.), December.

Sharma. K. (1999), "Understanding the Dynamics Behind Excess Capital Inflows and Excess Capital Outflows in East Asia ",in *Global Financial Turmoil and Reforms-UNU Policy Perspectives* edited by Barry Herman, United Nations, pp. 405-430.

Singh Y. P. (1996), "Emerging Dimensions of International

Financial Flows", *The Indian Journal of Commerce*, Vol XLIX, No. 189, Part IV, December.

Subrahmanyam. G. (1994), "Management of India's Capital Inflows", *CEPAL Review 53*, August, pp. 13-29.

Tang M. and Villafuerte. J (1995), "Capital Flows to Asian and Pacific Developing Countries: Recent Trends and Future Prospects", *Asian Development Bank*, Economics and Development Resource Centre, November.

Taylor, Mark, P. and Lucio Sarno, (1997), "Capital Flows to Developing Countries: Long and Short Term Determinants", *World Bank Economic Review* 11: 3, September, pp. 451-470.

Turner P. (19991), "Capital Flows in the 1980s: A Survey of Major Trends", *BIS Economic Papers No 30*, Basle, Bank for International Settlements, Monetary & Economics Department, April.

United Nations (1997). *Economic and Social Survey of Asia and the Pacific*, New York.

World Bank (1996), "*Managing Capital Flows in East Asia*," Washington D. C.

World Bank (1997), "Private Capital Flows to Developing Countries—The Road to Financial Integration", *World Bank Policy Research Report*, New York: Oxford University Press.

World Bank (1997). *Global Development Finance*, Washington.

Index

❑❑❑